Business Opportunities in the Pacific Alliance

"This book presents an analysis of the main factors to promote economic growth and development in selected Latin American countries."

—Arcadio A. Cerda, Dean, College of Economics & Business, Universidad de Talca, Chile

"This book is an excellent contribution to the Latin American literature on International Business, especially in times when protectionism seems to arise as a challenge to globalization."

—Carlos E. Ruiz, Associate Professor of Management, Georgia Gwinnett College, USA

"This book offers a timely and compelling view of the region's economic past, present, and future."

—John A. Parnell, Belk Chair of Management, School of Business, University of North Carolina at Pembroke, USA

"As the authors convey, the Pacific Alliance opens up many oportunities for its member countries to continue to achieve growth and reduce poverty through freer trade, in a world that is increasingly more complicated and uncertain."

—Aldo Defilippi, Executive Director, American Chamber of Commerce, Peru

"This book is an indispensable asset to the foreign investor who seeks to do business not just in the pioneering countries of the Pacific Alliance, but Latin America as a whole."

—Juan Pablo Carrasco, President, American Chamber of Commerce, Guatemala

John E. Spillan • Nicholas Virzi

Business Opportunities in the Pacific Alliance

The Economic Rise of Chile, Peru, Colombia, and Mexico

With contributed by Maria Alejandra Morales

palgrave
macmillan

John E. Spillan
University of North Carolina at Pembroke
Pinehurst, North Carolina, USA

Nicholas Virzi
Universidad Pontificia de Salamanca
Santa Catarina Pinula, Guatemala

ISBN 978-3-319-54767-1
ISBN 978-3-319-54768-8 (eBook)
DOI 10.1007/978-3-319-54768-8

Library of Congress Control Number: 2017941518

Printed on acid-free paper

This Palgrave Macmillan imprint is published by Springer Nature
The registered company is Springer International Publishing AG
The registered company address is: Gewerbestrasse 11, 6330 Cham, Switzerland

Preface

Globalization of Industry and commerce has brought many benefits and many changes in how goods and services are exchanged across borders in the Global economy. As such we are delighted to bring you *The Pacific Alliance: How Chile, Peru, Colombia, Mexico, and Costa Rica Offer Unique Business Opportunities for Both Insiders and Outsiders.*

Trade integration is not new. In fact, many countries in Latin America are ambitiously involved in a global network of trade arrangements and international business activity. The existence of the MERCOSUR, the Andean Pact, and other Free Trade Agreements (FTAs) have been active for a long period of time. The Pacific Alliance, or PA for short, is unique in that it brings together 4 countries which have demonstrated significant economic progress and offers major benefits to the 4 inside countries. The PA also offers significant opportunities for outsiders to participate in trade and global business with the PA members.

The PA is different than the other FTAs in the region because it includes other areas such as free circulation of labor, capital along with cooperation in other areas of business activity.

Because the PA includes the most stable and prosperous economies in the region, it can offer business and trade situations that are not available in other parts of the global economy. Since the members of the PA have substantial trade agreements with other countries outside the Alliance they can provide a strong connection with the globalization process, trade, foreign direct investment (FDI), and economic development.

The PA is a mechanism for deepening economic connections among the members while also recognizing the changing world dynamics that will inevitably affect all countries that participate in world trade. Latin America needs modernization and dynamic players who are strong enough and flexible enough to pivot quickly to meet the needs of their own country and those of the PA membership.

The PA members have consistently demonstrated economic and political stability while at the same time growing and developing new approaches that are benefitting their own populations and the Alliance itself.

Several attributes describe the essence of the PA. They are as follows:

- Innovative approach to trade
- Result-oriented approaches to cross-border activities
- An agreement among peers
- Shared commercial outlook
- Inherently open
- A dynamic model for regional integration
- Bridging agreements to Asia from which significant benefits can result
- Leveraging present agreements

So we are seeing five countries that are really the new stars in Latin America joining forces in order to produce more opportunities for its members and to enhance the business and quality of life for the populations that comprise each member state.

With the foregoing ideas in mind, this book is the first book on the topic. It provides a comprehensive discussion of what the PA is, what it does, and how it can be a strong trading entity that promotes the economic development, employment opportunities, and quality of life for all Latin Americans. The PA and Latin American environment is ever-changing and therefore needs new data analysis and a new perspective.

Contents

List of Figures

List of Tables

CHAPTER 1

Introduction

Overview

Pacific Alliance

The Pacific Alliance is a regional trade initiative of four countries: Peru, Mexico, Colombia, and Chile. It was established in 2011 with the *Declaración de Lima*. According to it, the members agreed to establish a trade alliance with aims to Asia and an economic integration with the *Mercado Integrado Lationamericano* (MILA).

These four countries have a population of 227.98 million, produce $1,749.73 billion and have a GDP per capita of $7,674.85, in current, nominal dollar terms. The primary aim of the Pacific Alliance (Pacific Alliance) is to promote and improve trade among Latin American countries and also to become a major trade group among the worldwide trade entities. Regional trade integration is not a new concept at all, even for protectionist oriented Latin America. For a long time, particularly in the postwar era, countries in several regions of the world have been gathering together to promote more trade among friends and neighbors. This was, in great part, due to the example and leadership of the democratic, capitalist, free trading United States. The Asian Tigers, places like South Korea, Taiwan, Hong Kong, Singapore, and Japan, which followed export-led growth models needed, of course, a main destination to send their exports, and the United States filled that role. Whereas often in the past the main impetus for trade has come from disparate regions

J.E. Spillan, N. Virzi, *Business Opportunities in the Pacific Alliance*,
DOI 10.1007/978-3-319-54768-8_1

seeking to penetrate the United States market, in the case of the Pacific Alliance, the different regions of the world seek freer trade among themselves in their own.

The notion of trade groups emerged to implement the idea that working together has more benefits than working along. To this end we see the Asian countries, the North American countries, the European countries and yes the Latin American countries constantly making deals through various trade groups in order to improve their trading techniques and to garner better goods and services at better quality and lower prices for its citizens. With this context in mind, this chapter outlines in detail what the Pacific Alliance is, who is part of the Pacific Alliance and why it was formed in the first place. The discussion is rich in contemporary information about the Pacific Alliance and also substantial economic analysis to show how the Pacific Alliance can contribute to the growth and development of not only its members but to all of Latin America.

Structure of the Book

The book is composed of 10 chapters that present the reader with a significant amount of detail about the origin of the Pacific Alliance and the economic benefit of it to its member countries, as well as to the general world economy. It also introduces the theoretical framework that provides the foundation upon which the Pacific Alliance was structured and essentially operates. From there the authors introduce the reader to an overview of modern economic history. This material provides a foundation for the next four chapters that individually analyze the Pacific Alliance members (Chile, Peru, Colombia, and Mexico). After a substantial discussion of the Pacific Alliance partners, the authors introduce a discussion of the logical next step for expansion of the Pacific Alliance. As such, a full chapter discusses how Central American countries can become part of and expanded Pacific Alliance both geographically and economically. Finally, the authors make some substantive comments about the future and some speculation on how trade integration in Latin America may play out over the short term even as the world becomes more dynamic. Overall, the book provides a comprehensive presentation of the Pacific Alliance and what it means to its partners and to the Latin American community.

Background

Some of the biggest economies in Latin America had united in an economic treaty like no another in Latin America, The Pacific Alliance is based on the principles of free market and trade with the objective of the creation of an economic bloc to trade and compete with big economies like Asia, Europe, and the United States. Chile, Colombia, Mexico, and Peru represents around the 37% of GDP of the countries in Latin America. All four countries in the Pacific Alliance have one major geographic characteristic in common, they all border on the Pacific Ocean. This feature makes it attractive to the Asian market because of the importance of the Pacific Ocean as a trade route.

Why the Pacific Alliance

The Pacific Alliance seeks for economic and commercial integration, growth, competitiveness, and the free movement of goods, services, resources, and people. The countries that comprise this initiative of regional integration are Chile, Colombia, Mexico, and Peru (alianzapacifico.net 2016).

This regional integration initiative was formed on April 28, 2011. The main purpose of this alliance is a trading bloc to have stronger economy. The United States plays a role in the Pacific Alliance in July 18, 2013 joined as an observer. The economic trade situtation of the United States with these four countries will continues to be positive. The Pacific Alliance will promote and integrate free trade agreements and significant trade policy among its members and with the United States.

The Pacific Alliance has the objective of building an economic integration, gradually increase the free circulation of goods, services, capital, and persons. The promotion of regional competitiveness and greater social welfare are also part of this Alliance. The main objective is to become a platform of trade integration with the rest of the world.

The role of the observers in the Pacific Alliance is important. "Being an observer country may help a country better understand the issues being negotiated and also provides opportunities for participation in activities such as trade forums and educational seminars" (Villareal 2016). As United States the other countries that are observers in this Treaty includes Australia, Israel, Japan, China, Canada, Turkey, and others. In total there are 42 countries that are observers.

The Pacific Alliance is the integration process in Latin America that is more like the Asian integration. Pacific Alliance is different from other

South America economic treaties because it is based in trade, liberalization, and promotes free circulation of labor and capital.

Why Chile, Peru, Colombia, and Mexico?

The actual four members share similar economic and political ideas. The success of the Pacific Alliance is evident over others initiatives such as MERCOSUR (Southern Common Market) because of the elimination of 92% of tariffs between the members. It has shown its practical success when, it created in 2014, the Additional Protocol of Framework Agreement, which was signed by the Presidents of the four States.

Chile, Colombia, Mexico, and Peru together represents a 35.4% of Latin America population and 36.3% of its total GDP and in the Trade market this countries also represent the 46.8% of the total imports of Latin America. "As a group, they represent the seventh-largest global market in terms of GDP" (Perry 2010).

The Pacific Alliance has the objective to negotiate with global markets like China creating an economic bloc to compete with Asian countries for trade with the USA by providing lower priced and better quality goods (Kotschwar and Schott 2013).

Latin America is going through challenges. A president toppled in Brazil, a next president to be removed in Venezuela, this in two countries that represent big economies in the region. Added to this, Central American nations, next logical partners, to join the Pacific Alliance, undergo massive corruption scandals, in Nicaragua, Guatemala, and El Salvador. These significant political factors notwithstanding, the Pacific Alliance countries focus on trade with each other which represents a step toward more free markets and better economic prosperity (Forbes 2016) (Fig. 1.1).

The Pacific Alliance taken as a region is expected to produce around $1,750 billion in 2016, over 35% of the economic production of Latin America. Its population is expected to report in at 227.98 million inhabitants for 2016. The region is expected to grow at a modestly robust 2.55% annual rate in 2016. This figure could and should be higher, but it must be taken into account that 2016 was a year in which the Latin American Region as a whole was forecast to come in at negative growth terms, due to corruption and economic setbacks in its principal economies, such as Argentina, Brazil, and Venezuela, countries which have suffered substantial setbacks due to flirtation with socialist economic policies.

Variables	2016
Gross domestic product, constant prices, % annual growth	2.55
Gross domestic product, current prices, $ billions	$1,749.73
Gross domestic product per capita, current prices, $	$8,015
Gross domestic product based on purchasing-power-parity (PPP) valuation of country GDP, $ billions	$3,834.86
Gross domestic product based on purchasing-power-parity (PPP) per capita GDP, $	$7,675
Total investment, % GDP	23.98
Gross national savings, % GDP	19.66
Inflation, % annual growth, end of period consumer prices	3.89
Volume of imports of goods and services, % annual growth	2.51
Volume of imports of goods, % annual growth	2.53
Volume of exports of goods and services, % annual growth	5.31
Volume of exports of goods, % annual growth	4.02
Unemployment rate	6.65
Population, millions	227.98
General government revenue, %GDP	22.95
General government total expenditure, %GDP	25.89
General government net lending/borrowing, %GDP	−2.94
General government primary net lending/borrowing, %GDP	−1.03
General government net debt, %GDP	24.30
General government gross debt, %GDP	37.33
Current account balance, %GDP	−3.13

Fig. 1.1 Pacific Alliance data as of 2016

Source: Calculations by authors based on International Monetary Fund data, 2016

In per capita terms, the GDP of the Pacific Alliance members represents $8,015 in nominal dollar terms, which is better than the regional GDP per capita, in similar terms. Adjusting for Purchasing Power Parity (PPP) among countries with different inflation and exchange rates, the GDP per capita of the Pacific Alliance countries of $16,821 bests the regional average of $15,259 for 2016, according to the most recent IMF data at the time of writing. This is also better than the figures for emerging countries, and emerging countries of Asia, both of which come in between $10,000 and $11,000, in PPP terms.[1]

Inflation is expected to be contained in the Pacific Alliance region, reporting in at about 3.89% per annum in 2016. Whereas total national savings as a percentage of GDP is calculated at an average annual rate of 19.66% of GDP, investment comes in at almost 24% of GDP, indicating greater potential economic growth in the future. Exports are expected to grow substantially over imports, as indicated by the 2016 reports. The current account balance for the region on average is expected to come in at −3.10% of GDP, for the four main countries of the Pacific Alliance. Government deficits are expected to be moderately high, at −2.94%

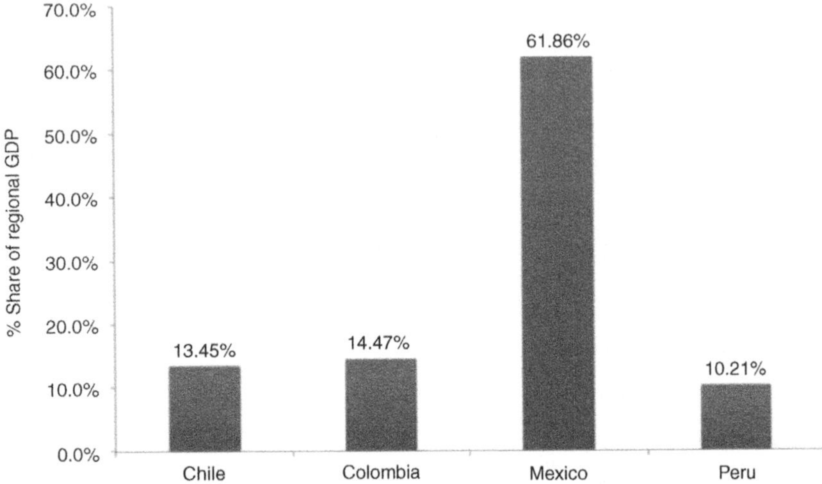

Graph 1.1 Share of GDP of the countries in Pacific Alliance

Source: Authors calculations based on World Bank, 2016 data

of GDP for 2016, on average. A worrisome factor is the relatively high level of gross debt in percentage terms of GDP for the region, which clocks in at 37.33% of GDP in 2016. This figure might seem low, especially as compared to the more developed countries of the world, such as the United States and the European Union, where countries show debt-to-GDP ratios close to or above 100% of GDP; however, in the case of Latin America, the tendency toward higher debt shows an unlearning of the lessons of the past, arising from the Latin American debt crises of the 1980s (Spillan et al. 2014).

The contribution of the countries from the Pacific Alliance to the combined GDP of this economic group is relatively similar in percentage terms for Chile, Colombia, and Peru, falling between 10% and 15% of the regional total. Mexico has the biggest economy in the Pacific Alliance, taking in 61.86% of the total. While Mexico is the largest country overall, it is Chile that provides the clearest lessons on how to achieve greater competitiveness through the basic factors of the rule of law, as other chapters will lay out.

Nonetheless, Mexico is one of the biggest economies in Latin America. As such, Mexico represents a benefit to the Pacific Alliance in no small part because nabbing a key regional player is a key selling point to the very idea of the Pacific Alliance. As well, the member countries are able to trade with Mexico with low tariff barriers and also can import the goods manufactured in Mexico with low costs. This spurs the competitiveness of the trade bloc as a whole, providing key incentives to trade with it, and imitate its success.

Contrary to what one might intuit of Latin American countries, their GDP value does not, on the whole, depend wholly on the exports of agricultural products. In value added terms, the Pacific Alliance countries have a big contribution in services, 62.3% of the GDP of the Pacific Alliance is based on services, 33.2% of the GDP of the Pacific Alliance is based on Industry and 4.5% of the GDP of the Pacific Alliance is based on Agriculture.

Agriculture represents a larger value of GDP share, in value added terms, for Peru (7.2%) and Colombia (6.8%), than it does for either Mexico or Chile (both under 4%). For the Pacific Alliance as a bloc, Agriculture and Services showed greater dynamism in 2016, growing at an annual rate of 2.9% and 3.5%, as compared to just under 1% for agriculture, which is due to a slowdown in world economic growth (Table 1.1 World Bank Data, 2016).

Table 1.1 Structural economic data for the Pacific Alliance

Variables	*CHL*	*COL*	*MEX*	*PER*	*PA*
Agriculture, % GDP	3.9	6.8	3.7	7.2	4.5
Industry, % GDP	32.9	34.0	32.7	35.2	33.2
Services, % GDP	63.2	59.2	63.6	57.6	62.3
Agriculture, % growth	4.3	3.3	3.1	−0.9	2.9
Industry, % growth	1.2	2.0	1.0	−1.2	0.9
Services, % growth	2.6	3.5	3.3	5.6	3.5
Exports, % GDP	30.1	14.7	35.3	21.0	30.2
Imports, % GDP	30.3	24.2	37.5	23.6	33.2
Exports, % growth	−1.9	−0.7	9.0	3.3	5.5
Imports, % growth	−2.8	3.9	5.0	2.4	3.5
Trade in services, % GDP	9.7	6.3	4.8	7.2	5.9
Travel services, % service imports	14.6	38.4	31.5	21.2	29.2
Logistics (5 best)	3.2	2.6	3.1	2.8	3.0
Days to start a business	5.5	11.0	6.3	26.0	8.9
Start-up costs, % GNI per capita	0.7	7.5	17.9	9.8	13.3
Customs burdens (7 best)	4.9	3.5	4.0	3.8	4.0

Source: Calculations by authors based on World Bank data, 2016

The balance of exports and imports in the Pacific Alliance is more inclined to be larger for imports than the exports. The imports represent a 33.2% of the GDP of this economic group and the exports represent a 30.2% of the GDP. Taken together, the external sector would represent an impressive 63.4% of GDP for the Pacific Alliance, a clear indicator of a trade bloc oriented toward greater trade liberalization (Table 1.1 World Bank Date, 2016).

The key here is not only export competitiveness, which can always degenerate into beggar-thy-neighbor policies, which shut down trade, instead of opening it up. The willingness of these Latin American countries to not only tolerate, but embrace, imports is a huge step forward, and a clear departure from the region's protectionist path. The signal is clearly conveyed that the protectionist stewards of the ECLAC[2] of the United Nations are losing sway over commercial policy in the region. This is a welcome move. Import openness means that a country can get better products at lower price. When a country imports goods it forces the internal market to innovate and become more specialized in their manufactures. Having better and cheaper goods also helps to improve the prosperity in those countries. This commonsense approach is novel to Latin American economies.

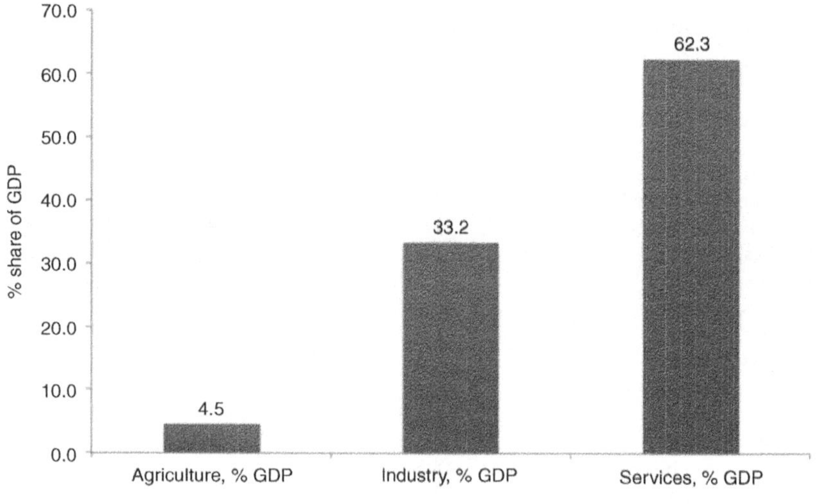

Graph 1.2 Economic structure of the Pacific Alliance

Source: Authors' calculations based on World Bank, 2016 data

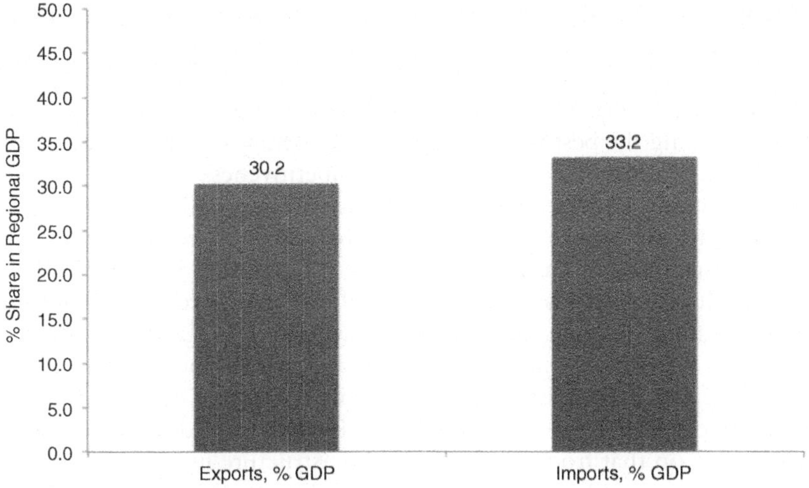

Graph 1.3 % of GDP of exports and imports in the Pacific Alliance

Source: Authors calculations based on World Bank, 2016 data

The Pacific Alliance Indicators

In this section, we do an overview for the Pacific Alliance to see how it fares as a region on several, commonly used indicators that are widely referenced by business sectors all over the world. These are the Global Competitiveness Index of the World Economic Forum (WEF 2016 data), the Ease of Doing Business Index of the World Bank (2016 data), and the Index of Economic Liberty, of the Heritage Foundation. As well, we include various other indicators; to wit: Index of Globalization, of the KOF institute in Switzerland (latest data as of October, 2016), the Human Development Index, of the United Nations Development Program (2016 data). Additionally, the Travel and Tourism Index of the World Economic Forum (WEF, 2016) and the Corruption Perceptions Index of Transparency International (2016 data) provide information on various trends that are occurring in the area.

Typically, what was done to generate regional scores was to take an average of each country's score on, for example, Global Competitiveness, or any of its 12 sub-pillars and weight each country score by that country's participation rate in regional GDP for the Pacific Alliance. This gives a rough, good-enough overview of a region's performance on key indicators, adjusting for the influence of radically different sized economies, as is the case between Mexico and Peru, for example.

The Pacific Alliance as a bloc is fairly competitive. All scores go from 1 to 7, 7 being the best score. Based on calculations using data taken from the World Economic Forum (Global Competitiveness Index), the Pacific Alliance scores 4.41 in the Global Competitiveness with strengths in the macroeconomic environment, with a score of 5.09, health and education (5.62, a standout in Latin America) and a big market size (5.23). Even higher education scores 4.3, and financial markets scores 4.63, reflecting relatively solid scores in these important areas (Table 1.2 WEF, 2016).

Strong investments in infrastructure, and health and basic education constitute key prerequisites to productivity growth. Therefore the relatively solid scores on the fourth pillar of Health and Education make for good news on that front, even though infrastructure investment needs to improve substantially. Macroeconomic stability is as important as ever, as Europe sloughs off into economic, political, and social decadence, and even the United States struggles to grow after 8 years since the economic crisis of 2008, due to fiscal and monetary mismanagement and gross overregulation. The Latin American region as a whole, having adopted the fiscal and monetary lessons of the Washington Consensus, confronted the 2008 economic crash with low deficits, debt, inflation, and a stable,

Table 1.2 Global Competitiveness of the Pacific Alliance

Global competitiveness index rank	*Pacific Alliance*
GCI Global Score	4.41
GCI Pillar 1 Institutions	3.47
GCI Pillar 2 Infrastructure	4.16
GCI Pillar Macroeconomic Environment	5.09
GCI Pillar 4 Health and Education	5.62
GCI Pillar 5 Higher Education and Training	4.30
GCI Pillar 6 Goods Market Efficiency	4.33
GCI Pillar 7 Labor Market Efficiency	4.01
GCI Pillar 8 Financial Markets	4.63
GCI Pillar 9 Technological Readiness	4.12
GCI Pillar 10 Market Size	5.23
GCI Pillar 11 Business Sophistication	4.15
GCI Pillar 12 Innovation	3.32

realistically pegged currency, and high international monetary reserves. Due to these neoliberal structural reforms, the Latin American economies resisted the crisis better than did other developing countries, and even better than the developed countries, and also recovered faster. The unlearning of these lessons has begun in earnest, in countries such as Brazil and, especially, Venezuela. However, the Pacific Pumas of the Pacific Alliance are among those countries, which still heed the hard-learned lessons of the past (Spillan et al. 2014).

The Pacific Alliance scores well on market size, due mainly to Mexico, a huge market, which, moreover, is right next to the United States. This factor cannot be ignored. Nonetheless, the Chilean economy is also relatively large, and fairly advanced, in efficiency and competitiveness terms. In particular, Chile holds promise of a past example of the benefits of sound fiscal and monetary management, more so than the rest of the countries in the Pacific Alliance. The good score of the Pacific Alliance on the financial markets item is important because foreign investors, in particular, want to know outright that their investment will be safe, that local money will hold its value, and that exchange rates will be stable.

On the first pillar of competitiveness, institutions, the Pacific Alliance score could, and should, be stronger, while in the area of economic innovation, the region still lags somewhat behind.[3]

In the Ease of Doing Business Index, according to calculations using the World Bank data, the Pacific Alliance would rank 49th out of 190 countries in the world, if it were, in fact, a single country. The best ranks for the Pacific Alliance are in getting credit (rank 20), protecting minority investors (rank 43), and dealing with construction permits (rank 45), as well as in registering private property (rank 48). Trading across borders, and enforcing contracts can also be considered as a source of information to measure this activity. The approximate rank of 64 in getting electricity might not seem a particularly strong ranking, but it would place the Pacific Alliance, as a "country," among the top third in the world in this all important category.[4] The fact is that there isn't one item on the Ease of Doing Business Index where the Pacific Alliance, taken as a single country does not come out in the top half of world rankings (Table 1.3 World Bank Data, 2016).

The Pacific Alliance project is designed to improve just the areas that need improvement, such as trading across borders, where the Pacific Alliance gets an approximate rank of 85. The entire Alliance is committed to improving scores on matters such as starting a business (approximate rank 87) and contract enforcement (approximate rank 80). Once these

Table 1.3 Ease of Doing Business scores of the Pacific Alliance

Doing Business, rank	*Pacific Alliance*
Ease of Doing Business Rank	49.08
Starting a Business	87.14
Dealing with Construction Permits	45.26
Getting Electricity	63.79
Registering Property	47.82
Getting Credit	20.71
Protecting Minority Investors	43.00
Paying Taxes	64.45
Trading Across Borders	84.86
Enforcing Contracts	80.46
Resolving Insolvency	60.78

processes are streamlined in each individual country and across the Pacific Alliance, the Alliance will become a force to contend with in Latin America.

The Pacific Alliance scores 67.9 out of 100 on the Economic Freedom Index. This is a fairly good score, particularly for Third World nations. Trade freedom within the region is great, with a score of 81.23. Other strong scores are in the areas of government spending and fiscal freedom (78 and 76.01, respectively), reflecting relatively low, predictable levels of government taxes and spending. Monetary freedom is another area where the Pacific Alliance scores strongly, with 79.10 over 100, indicating that the monetary sector is friendly to proper business concerns. Financial freedom as a subject area performs relatively well with 62.79. Freedom from corruption (40.71) and protection of property rights (53.69) have to improve if the Pacific Alliance is to achieve its full political and economic potential in the world.[5] It is precisely the move to institute the proper changes in the right direction that the Pacific Alliance represents (Table 1.4 Economic Freedom Index, 2016).

The Pacific Alliance scores 62.99 out of 100 in the Index of Globalization, an indicator which strives to measure how much a particular economy interconnects with the world, along three main dimensions, political, economic, and social globalization. Political globalization measures things such as how many countries a given country has embassies in, its participation in UN peace missions, its participation in international treaties, etc. Social globalization tries to measure how integrated and interconnected a given society is with the developed countries, and global society as a whole. It measures Internet, phone, mail connectivity, and

Table 1.4 Index of Economic Freedom of the Pacific Alliance

Index of Economic Freedom	*Pacific Alliance*
2016 Score	67.90
Property Rights	53.69
Freedom from Corruption	40.71
Fiscal Freedom	76.01
Gov't Spending	78.00
Business Freedom	71.68
Labor Freedom	62.31
Monetary Freedom	79.10
Trade Freedom	81.23
Investment Freedom	73.47
Financial Freedom	62.79

other cultural factors. The Pacific Alliance has relatively high political globalization (77.28) but the social globalization is still low (50.13). It is noteworthy that political globalization for the Pacific Alliance should be higher than its score for economic globalization, which basically measures the degree of free trade which exists among nations. This point is worthy of further study. Were it to be proven absolutely accurate that the countries of the Pacific Alliance were more politically integrated than economically integrated, it would be a strong statement on the need for a new economic vision among the Latin American economic elite (Table 1.5 Index of Globalization, 2016).[6]

The Human Development Index measures countries along a 0 to 1 interval, 1 being the maximal score. On the human development index, the Pacific Alliance score is of 0.76 for the region, based on the four original member countries.[7] The travel and tourism industry comes out relatively solid with a

Table 1.5 Scores of the Pacific Alliance on Various Indicators

Various Indicators	*Pacific Alliance*
Index of Globalization 2013	62.99
Index of Economic Globalization	65.50
Index of Political Globalization	77.28
Index of Social Globalization	50.13
Human Development Index	0.76
Travel and Tourism Index	4.17
Corruption Perceptions Index	39.91

score of 4.17 out of 7 in the World Economic Forum measure.[8] These scores are basically averages, and it must be taken into account that some countries offer much more than others in matters of tourism. Some countries simply have more tourist attractions, which they may, or may not exploit. Finally, we come to the term of corruption. Corruption is a disease, which negatively affects investment, employment, economic growth, and the standard of living. Unfortunately, corruption is widespread in the Third World. Thankfully, things are getting better, somewhat. As far as the Pacific Alliance countries are concerned, on average, the member governments are perceived as corrupt, scoring as they do 39.91 out of 100 in the Corruption Perception Index.[9]

Central America

The Central American economies as of yet do not form a part of the Pacific Alliance project. Yet, important countries of the Isthmus, such as Costa Rica and Guatemala, have expressed interest in joining the effort. It would

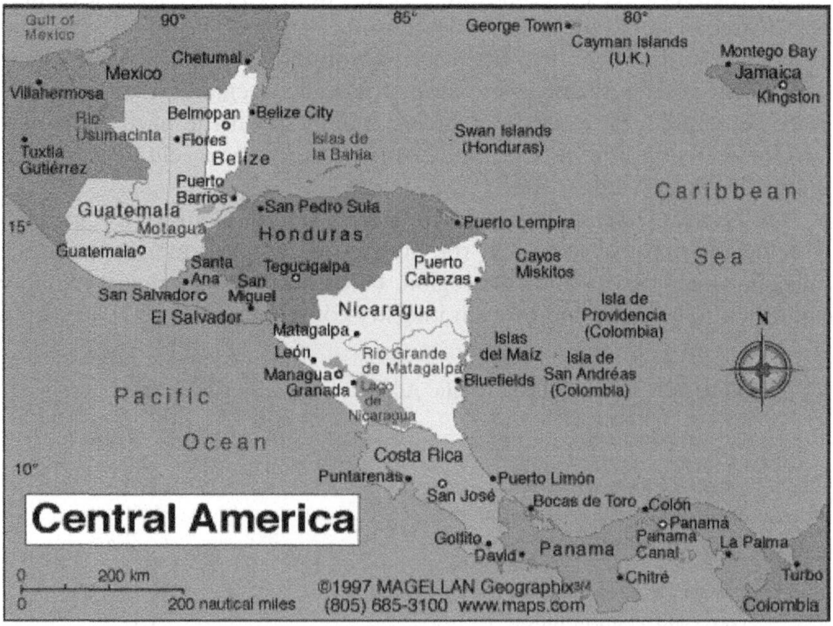

Map – Central America http://i.infopls.com/images/mapcentralamerica.gif

be a logical and positive move, both for the Central American countries, and for the Pacific Alliance project as a whole. All the countries of the Central American region have a Pacific Coast. Economic integration projects have been in the works for decades in Central America. The opportunities proffered by the Pacific Alliance project might just be the carrot that entices the political, economic, and business elites of the Isthmus to get their act together in order to spur competitiveness in the region and to finally achieve meaningful political and economic integration. The inclusion of Central America would bring the Pacific Alliance up from the southernmost part of South America in Chile up to the border of the United States.

Adding the Central American countries to the Pacific Alliance would be a smart move, not only for the original member coe original member countries of the Pacific Alliance, but also for the six nations of Central America. The six nations of Central America are Costa Rica, El Salvador, Guatemala, Honduras, Nicaragua, and Panama. On a simple sum basis, the Central American economy is expected to reflect a size, in billions of dollars of $241.67 in 2016, with a total population of just over 47 million inhabitants in 2016. In per capita GDP terms, the GDP per capita for the region of $5,141 translates into $9,258 in purchasing power parity (PPP) terms, below the average for both the region of Latin America and emerging economies as a whole (including emerging Asian economies as a category), according to the most recent IMF data (Table 1.6 International Monetary Fund Data, 2016). Nonetheless, the Central American region still remains strategically located on a geographical basis. Central America is between North and South America, and between Europe and Asia. The economic potential of the region as a trade and business hub for the whole world is readily appreciated. It may be that the prospects of inclusion into the Pacific Alliance, and the adoption of its market-friendly reforms, are just the type of orientation that the Central American economies sorely need.

Imports, on a volume basis, for Central America, exports are expected to grow over 4% for 2016, 4.18% for goods and services and 4.9% for goods, compared to exports, which are expected to grow at 3.57% for goods and services, and just over 1% for goods in 2016. The current account deficit for the region of –3.9% of GDP is modest by Latin American standards. Guatemala stands out with a near current account balance close to 0%, according to the latest IMF data. It needs be mentioned that this is also a reflection of lowered aggregate demand in 2016 versus prior years. As

Table 1.6 Central America data as of 2016

Variables	2016
Gross domestic product, growth rate, constant prices	4.14
Gross domestic product, current prices, $ billions	$241.67
Gross domestic product per capita, current prices, $	$5,141
Gross domestic product based on purchasing-power-parity (PPP) valuation of country GDP,$ billions	$435.22
Gross domestic product based on purchasing-power-parity (PPP) per capita GDP, $	$9,258
Total investment, % GDP	23.73
Gross national savings, % GDP	19.12
Inflation, end of period consumer prices, annual rate	3.29
Volume of imports of goods and services, annual rate	4.18
Volume of Imports of goods, annual rate	4.90
Volume of exports of goods and services, annual rate	3.57
Volume of exports of goods, annual rate	1.05
Unemployment rate	NA
Population, millions	47.01
General government revenue, % GDP	19.35
General government total expenditure, % GDP	22.16
General government net lending/borrowing, % GDP	-2.81
General government gross debt, % GDP	41.29
Current account balance, $ billions	-9.421
Current account balance, % GDP	-3.90

Source: Calculations by authors based on International Monetary Fund data, 2016

domestic consumption goes down in Central America, so does the demand for imports. For better or worse, the external, international economy weighs heavily on these small, open economies.

The economic potential of the Central American region and what it can add to the Pacific Alliance depends greatly on its business climate, which in turns depends on the fiscal and monetary situation of the individual countries, and the region as a whole. The region of Central America reflects, differentially, a somewhat polemical situation on taxes and spending. Countries like Costa Rica have followed patterns of public social investment recommended by international organizations, having achieved the highest level of human development according to the United Nations.[10] Many attribute this to a state presence of 15% in tax revenues and 20% in public spending, although increasing public deficits and debt are calling into question the sustainability of these fiscal practices. Meanwhile, countries like Guatemala, have tax revenues of 11% of GDP and public spending below 15% of GDP, which many attribute blame for the persistence of structural problems, such as poor infrastructure, generalized poverty, etc. It bears mentioning that Central America, like most Latin American nations, suffers from rampant corruption, where tax dollars go to waste, when they are not stolen. However, corruption is a given in Latin America. Inasmuch as it is not feasible that the developed world, or the American businessman in particular, should forego doing business altogether in Latin America, there will always be business enterprises willing to take the dive and do business in Latin America.

The good news is that, as a whole, the Central American region is not as tax-hungry as other regions of the world, like the United States, might be. For the region as a whole, government revenues, on a simple average in GDP terms, reflect a 19.35% of GDP, while spending accounts for 22.16% of GDP. Fiscal deficits, on average, in GDP terms, reflect –2.81% of GDP for the region (Table 1.6 International Monetary Fund Data, 2016). General government gross debt, again in simple average terms, reflects over 41% of regional GDP, a worrisome sign that the valuable lessons of the Washington Consensus, of fiscal discipline, are slowly being eroded (Spillan et al. 2014). Fortunately, the monetary lessons of monetary discipline are yet in place, with inflation being contained in 2016 at 3.57% in simple average terms for the Central American region in 2016.

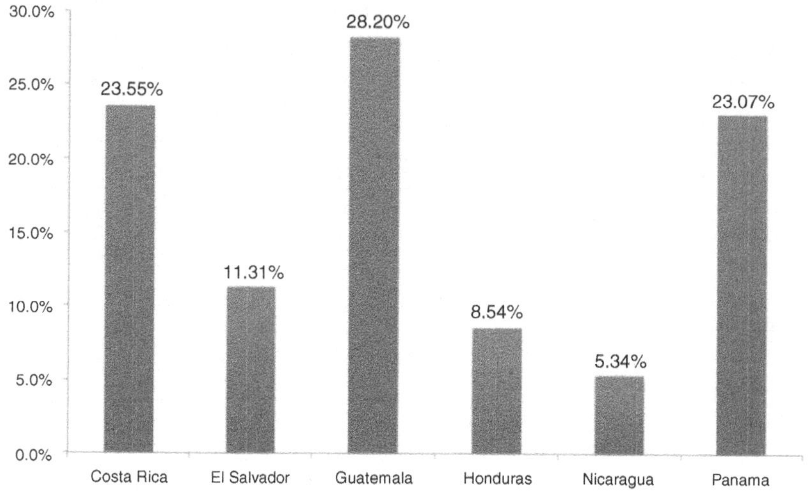

Graph 1.4 Share of GDP of the countries in Central America

The Central American economy, as a whole, is dominated by the countries of Costa Rica, Guatemala and Panama. Guatemala is the largest country of Central America, both in population terms as well as in production terms. However, whereas Guatemala represents some 35% of the regional population, Guatemalan GDP represents just over 28% of regional GDP, showing productivity lags due to structural problems pertaining to poverty, corrupt political institutions, etc. Costa Rica and Panama, with populations about one third of that of Guatemala's, both represent just over 23% of regional GDP (Fig 1.2).

If Central America as a region was added to the Pacific Alliance, the bloc could grow even further its exports to other big economic regions like Asia, which present strong demand for foodstuffs produced in Central America. Trade between the member countries of the Pacific Alliance would also be important, as tariffs approached zero on important foodstuffs, for instance.

When we compare the economic structure of the Pacific Alliance with other economic areas like Central America, we can see that these two economic blocs can be complementary to each other. In the Agricultural contribution to GDP, Central America has almost the double contribution of the same sector (8.6% of GDP) as the Pacific Alliance economy as a

Variables	CR	SLV	GTM	HON	NIC	PAN	CA
Agriculture, % GDP	5.6	11.3	11.1	13.9	18.8	2.89	8.6
Industry, % GDP	25.0	26.9	28.1	26.6	26.9	27.7	26.9
Services, % GDP	69.4	61.9	60.8	59.5	54.3	69.4	64.5
Agriculture, % growth	3.7	0.8	3.3	3.3	2.8	−0.66	2.2
Industry, % growth	2.4	3.2	3.7	3.2	2.5	5.93	3.7
Services, % growth	4.1	2.5	4.4	2.9	5.2	6.23	4.4
Exports, % GDP	35.1	26.0	21.3	45.1	37.5	53.6	35.4
Imports, % GDP	37.2	42.0	30.0	64.0	55.5	61.4	44.6
Exports, % growth	−1.7	2.4	4.0	1.5	−2.0	3.3	1.8
Imports, % growth	−4.0	3.2	8.9	4.9	11.6	2.96	3.7
Trade in services, % GDP	20.5	15.0	9.2	22.2	18.8	30.2	19.0
Travel services, % service imports	19.0	19.0	22.6	24.6	16.3	18.2	20.6
Logistics (5 best)	2.9	3.2	2.7	2.5	2.6	2.87	2.8
Days to start a business	24.0	16.5	18.5	14.0	13.0	6	16.0
Start-up costs, % GNI per capita	11.1	42.7	25.0	38.7	72.2	6.3	23.1
Customs burdens (7 best)	3.8	3.5	3.5	3.5	2.4	4.15	3.7

Fig. 1.2 Structural Economic Data for Central America

Source: Calculations by authors based on World Bank data, 2016

whole. Central America countries have a positive climate and geographical elements that contributes to the agriculture economy. In value added terms, Nicaragua presents the biggest agricultural sector on a national basis, representing as it does 18.8% of GDP. Honduras, El Salvador and Guatemala follow, with 13.9% of GDP, 11.3% and 11.1%, respectively. In value-added terms, services showed the highest level of growth for the region as a whole, according to World Bank figures for 2016, with 4.4% annual growth, followed by Industry with 3.7% growth, then followed by Agriculture with 2.2% annual growth. Costa Rica, surprisingly, shows the most robust growth for its agricultural sector, with 3.7% annual growth, followed by Guatemala and Honduras, each with 3.3% annual growth.

Both Panama and Costa Rica report a high of 69.4% of GDP for the Services sector, in value added terms, compared to a low of 54.3% for Honduras in the Services sector. For the region as a whole, Services showed the highest level of growth, according to World Bank figures for 2016, with 4.4% annual growth, followed by Industry with 3.7% growth, then followed by Agriculture with 2.2% annual growth. It was in Panama where Services grew the most, at 6.23% per annum, and in El Salvador where they grew the least, 2.5%. In Guatemala, growth in Services reported in at 4.4%, according to World Bank 2016 data.

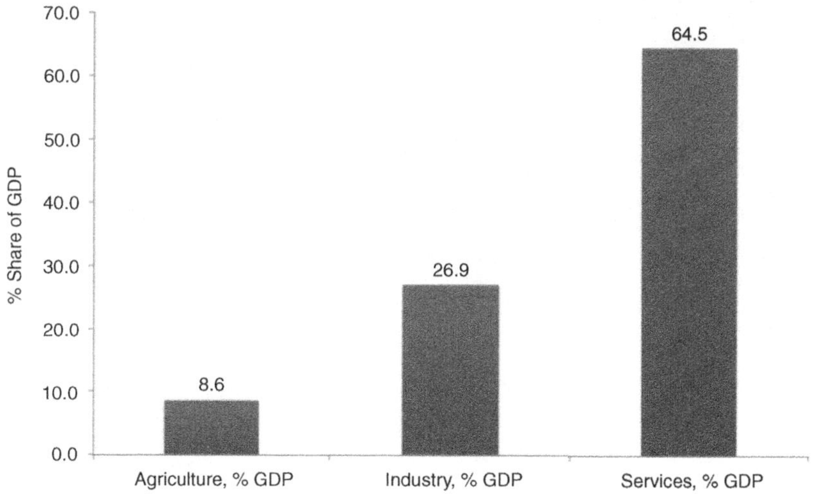

Graph 1.5 Economic structure of Central America

Source: Authors' calculations based on World Bank, 2016 data

In value added terms, Industry grew at 3.7% annual rate, according to 2016 World Bank data. Industry makes up about 26.9% of GDP for Central America, ranging from a low of 25% for Costa Rica, and a high of 28.1% for Guatemala. It was in Panama where Industry grew the most, at 5.93% per annum, and in Costa Rica where it grew the least, at 2.4%. In Guatemala, growth in Industry was reported in 2016 at 3.7%, according to 2016 World Bank data.

In value added terms, according to World Bank data, the Services economy accounts for some 64.5% of Central American GDP, Industry for 26.95% and Agriculture for 8.6% of GDP. These figures are weighted averages, wherein each country's particular contribution by sector was weighted by its economy's participation in regional GDP. It might seem surprising that the small, open Central American economies would be so services-oriented, but they are. Industry has been taking a larger share of the GDP pie, in value added terms, as well over the years. In short, what has been traditionally thought of as a backwards, agricultural outpost represents today a modernizing economy, a potential hub for business deals in all types of sectors for decades to come. This is what makes the Central American region a natural next step for the Pacific Alliance to incorporate.

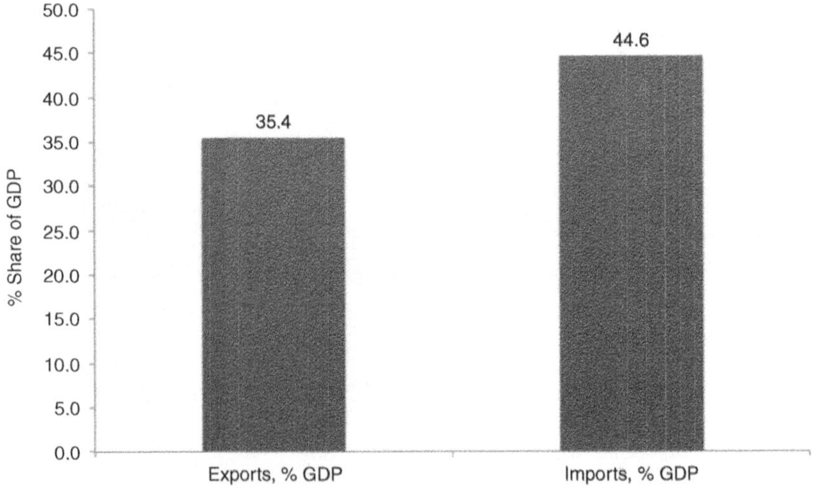

Graph 1.6 % of GDP of exports and imports in Central America

Taken together, Exports and Imports as a percentage of GDP make up a quick-use indicator that shows the degree of economic openness of a given economy. Exports and Imports account for 80% of regional GDP for Central America, according to our calculations using the latest World Bank data. This is a good figure, and it is to be expected, given that each and every one of the countries of Central America is classified as a small, open macro economy. The degree of economic openness is one that will surely rise as economic and political integration in the region get underway, a project that may well serve, and be served by, the incorporation of the Central American economies into the Pacific Alliance.

Who Will Benefit?

The world as a whole will benefit from the success of the Pacific Alliance. As the most pioneering, innovative Latin American countries forge together an economic alliance that shows the worlds the productive, political, and social benefits of market economics and freer trade, the seductive, disingenuous appeal of socialist models of development will fall off. Especially as the bloom comes of the rose for the disastrous basket case of an economy which resource-rich Venezuela has shown herself to be, and the Cuban model grows ever more dependent on tourism from capitalist countries, the Latin American countries need a development model that holds true promise for the future. This not only would benefit Latin American countries, but their trading partners all over the world, as greater productivity and competitiveness would translate into lower priced exports from Latin America and greater value added goods, as well. Efficiency benefits would propagate worldwide.

The International Monetary Fund (IMF) had said about the Pacific Alliance: "The combination of political and market enthusiasm may make the Pacific Alliance a more successful initiative than earlier regional attempts" (IMF 2016). This represents a departure in substance from earlier Latin American trade treaties that did not directly involve the United States. In these prior treaties, the impetus was more on protectionism than on free trade. The end result was that regional trade treaties, such as Mercosur, among large economies of South America, devolved into protectionist, rather than free trade, and today remain largely irrelevant as referents to the benefits of global, free trade.

The Pacific Alliance started as the ARCO del Pacífico initiative a trade agreement that wanted to include the Latin American Pacific Rim countries.

Since it was taking too long, these countries decided to create the Pacific Alliance. To talk about who will benefit from this treaty and the next countries that sign it we have to talk about importance of the Pacific Rim. There are several countries that belong to the Pacific Rim, countries from four continents: Asia, Australia, North America, and South America.[11] The name of Rim countries is delivered because it is ringed on one side by the Americas with North America, Central America, and South America and in the other side there is ringed on the other side Asia and Oceania.

The countries in the Pacific Rim have an important role in world trade and, taken together, they, too, represent a strong economy. The closeness to the Pacific Ocean has contributed to the movement of goods between countries, becoming one of the principal routes of trade and shipping. The vastness of the Pacific Ocean represents at once distance, but also connectivity and commercial potential. As the twenty-first century nears its third decade, and technological innovations in shipping, storage, logistics and infrastructure come into the fold and mature, having a coastline with the Pacific Ocean will prove invaluable. There are serious considerations of becoming part of the Pacific Alliance among countries like New Zealand, Taiwan, Thailand, South Korea, North Korea, Cambodia, Japan, Singapore, Australia, China, and Vietnam.

Counties situated in Central America will benefit from the Pacific Alliance because of the new possibilities of trade with much larger markets like Asia, Oceania, and Australia. This becomes even truer as the center of economic gravity moves from the stagnant Atlantic economies of Europe to the dynamic economies of emergent Asia and the Pacific. If the Pacific Alliance is composed by more Latin American countries a bigger market based on free trade will be available to the world. This will bring about concrete benefits such as greater economic specialization (division of labor among countries) and efficiency. Other benefits would naturally follow, such as the creation of jobs, the expansion of trade, innovation, the production of lower priced goods; eventually, there would be greater prosperity, and peace, among more counties (this is highlighted elsewhere in this book). Countries that are not members of the Pacific Alliance will certainly enjoy derivative benefits from trading with countries that are members of the Pacific Alliance or trade with the Pacific Alliance.

As always, alongside the question as to who will benefit from the Pacific Alliance surges the question of who will lose from the emergence of this trade pact. Although free trade benefits all signatory nations as parties in general, there will always be losers and winners. As a short answer, the winners are invariably the consumers. With freer trade, consumers get a larger quantity and greater variety of goods at lower prices. Importers get valuable inputs for production at more competitive terms. Winners may also include small businesses or established businesses seeking entry into previously untapped markets, or markets sub-optimally penetrated due to inordinately harsh regulations. Losers will include those sectors previously protected by law from competition. These will represent the strongest political opposition to freer trade treaties. On a grander scale, those who stand to lose from the success of the Pacific Alliance are those vested interests, which have always spoken on the benefits of protectionism and economic "management" from the government. These are to be found among the economic experts of the United Nations, in the Economic Commission for Latin America and the Caribbean (ECLAC, or CEPAL by its Spanish language initials), university experts throughout Latin America, who still extoll the benefits of mercantilist trade policies, and other such anti-market economic bodies of thought.

Is This Regional Trade Group Sustainable?

To talk about the sustainability of this Pacific Alliance regional trade group we have to know the size of the market that it represents globally. Essentially, the Pacific Alliance can be situated as being among the 10 largest economies in the world, and among the ten largest exporters in the world as well. The Pacific Alliance aims for deeper regional economic integration among its member economies, so as to facilitate the freer circulation of not just goods and services, and capital, but also people as well (The Pacific Alliance 2016).

The size of the market that the Pacific Alliance represents makes it a sustainable trade group because; the countries that are in this trade group can provide different benefits to other countries. The Pacific Alliance countries have different geographical and climate elements, which help to create more specialization, which can promote new "Asian Tigers" in the region. These have been called the Pacific Pumas. (George 2014).

In 2013 the four members of the Pacific Alliance signed an agreement to eliminate tariffs in 92% of merchandise trade. In the meantime, the member countries also eliminated visa requirements and created a regional Stock market, MILA (The Economist 2015). All of this shows that the Pacific Alliance is not like any other South America treaty, at least in the rapidity with which it has achieved the objective of a freer market. Insofar as the question of the sustainability of the Pacific Alliance is concerned, if the Pacific Alliance were a country it would be in the top 10 economy of the world, side to side with Russia and Brazil, and in front of United Kingdom; so, the size is there. As far as reducing barriers to starting businesses, and trading across countries, the Pacific Alliance seeks to revolutionize the way of doing things, along market economy lines. If the Pacific Alliance strives to streamline business processes and free up trade between countries, not just in Latin America, but among all countries with a Pacific Ocean coastline, and, indeed, the world, it will not only be sustainable, it will be a model of economic development for decades to come.

The Current State of Globalization and Trade

There are several factors that can influence global trade. World Trade Organization for 2016 has declared that with regard to merchandise trade in volume terms:

> The regional and product composition of export and import growth has changed in recent years. In 2012–13, strong demand for imported goods and services on the part of China and other developing economies helped cushion slow GDP growth and weak import demand in developed countries, particularly in the euro area. However, in 2015 a recovery of imports in Europe and North America compensated for weak import demand in developing countries including Asia, especially among natural resource exporters. (World Trade Statistics 2016)

Globalization is here to stay. In 2016, according to IMF data, the trade volume for goods and services will come in at a figure between 2% annual growth and 2.5% annual growth. The same is true for the volume of imports of goods and services, and the volume of exports of goods and services.[12] There can be no doubt that trade in Goods and Services is important to the Pacific Alliance countries. Moreover, trade treaties among the Pacific Alliance countries, and between them and their trading partners, abound all around the world. The more powerful and biggest economies have more trade between them and that is one of the reasons they grow rapidly. Following this example, the Pacific Alliance has ample potential and prospects to grow.

Conclusions

Free trade, and its corollary, regional trade integration, is not new concepts. Around the world there are many trade blocs that on a daily basis exchange goods and services that allow economies to achieve their goals of satisfying their citizens with the wherewithal to meet each days demands. The Pacific Alliance would be just one more of the regional trade integrators that have much to offer the Latin American countries.

Although the Pacific Alliance would just follow through on other prior commitments to free trade, this particular entity offers more than the others. First, it not only provides a mechanism for trade of goods and services among its members but also capital and labor. This is a significant difference and a major contribution to economic development and prosperity for these four Latin American countries. Secondly, it is structured to become a platform for much larger trade activities like competing with the big Asian, European, and American trade groups. Since the four members of the Pacific Alliance represent about 37% of the GDP in Latin American, their economic impact can be substantial. The potential that this Alliance presents is substantial and brings Latin America into a new era of world trade and economic development. How each of the Pacific Alliance country members manage their economies will have a major determination as to the future success of this regional trade integration group. The recent analysis indicates that the future is bright and progress toward including more countries especially from Central America could strengthen the Pacific Alliance even more.

In real term it is important to think of the Pacific Alliance not as an outsider but as an integral component necessary for both short- and long-term economic stability and prosperity among not only the members of the Pacific Alliance but for other countries in Latin America. It has been substantially demonstrated that Latin America has had both a turbulent economic and political history. With the formation of the Pacific Alliance we are seeing more economic development, more political stability and more opportunities for prosperity than ever before. The leaders of the Pacific Alliance need to keep their eyes on the prize and continue to thing about mutual benefit rather than individual success. With this approach there are many more opportunities for all of Latin America to benefit from this important Regional Trade Integration with the existence of the Pacific Alliance.

Notes

1. International Monetary Fund. 2016. World Economic Outlook indicators. Online database. http://www.imf.org/external/pubs/ft/weo/2016/02/weodata/index.aspx. Last accessed December, 2016.
2. The Economic Commission for Latin America and the Caribbean (ECLAC).
3. http://databank.worldbank.org/data/reports.aspx?source=world-development-indicators. Accessed October 2016. World Development Indicators. World Bank.
4. http://www.doingbusiness.org/data. Accessed October 2016. Ease of Doing Business Index. World Bank.
5. http://www.heritage.org/index/explore. Accessed October 2016. Index of Economic Freedom. The Heritage Foundation.
6. http://globalization.kof.ethz.ch/. Accessed October 2016. Index of Globalization. KOF.
7. http://hdr.undp.org/en/content/human-development-index-hdi. Accessed October 2016. Human Development Index. United Nations Development Program.
8. https://www.weforum.org/reports/travel-and-tourism-competitiveness-report-2015 Accessed October 2016. Travel and Tourism Index. World Economic Forum.
9. https://www.transparency.org/country/. Accessed October 2016. Corruption Perceptions Index. Transparency International.
10. See the chapter on Central America for the precise indicators.
11. For the most part, the analysis in this book will exclude Australia, seeking to emphasize the lessons of trade exported by Western countries to other cultures, such as those found in Latin America and Asia. Australia, for practical intents and purposes, is taken as a Western country. Adding Australia to the political and economic analysis made herein would only add to the central argument of the book, that Western free trade principles add positively to the efforts of Third World countries to develop via freer markets and trade.
12. See International Monetary Fund. 2016. World Economic Outlook databases. http://www.imf.org/external/pubs/ft/weo/2016/02/weodata/weorept.aspx?pr.x=88&pr.y=8&sy=2000&ey=2021&scsm=1&ssd=1&sort=country&ds=.&br=1&c=001%2C05%2C205&s=TRADEPCH%2CTM_RPCH%2CTX_RPCH&grp=1&a=1.

References

Alianza del Pacifico. (2016). https://alianzapacifico.net/.

Authors' calculations using IMF data. International Monetary Fund. World Economic Outlook databases. (2016). Online database. http://www.imf.org/external/pubs/ft/weo/2016/02/weodata/index.aspx. Accessed October 2016.

Forbes. (2016). http://www.forbes.com/sites/nathanielparishflannery/2016/05/30/what-should-investors-know-about-latin-americas-pacific-alliance/print.

George, S. (2014). *The Pacific Pumas: An emerging model for emerging markets.* Washington: Bertelsmann Foundation. http://www19.iadb.org/intal/intalcdi/PE/2014/14383.pdf.

International Monetary Fund. (2016). World Economic Outlook, online database. www.imf.org. Accessed October 2016.

Kotschwar, B. & Schott, J. J. (2013). The next bigh thing? The trans-Pacific partnership and Latin America. http://www.americasquarterly.org/next-big-thing-trans-pacific-partnership.

Perry, G. (2010). *Financial integration in the Pacific Alliance* (p. 3), IDB Monograph Washington, D.C.: Inter-American Developmental Bank.

Spillan, J., Virzi, N., & Garita, M. (2014). *Doing business in Latin America: Challenges and opportunities.* New York: Routledge Publishers

The Economist. (2015). Available in: http://www.economist.com/news/americas/21646273-pacific-alliance-great-brand-search-shared-product-how-deep-their-love).

The Pacific Alliance Consolidating Regional Integration and Cooperation. (2016). http://www.iadb.org/en/topics/trade/the-pacific-alliance-consolidating-regional-integration-and-cooperation,8827.html.

Villareal, A. (2016). *The Pacific Alliance: A trade integration initiative in Latin America.* Washington, D.C.: Congressional Research Service. Available in: https://www.fas.org/sgp/crs/row/R43748.pdf.

WEF. (2016). The Global Competitive Report 2016-2017, https://www.weforum.org/reports/the-globalcompetitiveness-report-2016-2017-1.

World Trade Statistical Review. (2016) p. 19. Available in: https://www.wto.org/english/res_e/statis_e/wts2016_e/WTO_Chapter_03_e.pdf.

CHAPTER 2

Theoretical Framework

Introduction: The Benefits of Free Trade

The free trade as an economic policy seeks to eliminate discriminations of imports and exports from foreign countries. In a free trade policy the government does not apply tariffs, quotas, prohibitions, or subsidies so buyers and sellers can trade without these restrictions.

A free trade policy promotes innovation and competition. These elements exist because the goods can be acquired with more ease. With this type of policy there are more goods in the market because there are less obstacles preventing the import of goods. When it is easy to import and export, the access to a variety of goods and services for costumers increases thus having a positive impact in the standard of living. When there is free trade policy national and international companies have to innovate to develop better products at lower prices and high quality to keep or increase their market share.

The free market and reduces the time needed to produce innovations. This situation exists because the flow of trade produces new ideas. Many times failures become more obvious and great inventions turn out to be part of the national market making effort and a major benefit for companies and costumers.

In 1999 Charlene Barshefsky a US Trade Representative observed "The European CAP, including $60 billion in trade-distorting subsidies, and 85% of the world's agricultural export subsidies, is among the largest distortions of world trade in any sector. Reform is in everybody's

J.E. Spillan, N. Virzi, *Business Opportunities in the Pacific Alliance*,
DOI 10.1007/978-3-319-54768-8_2

interest. The combination of high tariffs and subsidies make European consumers pay prices far above world markets for food. Export subsidies, in particular, place an immense and unfair burden on farmers in other countries, especially developing countries" (Barshefsky 1999). This astute observation shows the negative impact of protectionist policy that opposes free trade policy.

Free trade also promotes the economic growth. One example of this is in the United States. "Since NAFTA took effect, total U.S. trade with Canada and Mexico has risen more than 86% – from $299 billion in 1993 to more than $550 billion in 1999. U.S. exports surpassed $2,350 billion in 1999, making up slightly more than 25% of overall GDP and more than 15% of all global trade" (Froning 2000). This economic growth benefits people of the countries with free trade policy with more jobs, savings, higher incomes and more goods at lower price.

The free trade also promotes the rule of law. World Trade Organization an organization that seeks trade opening and a place to settle trade disputes compels the State members to honor trade agreements. The rule of law becomes supported by the free trade because contracts have to be enforced. Alejandro Chafuen, President of Atlas Economic Research Foundation, noted "True economic freedom is possible only under a system of limited government with a strong rule of law" (Chafuen and Guzman 2000).

The rule of law is also supported by the free trade because the Country that follows this policy have to abide their international agreements of free trade with other countries and with International Organizations having a positive impact in their international public and private law.

The impact of economic growth that brings the free trade also contributes to enforce the Rule of Law. The customs become more effective because with free trade makes process more simple. Adam Smith in the eighteenth century said that a culture of freedom can flourish whenever a great society.

The free trade has a direct in economic freedom. Hong Kong, Singapore, New Zealand, the United States, Australia, and Canada are counties that have adopted free trade policies to be open to international trade and investment.

The benefits of free trade for a country are clear. These benefits are more goods with better quality and lower prices, more work opportunities, induces faster innovation and better competition. The benefits of free trade are enjoyable by citizens of countries that have adopted this policy.

Strategic Trade Theory: Premises and Predictions

The Strategic Trade takes place when the government helps the domestic companies. This help can be by subsidies on research and development costs, having products subsided by the government or having higher tariffs for the import of the same product.

Strategic Trade Policy is defined as "government policy, which attempts to shift excess profits in a oligopolistic international markets towards the home country firms" (Lecture, 28, na). These Policy usually involves subsides, outright grants, loans at lower than market interest rates, purchase from government, etc.

There are several reasons that have been pointed as negatives when applying this policy. These negative include items such as: huge informational requirements, beggar thy neighbor policy, political economy problem such as protecting the wrong industries and retaliation a problem.

One of the biggest problems of Strategic Trade Policy is that if a government protects and subsidizes their firms it is possible that the rival government applies the same policy and thus lead both countries to have a bad economy. The cooperation in economy between countries helps governments to achieve better economies through growth and economic development instead of having high subsidy costs.

The Strategic trade promotes "competitiveness of domestic firms in key industries at the expense of foreign firms" (Nollen and Quinn 1994). Several times governments have applied these policies saying they are necessary because of the existence of oligopolies. This type of policy became more popular during the 1980s. In the middles of 1980s the Strategic Policy concept became popular and several governments began to apply this type of policy. The objective of these governments was to have higher domestic welfare but eventually it became clear that it morphed into a policy of protectionism under free trade. Domestic welfare is obtained through trade and the protectionism policies, which seek to protect the national firm. The protection of national firms by governments results in imperfect competition compared with companies with the same products in other countries.

One of the main issues associated with the Strategic Trade Theory is the definition of a strategic sector. Without a solid definition then other unwanted situations emerge. One of the results of Strategic Trade Theory is the creation of lobbyist that pressure government officials in order to obtain the benefit(s) of the rent that the government is giving.

Another difficulty of applying Strategic Trade Theory relates to the fact that every company need a different policy "different industrial structures will need specific policies and incentives, and even inside the same sector of a country, firms will react differently. In these circumstances, it is very challenging to have a strategic policy that can be appropriate for all countries, and in all sectors" (Postolachi and Liviu 2012).

Liberal Trade Theory: Premises and Predictions

Liberal Trade Theory seeks rewards such as producing best products, best price, and with the best design. Unrestricted and non-discriminatory are the main objective of the Liberal Trade Theory.

The Liberal Trade Theory made an important contribution to International Law and organization. In 1947 several States signed the General Agreement on Tariffs and Trade (GATT) an international trade agreement. GATT system is based on various premises like that multilateral negotiations among all nations are preferable to bilateral arrangements, the international trade has to be made by private actors who freely set the prices to their products, and the intervention of government in economies is a distortion of the market. This international trade agreement in 1994 included the creation of the World Trade Organization (WTO) an important obligation to its signatories. All of these have had the impact of lowering the tariff rates between countries.

The benefits of Liberal Trade Theory have become popular among those countries that apply this policy. "This resulted in greater specialization of production, and undoubtedly contributed to the long period of economic expansion" (Cooper R. 1968). Liberal Trade Theory also contributes to have strongest democracies around the world because their economies depend on the exchange of products between countries.

Gains from trade are a basic principle of the Liberal Trade Theory. "The widespread support of liberal trade by professional economist is because theory and evidence persuade them that there are gains from trade in an average sense in all these models of the determinants of trade" (Anderson, na). The gains from trade are for the foreign country as well as for the home country too. The Liberal Trade Theory helps and motivates the companies to specialize more in their work.

The benefits from Liberal Trade Theory are clear to several countries. Nations these days are looking to participate in organizations as WTO because of the economic benefits that bring to their country.

The Democratic Peace Literature

This refers to the Theory that countries in democracy tend to respect the democracies of other countries. The public opinions of citizens have an important role to play in influencing the attitudes and disposition of country leaders. The leader who wants to have stabilization tend to respect the opinion of citizens because going against it puts at risk of their charge. Leaders also respect the public opinion because they want to be popular so they can remain at charge or have influence.

The voters of a country are the ones who suffer the costs of war. Kant in 1991 wrote Perpetual Peace declaring, "If the consent of the citizens is required to decide whether or not war is to be declared, it is very natural that they will have great hesitation in embarking on so dangerous an enterprise. For this would mean calling down on themselves all the miseries of war and its accompanying miseries. But under a constitution where the subject is not a citizen, and in effect has not say in any part of government decision making, it is the simplest thing in the world to go to war."

Democracies tend to be restrained from going to war and it is more restrained if the other country is a democracy also. Before going to war the leaders make a valuation of threat perception, deterrence, and morality.

Threat Perception is the first thing leaders evaluate before going to war. Leaders see less military threat from democracies than from autocracies. This perception of threat is going to play an important role in the theory of democratic peace. The citizens who live in a democracy as they resolve their disputes peacefully reject violence. The peaceful way to resolve disputes by citizens in a democracy is reflected also in an international way by them. Another important perception for absence of threat in a democracy is to share interests with the other democracy. If the citizens of a country and leaders believe they the common interests they will not feel threaten by them.

Deterrence as the possibility of success and the cost of fighting is also an important valuation leaders make before going to war. The cooperation between democracies, high mobility of goods and resources makes a

Democracy more difficult to defeat than an autocracy where it doesn't exist a free and high mobility of goods and resources. So the possibility of winning a war against a democracy several times is found to be low or even uncertain. The idea of low possibilities of winning and high costs of fighting also influence in the decision of not going to war against a democracy.

The morality also plays an important role in the valuation of going to war or no. Democracies usually have educated it populous about avoiding violence. Democracies can have the perception that the use of military violence against other democracies would be morally wrong. Several democracies do not use their military force to resolve problems inside their country even some of modern democracies doesn't have a military force.

There has been several studies and experimental research about the Theory of Democratic Peace. The research about this topic has shown that "Democracy reduced support for strikes not only on average, but also for each combination of alliance, power, and trade." (Tomz 2013).

Ordoliberal Contributions to Trade Theory

While the term "ordoliberalism" is relatively unknown in essence it describes something of great importance: property rights, freedom of contract, stability in prices and economic policies, and the promotion of market competition (Stark 2008). Contrary the popular conception of neoliberalism, an ordoliberal state has a role when it comes to markets: it stabilizes them, neither seeking to counter nor to further them. Its motivation is to ensure that markets work as close as possible to their competitive ideal. Its central tenet: the regulation of markets to achieve their maximum theoretical outcome in a state of perfect competition (Dullien and Guerot 2012).

Although economists generally agree on the social benefits of competition, a strong case for its natural prevalence is yet to be made. From public policy to private machinations many factors may obstruct competition in detriment to social and consumer interests alike. On one side Angela Merkel champions Ordoliberalism for the Eurozone as a whole as a way to guarantee rigid rules and legal frameworks that are beyond the reach of democratic decision-making (Muller 2012). On the other, many Europeans criticize it's influence on German economic thought and, thus, over Europe (Young 2014).

New Institutional Economics and Trade

The form a state adopts is crucial to its ability to be a guarantor of the conditions of free markets. This is specially so considering that threats to their proper functioning can arise from both the public and private sectors. The Ordoliberal solution to this is to have economic constitutions that proscribe public and private interference with market processes. Much like Public Choice Theory it reminds us of the dangers of a private interest capture of public interest processes.

German-inspired Ordoliberalism demonstrated its tremendous influence over European economic policy in the crisis of 2009. The Eurozone's reaction was one of austerity rather than one of inactivity or Keynesian deficit spending. German rules-based ordoliberalism rejects notions of centralized economic planning, pure laissez-faire, and also Keynesian demand management. Ordoliberalism believes in capitalism; but also in strong governments that lay down the framework of rules needed to create the order that free markets require in order to function according to their theoretical promise. Ordoliberalism focuses on the importance of a conservative monetary policy that solely aims to curtail inflation, as it does on the preservation of competition as the main selling point of the market economy (The Economist 2015).

Public Choice and Trade

The economic crisis not only served to demonstrate the influence of Ordoliberalism over German policy, and through it, over the Eurozone at large; it also served to prove its importance. At the time of the crisis the United States, the United Kingdom, and Germany all responded with Keynesian fiscal stimulus. Two years later only Germany had bounced back, returning to fiscal balance and reducing its debt, while the United States has yet to do so, eight years later.

On matters of trade Ordoliberalism favors open policies, reduced tariffs, and greater competition. It believes that countries with trade surpluses are simply more competitive. Such ideas were important in the eventual rejection of industrial policy thinking in the European Union (Gerber 1995). In a speech to the Executive Board of the European Central Bank, Jürgen Stark spoke on the influence of Ordoliberalism on the region's integration and trade policy, specifically mentioning the theory's father: "Eucken's main insight was that a market economy can only flourish in a sustainable manner if certain timeless principles are adhered to – and, importantly, all at the same time, because of what he called 'the interdependence of orders'" (Stark 2008).

Stark even proposed that given that there exists an "interdependence of international orders," that these principles should be adhered to around the globe. The recent wave of globalization and rapid financial market integration has only reinforced the need to account for international interdependence in formal trade treaties (Stark 2008). And given that Ordoliberalism emphasizes competition it's especially suited to inform the clauses of free trade enterprises such as the Pacific Alliance (Joerges and Petersmann 2006).

Discussion: Toward an Ordoliberal Theory of Trade

Under Ordoliberalism international trade policy and competition law complement each other as mechanisms that spur competition. Competition law fosters it domestically by removing obstacles to market entry, while trade policy aims to remove barriers between countries. Under the Ordoliberal watch, import controls, export subsidies, and the like would generally be frowned upon. Ideals that are strictly protectionist are also considered inconsistent with the spirit of a free trade union (Gerber 1995).

Competition Law is prevalent in all of the countries that form the Pacific Alliance. Where ideally it tries not to distort trade and investment flows across the external borders of the Alliance. Such also seeks to advance the cause of competition generally rather than confining it to local trade. Therefore, State authorities are bound to the equal treatment of foreign and domestic firms alike, and must decide against protectionism, generally. (Gerber 1995). Care must be taken not to let other well-intentioned policies work against the promotion of competition. For instance, although well meaning, environmental regulations may work to the benefit of dominant, entrenched industries by dissuading the entry of new competitors (Gerber 1995).

The European Union also serves to demonstrate that the values of competition must be represented in in trade policy decisions. This as shown in article 110 Rome Treaty on the European Union's common commercial policy: "common commercial policy [must] contribute, in the common interest, to the harmonious development of world trade, the progressive abolition of restrictions on international trade and the lowering of customs barriers" (Gerber 1995).

Discussion

Theories provide the models, structures or assumptions upon which people can make decisions. In most cases when there is a theory involved then the decision maker has a guide toward better decisions. Throughout history people have used theories to help them navigate various pathways in their decision-making. When it comes to international trade and policy-making, theories can be one source of guidance or at least a framework for thinking about policy development and implementation. The afore-mentioned discussion of Trade theory whether it be Strategic Trade theory or Ordoliberal theory provides the decision maker, especially those in governments that control trade, a thoughtful mechanism to help them analyze trade policy and how it can be implemented. We have seen from the information about theories that they generally work in democracies where free expression of information and ideas exist. When there are opportunities for the citizens of a country to voice their concerns or agreement of a certain direction then there is an enhanced ability to make policies work successfully. Trade theories have demonstrated that there are major gains to be made from the exchange of goods and services among countries. What is one country's expertise is another country's needs. So cooperation and exchange of good, ideas, labor, capital and information all are extremely helpful in giving one country a better quality of life than if that trade or exchange of items did not exist. Cleary, knowing the theories provides the confidence, the rationale and the motivation to enter into international trade and development.

Conclusion

It becomes very clear that the more we think about trade, the more we participate in trade the more we benefit. Yes, there are situations that could cause negative results but if one studies the theories, understands the business environments that he or she is working in, then they can call upon the theories as major guidebooks for helping with the practice of trade. Those Pacific Alliance (PA) partners have the human resources, the knowledge workers and the economic and political structures to allow them to be successful in regional trade integration. Having these talents and skills will provide the vehicles for achieving good results that are mutually beneficial for all the Pacific Alliance partners and hopefully all of Latin America.

References

Anderson, J. (na). International trade theory, Boston College, p. 11. A: https://www2.bc.edu/james-anderson/palgravetrade.pdf.

Barshefsky, C. (1999). U.S. trade representative, testimony on U.S. priorities at the WTO ministerial in Seattle, Committee on Agriculture, Nutrition and Forestry, U.S. Senate, 106th Cong., 1st Sess., June 24, 1999.

Chafuen, A. A., & Guzmán, E. (2000). Chapter 3, Economic freedom and corruption. In G. P. O'Driscoll, Jr., K. R. Holmes, and M. Kirkpatrick (Eds.), *2000 index of economic freedom*. Washington, D.C.: The Heritage Foundation and Dow Jones & Company, Inc.

Cooper, R. (1968). *The economics of interdependence: Economic policy in the Atlantic community* (p. 70, 269) New York: McGraw-Hill.

Dullien, S., & Guerot, U. (2012). *The long shadow of ordoliberalism: Germany's approach to the euro crisis. Policy Brief.* European Council on Foreign Relations. February, 2012. Available in: http://www.ecfr.eu/article/commentary_the_long_shadow_of_ordoliberalism.

Froning, D. H. (2000). The benefits of free trade: A guide for policymakers. http://www.heritage.org/research/reports/2000/08/the-benefits-of-free-trade-a-guide-for-policymakers.

Gerber, D. (1995). Competition law and international trade: The European Union and the neo-liberal factor. *Pacific Rim Law & Policy Association*, *4*(1), 38–57.

Joerges, C., & Petersmann, E.-U. (2006). *Constitutionalism, multilevel trade governance and social regulation* (p. 243). Oregon: Hart Publishing.

Lecture 28. (na). Economics 181, International trade, Berkeley. Available in: http://eml.berkeley.edu/~webfac/harrison/e181_s04/181s04lect28nts.pdf.

Müller, J.-W. (2012). What do Germans think about when they think about Europe? *London Review of Books, London*, *34*(3) 9 February 2012, 18–19.

Nollen, S. D., & Quinn, D. P. (1994). Free trade, fair trade, strategic trade, and protectionism in the U.S. Congress, 1987–88. *International Organization*, *48*(3), 497.

Postolachi, A., & Liviu, M. (2012). Theoretical controversies on strategic trade policy, p. 50. Available in: http://www.ugb.ro/etc/etc2012no1/40fa.pdf.

Stark, J. (2008). Executive board of the ECB, 11th Euro Finance Week in Frankfurt, Germany. http://www.ecb.europa.eu/press/key/date/2008/html/sp081118_1.en.html.

The Economist. (2015). *Germany and economics: Of rules and order*. Berlin: The Economist.

Tomz, M. (2013). Public opinion and the democratic peace. *American Political Science Review*, *107*(3), August 2013, Stanford, 16.

Young, B. (2014). German ordoliberalism as agenda setter for the euro crisis: Myth trumps reality. *Journal of Contemporary European Studies*, Jul 2014, *22*(3), 276–287, 12p.

CHAPTER 3

The Modern Economic History of Trade

Globalization's Successive Waves

Globalization waves are specific periods of time where important advances in economic activity such as infrastructure, transportation, capital flows, or trade occur that benefit all parts of a country's society. The first wave of globalization occurred between 1870 and 1914. This first wave of globalization is known by a drop in prices of transportation, the lifting of many barriers, and the use of abundant land. This wave of globalization was also important to the growth in trade, and financial integration. The production of commodities increased dramatically due to the demand of large increase in exports. The increase of per capita income was evident – "Per capita incomes, which had risen by 0.5 percent per year in the previous 50 years, increased by an annual average of 1.3 percent" (World Bank Policy, 2002).

The second wave of globalization took place between 1945 and 1980. After the first wave of globalization a big nationalism policy occurred. This had some impact on trade and international business activity. There was also a reduction in the trade barriers, which created a more active import and export environment. The second also produced a reduction in inequality.

The third wave of globalization began in 1980 where "only 25% of the exports of developing countries were carried on by manufactures. By 1998 this type of trade had risen to 80%" (World Bank Policy 2002, p. 32). In this last wave of globalization there was clearly an increase in the

J.E. Spillan, N. Virzi, *Business Opportunities in the Pacific Alliance*,
DOI 10.1007/978-3-319-54768-8_3

manufactures export of goods and a decrease in the agriculture areas. New technologies and information have played an important role in the third wave of globalization. With all of its import and export activity, the globalization process makes an important contribution to society. It does this because there was an increase of property rights and rule of law in the more globalized States. Frankel and Romer in 1999 conducted a study that concluded that States with a more open economy to the world caused by reduced tariffs tend to have better economic institution and property rights.

Trade and Prosperity

The increase of trade in a State is not pursued for its own sake but is pursued for the benefits that it brings. Essentially, there are three benefits that are closely related to or can be achieved by trade: (a) economic growth, (b) more employment and paid jobs, and (c) higher incomes.

One positive link between trade and prosperity is the economic growth that trade brings. This economic growth includes an increase of capital and the incentive of labor in areas with better return. Trade also contributes to innovation in goods, services and investments. Additionally, an "open trade environment encourages competition and thereby provides an incentive to supply the best price/quality ratio of goods to consumers along with an increase productivity" (trade.ec.europe 2010).

The prosperity created by trade is also connected with the creation of lager markets that have lower consumer prices, higher productivity, and lower inflation. "Tariffs cuts lead to lower consumer prices, although the pass-through effect of this price transmission is usually imperfect. For instance, during the period 1996–2006 import prices for textiles and clothing fell by 27.5 and 38.4% respectively in real terms. For the same period the import price of consumer electronics fell by around 50%" (Trade Growth EU 2010).

This is a clear indication that the globalization process through increased trade has a positive benefit to a country's citizens.

Trade and Human Development

There is a large body of economic literature that links trade with more jobs. Trade brings globalization to the State, which creates more competitive markets on one hand while on the other hand protectionism reduces the size and the competitiveness in national markets thereby reducing the opportunities for job creation.

Human development relates to the enhancing of a human's capabilities such as knowledge, long and healthy life, and a decent standard of living. The United Nations declared, "Work enables people to earn a livelihood and be economically secure. Work is also critical for equitable economic growth, poverty reduction and gender equality. It also allows people to fully participate in society while a giving them a sense of dignity and worth. Finally, work can contribute to the public good, by caring for others which builds cohesion and bonds within families and communities" (United Nations 2015).

The Human development in a State is clearly connected with the jobs opportunities. Trade policy creates more job and better jobs because through innovation and competition. Trade brings more choices to people that can increase the richness in their lives. Trade also helps to increase the quality of work because there is a demand or necessity to innovate in order to successfully compete in an open market.

The United Nations has declared that work is fundamental to achieve human development and that it is imperative and important for Nations to develop policies and strategies for creating work opportunities, and ensuring worker's well-being. When there are coherent and equitable trade policies then country policies that seek national employment strategies can be achieved more quickly and easily.

Trade and Peace

When other conditions remain the same trade makes conflict less likely. The World Trade Organization (WTO) has declared a list of 10 benefits that trade creates between and among economies. The first benefit from that list is that the system helps to keep the peace because sales people are usually reluctant to fight their customers. Peace is fundamental to trade because it helps to flow of goods and creates confidence between economies. In the 1930s a trade dispute contributed to the starting of a war. Protectionism became a popular national tool. According to this public policy each country tried to protect its domestic products and producers by raising tariffs. Ultimately this approach caused other countries to reciprocate by increasing their trade barriers. These actions eventually had a part in the start of World War II.

The General Agreement on Tariffs and Trade (GATT) was created at the end of World War II to help avoid tensions that had precipitated the war in the first place. GATT eventually evolves into the WTO (World Trade Organization) which functions as an arbitrator for trade agreements among countries around the world.

The protectionism previously mentioned creates tension with other countries because it ignores how other others countries are going to react to this action. In the long term economic protectionist generally results in retaliation between countries. The WTO tries to mitigate these tensions by developing agreements by consensus, and solving the controversies.

Another benefit from trade that contributes to peace is that the system of trade treaties allows disputes to be handled constructively. Trade is usually established through treaties between countries. These treaties generally obligate each party to resolve the dispute in using an international organization such as WTO. Before these organizations existed the countries tended to resolve disputes unilaterally. This approach sometimes created friction and from time to time caused a war between countries. If the actual method of resolving disputes that comes from trade treaties is friendly and does not increase tension between countries then everyone involved receives positive benefits. This dispute resolution between countries contributes to world peace (WTO 1999).

Smaller and poorer countries have more voice, power, and development when they Trade. Trade reduces the cost of living in most countries around the world. Goods like food, clothes, and services are lower in countries where Trade is involved. As such, this helps to increase the peace because as economic inequality and instability increases so do the incidents of violence. This causes national security problems and fear among its citizens. As mentioned previously, trade can increase economic growth, which in turn generally produces more jobs and economic stability.

A Brief Political Economic History of Latin America

Latin America is composed of countries that, in the main, speak Spanish. Some of the citizens of other countries speak Portuguese such as Brazil. There are 20 countries in Latin America excluding the Caribbean countries. These counties pretty much are based from Mexico to South

America excluding Belize and the three Guineas. By 1820 most of countries of Latin America were already independent from the Spanish crown.

In the nineteenth century the trade pattern in Latin America focused on exchange of manufactured and industrial goods. Products such as gold, fruit, lumber, dyes, sugar, tobacco, and coffee provided value in the trade with the North Americans and Europe. In these years the economies in Latin America depended on export of commodity goods produced in national territory because the export economy were not sufficiently diversified.

The exports in the Latin American provided economic growth but not enough because they didn't have strong financial centers to attract capital. The principal products in this century were agricultural products. The political environment in this century did not contribute to the progress in international trade because the commercial, monetary, and fiscal policies were not well developed. Nevertheless, trade policies, even though crude, caused Latin America to have access to more knowledge and technologies, which helped producers develop better products.

The 1870s were interesting years for exports from Latin America. The occurrence of World War I and the Great Depression caused major growth in export around the world. The land in Latin America played an important role because the goods that they were being exported came from the extraction of existing resources and were not from the production of non-existing ones.

The geographical place of Latin America with access to the Atlantic and Pacific Oceans have been an important factor for their Economy. Each country of Latin America has different attributes that have contributed to the diverse commodities for exporting. "The geological diversity of Latin America meant that each republic had only a limited choice of commodities to export. Chile, a temperate country, could export wheat but not coffee. It has huge deposits of copper but little oil and therefore has to trade one for the other. The commodity lottery dictated that Chile would be integrated into the world economy on the basis of products that were very different from, say, Colombia, where the tropical climate and mountainous terrain make coffee production particularly appropriate" (Blumer 2003).

The Rise and Fall of The Import-Substitution-Industrialization (ISI) Model in Latin America

Latin America had an important change in their trade model because of the Great Depression. The collapse of Europe and United States economy during this time caused a drop in the prices of commodities that were the main export for Latin America. The Great Depression created pressure in Latin America to take actions. Because export trade was increasing, the financial sector had to establish structures to accommodate the accounting for these international transactions that were occurring. As such, new economic models had to be created to assess and predict the business activity that this new mode of commerce was presenting.

The response to Great Depression in Latin America was the implementation of import substitution industrialization (ISI) structures. ISI is an economic policy based in transfer of riches and commercial protectionism so industries would tend to local demand. ISI policy was focused on creating self-sufficient development. The policies to achieve this goal consisted of protectionist trade, state-led regimes, subsidized strategic industries, and nationalization of key industries.

The initial leaders in this ISI policy were the big countries en Latin America and then followed by the medium and small counties in the area as well. The industrialization in this model focused on the domestic consumer rather than trade with the global market. "Import substitution consists of establishing domestic production facilities to manufacture goods which were formerly imported" (Werner 1972). ISI policy in Latin America also focused on keeping the goods they used to export available for the internal domestic market.

To implement ISI policy, Latin America countries used the pro-interventionist policies known later as Keynesian economics. In the short term the domestic demand provided only part of the economic success it anticipated. As such, there was an increase in greater levels of state intervention. In the long run, however, the costs of state interventionism made Latin American were too high and governments stopped implementing the ISI approach. As a result of this decision, the governments returned to its previous approach to trade policy that seeks industrialization and growth from the export sectors.

Cuba's commitment to communism caused the US to pay attention to the economic problems of underdevelopment in Latin America. The Alliance for Progress was created in 1961 to improve US relations with Latin America. It focused on improving the economic growth and political development to decrease the interest in radical communist political programs in the area at that time. All of this political activity had an impact on the development and progression of international trade among Latin American countries.

The Failure of ISI Models

In the short term, ISI models created increased economic growth rates in Latin America, but unfortunately the productivity, capital goods investment, and research and development were disappointing. Latin America's lack of productivity and efficiency was made evident when the economic crises hit at the end of 1970s (Yanex et al. 2010).

The ISI economic policy of intervention brought social welfare policies in education, health, and strongest and radicalized labor unions. The labor unions achieved several concessions affecting the competitiveness and efficiency in the markets. Another result of ISI policy was the emergence of rent seeking mercantilism practices. This mercantilism by rent seeking became the way of life for businesses and politicians in those days. The public investments in infrastructure were a waist time and money.

The leak of efficiency in Latin America countries that followed ISI policy was evident, when big national companies with goods such as power, telephony, banking, and airline were not providing good or services inexpensively. This ultimately affected the prosperity of the Latin American population.

ISI in large countries with big markets had some moderate increases in economies of scale. Countries like Mexico and Brazil had experienced success from ISI policy but every other country with small or big market reflected differing levels of success with ISI policy. An important achievement was the impetus to create regional economic integration to trade goods.

ISI policy did help to industrialize some areas of Latin America and this created an active middle class. This middle class has played an important role as demander of health and education services provided by the state. This action has helped to create a productive class.

The economic results of ISI policy are questionable for several reasons. When the growth in incomes during time from Latin America area is compared with other economic areas we can see an important delay. When compared with the US it barely outpaced it. When compared with Asia it fell way behind, and more behind with Japan.

During the time ISI policy was being implemented in Latin America the economy was refraining from trade and therefore it didn't have any significant advance in innovation and competitiveness. This resulted in government intervention for protection and benefits. The ISI policy in Latin America also had a negative impact on the institutions of governments because emanating from the promotion of mercantilism and rent seekers between government employees and businessman. This type of economy weakened the institutions of government.

The Bankruptcy of *Dirigisme* Models in Latin America

Latin America several times attempted to create an economic bloc but was unsuccessful. When Latin American countries tried to create an economic integration they essentially created more protectionism, mercantilism, and difficulties for commerce to operate. One of the lasts regional efforts to create an economic bloc was the CELAC, Comunidad de Estados Latinoamericanos y Caribeños. Raúl Castro was elected as president of this entity in 2013. Having Raul Castro, a dictator of failure economy, head of this organization demonstrates the lack of serious economic policy. This model had been based on ISI policies that already had been in Latin America in the 40s and 80s.

It is clear to see the bankruptcy of dirigisme models in Latin America when we compare it to Asia. In 1980 Latin America was representing 7.8% of the world production and Asia was representing 6.8% of it. In 2016 Latin America represents a 6.7% of the world production and Asia represents a 21.6% of the world production (IMF 2016). This shows how the Latin America model of protectionism based in ISI policy has failed.

History of Regional Trade Groups in Latin America: Atlantic-Centered and Protectionist

Latin America countries have been susceptible to socialist and populist governments. The governments in Latin America have exploited poverty and inequality that increased by the lack of job opportunities, due to the push toward anti-capitalist and anti-democratic agenda. The agenda of these populist and socialist governments in this area have been hostile to internal or external investment. Populist and protectionist governments have been elected in several Latin American countries in Latin America with larger economies like Argentina, Ecuador, Venezuela, Bolivia, and Ecuador and small counties like Nicaragua too. In the late 1980s and beginnings of 1990s, several leaders from socialist parties in Latin America gathered to establish the socialism of the twenty-first century. Many leaders of these governments came from applying ISI policies in their countries and now had to obtain their richness using protectionism, national enterprises, and mercantilism.

Hugo Chávez, Rafael Correa, Evo Morales, Luiz Inácio Lula da Silva, and others formed the Socialism of the twenty-first century political movement. The fundamental argument in this movement is that free-market and twentieth century socialism didn't resolve the problems of economic. This movement seeks to attack the notion of private property to give more economic power to government. It is mainly based on protectionism and it blocks the trade policy with other countries that do not participate in this political movement and also excludes trade with North American countries.

In 1986 Brazil and Argentina signed the PICE agreement for Integration and Economics Cooperation Program. This agreement was the background to the formation of MERCOSUR (Mercado Comun del Sur-Common Market of the South). In 1991 with the Treaty of Asunción Brazil, Argentina, Brazil, Paraguay, and Uruguay established MERCOSUR with the goal of a common market by 1995. Chile joined in 1996, Peru joined in 2003. A Fund for the Structural Convergence of MERCOSUER (FOCEM) was funded as a Structural Convergence of MERCOSUR with the objective of promotion of social cohesion. Venezuela full admission was in 2006. In 2012 in MERCOSUR there was an accession of Venezuela and suspension of Paraguay. Paraguay was suspended based on the application of the "Democracy Clause" and Venezuela granted the treaty with the consent of Argentina, Brazil, and Uruguay (Nitin 2013).

MERCOSUR has very limited trade activity with North America. As of 2001 only 14% (Nitin 2013) of the merchandise trade has been with this important trade market. MERCOSUR has used the Import-Substitution model (ISI) where the State has an important role as the main investor in economy. MERCOSUR is not a free trade area like the European Union or other treaties. It has selected economic integration according to selected features such as economic isolation where consumption is restricted to domestic production and limited trade.

In the beginning MERCOSUR started as a liberalization project but the countries were applying macroeconomic stabilization plans that were not synchronized with the liberalization of economy. The country members "have unilaterally changed tariff levels and non-tariff too many times thus creating a poor environment to consolidate gains and move toward higher levels or integration" (Pavia and Gazel 2004). The decisions taken in MERCOSUR where not based on an Institutional dispute resolution but based in diplomatic and political actions.

Another regional trade group in Latin America is called UNASUR (The Union of South American Nations). It is an integration group in South America based on multilateralism with poor progress because it doesn't have any organizational structure or institutionalization. UNASUR has failed because it has validated the political decisions in Venezuela and they haven't question the violations of human rights and democracy that some countries like Venezuela commit.

UNASUR in 2013 endorsed the victory of Nicolás Maduro in Venezuela when there were serious questions about the legitimation of those elections. Venezuela validated their electoral process with UNASUR and didn't invite other important international organizations like OAS or EU. Socialist leaders have used this group to validate their actions against democracy.

A Brief Political Economic History of Asia

Asia has can present a lesson of political economy to the world. Communist China has moved from the nation where 45 million people were killed and starved to the Capitalist China where trade and property have played an important role in it becoming one of the largest economies in the world. Asian countries are well known by their trade policy and domination in the export world. The impressive growth that Asian countries like Hong Kong, Singapore, South Korea, and Taiwan went through from the 1960s to the 1990s is impressive.

Communist China, a Lesson in Failure

The Communism in China started in 1929 with the founding of the Socialist Youth Corps and later in 1921 the Communist Party of China was founded. Mao Zedong led a revolution in 1927 and the Communist Party of China began governing in 1947. At the end of 1949 it declared the creation of Peoples Republic of China. This act created friction with the Nationalist Party. During this time the diplomatic relationships between China and United States were suspended.

The dictatorial government of the Communist Party of China suppressed the members of the Nationalist Party. World War II played an important role in increasing the power of the Communist parties in China. With coordination by way of the Soviet forces they were able to extend their territory. The Marxist doctrine especially focusing on the social class was a problem in the Chinese context because the theoretical emphasis on the working class was totally out of context for China. The war between China and Japan fought for eight years and in 15 August 1945 the Japanese surrender having as result a reinforcement of the power of the Communist Party. The Communist Party of China reached power with "a combination of redistribution of land to win peasant support, ideological conviction, strong party discipline, impressive organizational capacity and military prowess brought the Communist to power" (Brown 2011, p. 184).

Communist China followed the Soviet Union political model. During that era, China was looking to apply the Soviet model of political, social, and economic development with the "undivided power of a strictly centralized and hierarchical Communist Party, the unbounded cult of the party leader, all-encompassing control over the political and intellectual life of citizens by the organs of public security, state seizure of private property, strictly centralized planning, priority security, state seizure of private property, strictly centralized planning, priority given to the development of heavy industry and huge resources devoted to national defense" (Brown 2011 p. 184).

During Mao Zedong administration there was one of the greatest mass murderer in the history of the world. There was starvation, killing of Chinese peasants, and tortures. It is estimated that around 4 years there was 45 million people were starved or beaten to death in China.

When Mao the leader of the Communist Party of China died the Gang of Four, the political faction of four Chinese Communist Party officials, were arrested. Deng Xiaoping, the little man, became the new leader of China. He didn't follow exactly the Communist ideas of Mao. In the early 1990s Deng dismantle the ideas and legacy of Mao. FroDeng introduced important market economy reforms into China. There are historians who say that Deng wasn't really a Marxist but a revolutionary who wanted to see China as a great global power. Around 1978 Deng implement economic reforms in China that would be the end of Communism. He accelerated the market model and as such there was more freedom in the markets and China opened itself to world trade.

The Sustained Success of the Export-Led-Growth Model in Asia

One of the most remarkable things about the countries of East and Southeast Asia is that they lead the group of countries that have come to dominate exportation around the world. In the beginning, the exports where based on primary products, the ones that are available from activities like agriculture or simple processes that doesn't involve manufacturing or composed processes.

Nowadays, the exportations in Asia are the complete opposite; they have shifted to electronics, apparel, etc. Textiles and electronics are the most important products regarding Asia exports. Textiles, for example, isn't something new in their market, unlikely electronics, they have been exporting textiles for centuries, beginning in Japan in the nineteenth century, following Shanghai, in the twentieth century, and from that moment, this activity was settled as a strength for Asia. The electronics area is more recent and it began in the 1960s when the US firms were searching for offshore production location, and even though Caribbean and Latin American countries seemed like an obvious choice, they weren't because of political instability, hostility to foreign investment, nationalization of private countries, etc. Asia, on the other hand, had countries with these types of disadvantages but also had countries, like Hong Kong, that were attractive location for US firms.

The success of these countries had encouraged others to do the same and that's the reason nowadays Asia has a very concentrated electronics exports. "The recent experience of manufactured exports and economic growth in developing countries suggests that two elements are crucial for success: free trade (at least for exporters), and government institutions that help markets to work effectively [. . .] governments in East and Southeast Asia created several innovative programs and institutions to provide the means by which firms could overcome these distortions and become competitive exporters. These facilities included subsidized credit, tax breaks, export processing zones, bonded manufacturing warehouses, duty drawback programs, privatization of customs administration, and direct export subsidies" (Radelet et al. 1997, p. 33).

The Asian Tigers

Hong Kong, Singapore, South Korea, and Taiwan are a group of Asian countries that went through an impressive growth from the 60s to the 90s. The following factors determined their success: (1) human capital – measured in terms of years of schooling, proving that a more educated country has more skilled to produce, the Asian tigers were found to have 1.5 more years of schooling than the other countries. Education is the most important strength a country needs in order to achieve success in any type of activity. (2) Exports and productivity – these countries started promoting this activity and started trading with other continents like Europe and America. (3) Foreign direct investments – the Asian Tigers had the most foreign direct investments during the 70s, along with the exportations; the investments became very attractive for firms around the world. "The East Asian Tigers did not have "extraordinary" features that enables them to grow that much. Surely, the four governments spending on education and investing in physical capital positively affected the production of output. However, they were provided with rather favorable geographic conditions that allowed them to experience an extremely fast development based on trade. Indeed, the vicinity with the sea permitted them to develop their export-oriented strategy more efficiently due to reduced transport costs. Moreover, the particularly high inflows of foreign direct investments predisposed positively their growth rates" (Mascelluti 2015, p. 42).

Capitalist China, a Lesson in Success

The capitalist in China have had major success. According to World Bank data, China in 2016 is ranked in the second place in GDP (Gross Domestic Product) with $11,391.620 billions of dollars and in 1996 they were ranked seventh. So they were able to grow their GDP more than countries like United Kingdom, Italy, France, Germany, or Japan. There are several ranges of developments of commodification of land, emerge of private firms, and formation of finance capital that prove the success of capitalism in China.

China has a large emerging working class with three major regions of industrialization. They Yangtze River Delta, the Yellow River Valley and, the Pearl River Delta where around 20 to 25 million people work. It is an estimated that there are around of 200 million working in manufacturing and 770 million people in China's working class population.

Capitalism has the element of the freeing land and creating property. The urban market in China has emerged since the privatization of lands has become public policy. The property developer in China can be by identified as state enterprises, a foreign company and a private company. The flow of capital in property development in China proves the success of Capitalism in this country. "In Shanghai, real-estate investment rose from around $100 million per year in 1990 to an astounding $7.5 billion in 1996, falling at the end of the decade only to reach $7.6 billion in 2001 and over $11 billion in 2002" (Walker and Daniel 2007).

The building of a capitalist industry and agriculture demand a development of the home market in China. China changed from household products to manufacture goods and to fulfill the market the home market grown and there was import international trade. This growth of the market with rising incomes and lower commodity prices benefited all social classes. Since 1980 China has created foreign-trade zones and this has helped to develop the export market. This country has a major force in trade and exports. "After 2000, with China entry into WTO, the figure leapt to 35% – a level comparable to that of Korea. But most of this is driven by foreign-owned firms and joint ventures" (Walker and Daniel 2007, p. 52). The main market of China firms is the internal market where around 50% of GDP is to internal consumption.

Southeast Asia, the New Tigers

ASEAN (Association of Southeastern Asian Nations) is a geopolitical and economic organization formed by Indonesia, Malaysia, The Philippines, Singapore, and Thailand. This group of countries, like the group of Tigers, also has a strong economic growth, social, and cultural progress. For example, in 1992 the CEPT (common effective preferential tariff) was signed by them in order to adjust the region competitive production tariffs to make themselves more attractive to the world market. Other features of this group are the elimination of all their tariffs on their goods, services, liberalization of their financial services sector and opens to all industries that want to invest in the ASEAN group. This group has also promoted and negotiated free trade agreements. "Free Trade Agreements (FTAs) have been a hot topic in the world economy, and are considered by many to be one of the most effective tools to promote and enhance cross-border trade between countries. Especially in recent years, FTAs have taken a central role in the development and management of trade, as measures implemented by the World Trade Organization to further promote trade liberalization have slowed over time" (PWC 2002, p. 15). ASEAN has the ASEAN free trade agreement, which was created 20 years ago and has the benefit of making them a free trade area. The duty rates between them for most products expectation for 2015 was to be reduces to almost 0%. ASEAN has also established more FTAs (Free Trade Associations) with other countries, for example:

1. China (ASEAN-China FTA)
2. India (ASEAN-India FTA)
3. Japan (ASEAN-Japan Economic Partnership Agreement)
4. Korea (ASEAN-Korea FTA); and
5. Australia and New Zealand (ASEAN-Australia/New Zealand FTA).

Asia is a more dynamic region than Latin America and the Caribbean (LAC). Emerging Asia includes countries like Taiwan, Korea, Singapore, Indonesia, Malaysia, Philippines, Thailand, and Vietnam. Emerging Asia share of GDP from the world has been increasing at an astonishing peace from 7.77% from 2002 to 22.69% in 2017 and according to IMF projections it will have a share of 26.43% in 2021. LAC has a different increase of share of GDP in 2002 7.77% in 2017 5.98% and according to IMF projections it will have a share of 5.92% in 2021 (Table 3.1 IMF Data, 2016).

Including the more developed economies in Asia, the region has even more important, and significant, economic results. In 2017 the region taken together will represent an estimated 26.74% of the World GDP. According to IMF projections they will represent a 28.96% of the World GDP by 2021. This will represent an increment of 8.30% of the region's share of the World GDP.

The total of Gross domestic product, current prices in billions of dollars for developed Asia countries in 2017 is $20,795.54 and according to IMF projections in 2021 it will be a total of $27,914.14 this will mean an increment of 34.23% in that time frame. In the first place, China in 2017 will have a GDP of $12,263.43 billion and according to IMF projections in 2021 it will be a total of $12,762.01 billion; this will mean a growth of 44.84% in her GDP.

Table 3.1 The economies of Asia in numbers: Quantifying the economic potential of trade

% World Total	*2002 (%)*	*2017 (%)*	*2021 (%)*
Emerging Asia	7.77	22.69	26.43
LAC	5.49	5.98	5.92

Source: Table and calculations by authors using I.M.F. data, from World Economic Outlook online database. Accessed on Saturday, November 19, 2016, available in: http://www.imf.org/external/pubs/ft/weo/2016/02/weodata/weoselgr.aspx.

Table 3.2 Gross Domestic Product (GDP) levels for Selected Asian Countries

Country	*Variable*	*2017*	*2021*
Cambodia	Gross domestic product, current prices, billions $	21.015	29.21
China	Gross domestic product, current prices, billions $	12,263.43	17,762.01
Hong Kong	Gross domestic product, current prices, billions $	337.1	409.768
Indonesia	Gross domestic product, current prices, billions $	1,024.00	1,427.88
Japan	Gross domestic product, current prices, billions $	4,513.75	4,895.42
Korea	Gross domestic product, current prices, billions $	1,379.32	1,628.61
Macao	Gross domestic product, current prices, billions $	44.839	52.821
Malaysia	Gross domestic product, current prices, billions $	344.848	531.298
Philippines	Gross domestic product, current prices, billions $	345.308	527.798
Singapore	Gross domestic product, current prices, billions $	304.097	347.317
Vietnam	Gross domestic product, current prices, billions $	217.838	302.01
Total	Gross domestic product, current prices, billions $	20,795.54	27,914.14
	% World total	26.74%	28.96%

Source: Table and calculations by authors using I.M.F. data, from World Economic Outlook online database. Accessed on Saturday, November 19, 2016, available in: http://www.imf.org/external/pubs/ft/weo/2016/02/weodata/weoselgr.aspx

Other countries are not far behind in growth performance. Indonesia in 2017 will have an estimated GDP of $1,024.00 billion. According to IMF projections in 2021 it will total $1,427.88 billion, representing a remarkable growth of 39.44% in her GDP (Table 3.2 IMF Data, 2016).

South Korea in 2017 is projected to have a GDP $1,379.32 billion. According to IMF projections, it will total $1,628.61 billion in 2021, which translated into a percentage growth of 18.07% in her GDP.

Malaysia in 2017 is projected to have a GDP of $344.848 billion. According to IMF projections, Malaysian GDP will total in 2021 an estimated $531.298 billion, representing a rate of economic growth of 54.07% in her Gross Domestic Product.

The Philippines will have a GDP of approximately $345.308 billions in 2017. According to IMF projections her GDP will total $531.298 billions. This translates into a total growth of 52.85% her Gross Domestic Product in that short time frame.

In terms of population, the above economies in Asia represented a total of 1,880.41 million people in 2002, an estimated 2,089.37 million in 2017 and, according to IMF projections, in 2021 they will have a total population of 2,145.94 million. This is undoubtedly a huge market, not just in terms of population but increasing economic clout and purchasing power.

China, of course, has the largest population, not just among the economies in Asia, but the world. In 2002, China had a population of 1,284.53 million, in 2017 1,388.32 million and, according to IMF projections, in 2021 it will have a total of 1,416.136 million inhabitants. Population growth is greater in other parts of Asia. Vietnam in 2002 had a population of 79.727 million. In 2017, its population is projected to be 93.607 million people. According to IMF projections, Vietnam will have a population total of 97.253 million people by 2021. For its part, Indonesia had a population of 212.19 million in 2002. By 2017, the Indonesian population total reached 262.19 million. According to IMF projections, in 2021 it will have a total population of 276.168 million people (Table 3.3 IMF Data, 2016).

In terms of Gross Domestic Product per capita in Asia we can appreciate an important increment overall in the last years. According to IMF projections GDP per capita is slated to continue to increase in the years to come.

Hong Kong in 2002 had a GDP per capita of $24,729.583 in current dollar terms. By 2017 Hong Kong's GDP per capita had reached $45,540.109. According to IMF projections in 2021, Hong Kong will have a GDP per capita of $54,008. Singapore's GDP per capita grew from $22,107 in 2002 to $54,053 in 2017, with a GDP per capita in current dollar terms of $59,870 projected for 2021 by the IMF (Table 3.3 IMF Data, 2016).

China in term of Gross domestic production per capita, in 2002 had a GDP per capita of $1,143.50. In 2017, China reflected a GDP per capita of $8,833.28 in current dollar terms. According to IMF projections in 2021, China will have a GDP per capita of $12,542.59.

Table 3.3 Population Growth for selected Asian Countries

Country	*Variable*	*2002*	*2017*	*2021*
Cambodia	Population, millions	12.709	16.013	16.995
China	Population, millions	1,284.53	1,388.32	1416.136
Hong Kong	Population, millions	6.726	7.402	7.587
Indonesia	Population, millions	212.19	262.19	276.168
Japan	Population, millions	127.40	126.11	123.917
Korea	Population, millions	47.62	51.04	51.877
Macao	Population, millions	0.441	0.731	0.879
Malaysia	Population, millions	24.727	32.059	34.295
Philippines	Population, millions	80.16	106.279	115.04
Singapore	Population, millions	4.176	5.626	5.801
Vietnam	Population, millions	79.727	93.607	97.253
Total	Population, millions	1,880.41	2,089.37	2,145.95

Source: Table and calculations by authors using I.M.F. data, from World Economic Outlook online database. Accessed on Saturday, November 19, 2016, available in: http://www.imf.org/external/pubs/ft/weo/2016/02/weodata/weoselgr.aspx

In terms of GDP per capita Indonesia had a GDP per capita in 2002 of $1,002.907, in nominal terms. In 2017, Indonesia had a GDP per capita of $3,905.636; according to IMF projections in 2021 the country will have a GDP per capita of $5,170.307 (Table 3.4 IMF Data, 2016).

In terms of key Asian nations' individual share in the world's GDP, based on purchasing-power-parity (PPP), it has grown in the last years. According to IMF projections the Asian economies will keep increasing their share of the world's total product. In the years between 2002 and 2002 they went from 20.414% to a 29.13% of the world's total product, with total world product share increasing another percentage point by 2021 to 30.63% (Table 3.5 IMF Data, 2016).

China in term of GDP based on PPP, in 2002 had a PPP of 8.287% share of the world total, a share of 18.11% of the world total in 2017, and according to IMF projections in 2021 it will have an astonishing 19.76% share of the world total product, just that one country alone.

Japan went from a world share of 6.241% in 2002, to 4.01% in 2017, a share that is projected by the IMF to fall to 3.55% by 2021. Similarly,

Table 3.4 Per Capita Gross Domestic Product(GDP) for Selected Asian Countries

Country	*2002*	*2017*	*2021*
Cambodia	337.501	1312.421	1718.676
China	1,143.50	8,833.28	12,542.59
Hong Kong	24,729.583	45,540.109	54,007.546
Indonesia	1,002.907	3,905.636	5,170.307
Japan	31,247.149	35,793.706	39,505.608
Korea	12,788.523	27,023.236	31,393.398
Macao	16,622.924	61,365.288	60,100.911
Malaysia	4,379.641	10,756.834	15,492.140
Philippines	1,014.941	3,249.070	4,587.963
Singapore	22,016.985	54,052.853	59,869.879
Vietnam	440.209	2,327.156	3,105.409

Source: Table by authors based on IMF data, accessed on Saturday, November 19, 2016, available in: http://www.imf.org/external/pubs/ft/weo/2016/02/weodata/weoselgr.aspx

Table 3.5 Gross Domestic Product and Purchasing Power of Parity (PPP)

Country	*2002*	*2017*	*2021*
Cambodia	0.029	0.051	0.058
China	8.287	18.11	19.76
Hong Kong	0.352	0.358	0.347
Indonesia	1.989	2.59	2.81
Japan	6.241	4.01	3.55
Korea	1.664	1.61	1.57
Macao	0.031	0.05	0.047
Malaysia	0.61	0.737	0.772
Philippines	0.534	0.689	0.764
Singapore	0.326	0.405	0.389
Vietnam	0.35	0.515	0.566
Total	20.413	29.13	30.63

Source: Table and calculations by authors, based on IMF data, accessed on Saturday, November 19, 2016, available in: http://www.imf.org/external/pubs/ft/weo/2016/02/weodata/weoselgr.aspx

[South] Korea's world share fell slightly in the 2002 to 2017 interval, from 1.664% to 1.61%, and also is projected to fall to 1.57% of the world total product by 2021, according to the IMF.

Other smaller countries continue growing their share of the world total product. Indonesia, for example, went from a 1.989% share of world total in 2002 to 2.59% by 2017, with a projected share of world total product in 2021 of 2.81%, according to the IMF (Table 3.5 IMF Data, 2016).

The Pacific Alliance countries do right in focusing on the Asian economies, not just because of their size, but also their dynamism and growth rates which can only be called exceptional. China in terms of GDP showed an astonishing average annual growth rate of 9.9% between 2002 and 2007, a rate of 3.4% in the recession years of 2008–2009, rebounding to an average annual rate of 7% between 2010 and 2015. According to IMF projections, between 2016 and 2021 China will have an average annual growth rate of 6.1%. It is important to point out the deceleration it projected in the last period. However, this is widely considered to be a positive development as China transitions from a developing economy to a more mature, developed economy (Table 3.6 IMF Data, 2016).

Table 3.6 Gross Domestic Product (GDP) Growth Rate for Selected Asian Countries

GDP Average Annual Growth Rate	*2002–2007*	*2008–2009*	*2010–2015*	*2016–2021*
Cambodia	9.9	3.4	7.0	6.9
China	11.2	9.4	8.3	6.1
Hong Kong	5.7	-0.2	3.6	2.7
Indonesia	5.3	6.1	5.7	5.6
Japan	1.6	-3.3	1.3	0.5
Korea	5.0	1.8	3.5	3.0
Macao	13.9	2.4	7.7	0.2
Malaysia	5.8	1.7	5.7	4.8
Philippines	5.3	2.7	6.2	6.3
Singapore	7.3	0.6	5.8	2.4
Vietnam	7.3	5.5	6.0	6.2

Source: Table and calculations by authors based on IMF data, accessed on Saturday, November 19, 2016, available in: http://www.imf.org/external/pubs/ft/weo/2016/02/weodata/weoselgr.aspx

Hong Kong showed an average annual growth rate of 5.7% between 2002 and 2007. Between 2008 and 2009, Hong Kong reflected on average annual terms a recessionary negative growth rate of -0.2%. Hong Kong's average annual growth rate rebounded to 3.6% between 2010 and 2015. According to IMF projection, Hong Kong is projected to grow between 2016 and 2021 at an average annual growth rate of 2.7% (Table 3.6 IMF Data, 2016).

Vietnam is another case of stellar average annual growth. It averaged a growth rate of 7.3% between 2002 and 2007, a still high and healthy growth rate of 5.5% between 2008 and 2009. Vietnam's average annual growth rate rebounded to 6% between 2010 and 2015, similar to the average annual growth rate of 6.2% that the IMF projects for this country in the 2016–2021 time frame.

Cambodia similarly shows exceptional average annual growth rates. Cambodia grew at an average rate of 9.9% in the 2002–2007 period, decelerating to 3.4% in the crisis years of 2008 and 2009. Cambio then rebounded to 7% average annual growth rate in the 2010–2015 time frame, a pace it is expected to maintain in the 2016–2021 time frame (6.9%). Malaysia and the Philippines also show healthy past and future growth trends. Malaysia grew at an average annual rate of 5.8% in the 2002–2007 time period, compared to 5.3% for the Philippines. While Malaysia grew at a rate of 5.7% in the 2010–2015 time period, the Philippines grew at an average annual rate of 6.2%. Similarly, the projected Philippine average annual growth rate for the 2016–2021 time frame of 6.3% exceeds the Malaysian estimate of 4.8%, which is still a healthy figure for average annual economic growth.

South Korea is a more mature economy, so it is expected that its growth rates would decrease as its income level increased. This country grew at an average annual rate of 5% in the 2002–2007 interval, 3.5% in the 2010–2015 time frame, and is projected by the IMF to grow at a healthy 3% the time interval of 2016–2021. Other Asian economies have seen better years, although they still represent important markets. Japan is still the third largest economy in the world, but has entered into a steady state of very low growth. Japan only grew at an average annual rate of 1.6% in the 2002–2007 time period, but contracted a significant -3.3% in the recession years of 2008–2009. Japanese growth averaged only 1.3% between 2010 and 2015, and is projected to barely grow, at 0.5% in the 2016–2021 time frame, according to IMF data (Table 3.6 IMF Data, 2016).

Table 3.7 Current Account Percent (%) of Gross Domestic Product (GDP)

Current Account, % of GDP	*2002–2007*	*2008–2009*	*2010–2015*	*2016–2021*
Cambodia	-2.4	-6.8	-10.6	-7.2
China	5.5	7.0	2.4	1.4
Hong Kong	11.0	12.4	3.3	3.3
Indonesia	2.2	0.9	-1.7	-2.9
Japan	3.7	2.9	2.0	3.7
Korea	1.5	2.0	4.7	6.7
Macao	27.1	25.1	39.1	20.5
Malaysia	12.3	15.8	6.1	1.8
Philippines	2.5	2.5	3.3	2.1
Singapore	21.1	15.6	19.6	19.6
Vietnam	-3.4	-8.7	2.2	0.5

Source: Table and calculations by authors based on IMF data, accessed on Saturday, November 19, 2016, available in: http://www.imf.org/external/pubs/ft/weo/2016/02/weodata/weoselgr.aspx

The most important economies of Asia have different values in terms of Current Account, expressed as a percentage of GDP. There are several countries with a current account surplus; this can be a challenge to the countries of the Pacific Alliance that seek to outcompete these dynamic Asian economies. Important countries of Asia have trade surpluses, countries such as China, Hong Kong, Japan, [South] Korea, Macao, Malaysia, the Philippines, Singapore, and even Vietnam have run or are projected to run surpluses in their Current Accounts, according to IMF data.

Macao in terms of current account had a surplus of 27.1% of GDP between 2002 and 2007 a value of 25.1% between 2008 and 2009, a value of 39.1% between 2010 and 2015, and according to IMF projections between 2016 and 2021 it will have a current account surplus of 20.5% of its GDP. Singapore in terms of current account had a surplus of 21.1% of GDP between 2002 and 2007 a value of 15.6% between 2008 and 2009, a value of 19.6% between 2010 and 2015, and according to IMF projections between 2016 and 2021 it will have a Current Account surplus equivalent to 19.6% of its GDP (Table 3.7 IMF Data, 2016).

Importantly for world commerce, but especially for the Pacific Alliance economies seeking to pivot to Asia, the Asian Current Account surpluses are decreasing. China is expected to go from an average annual Current Account surplus of 5.5% of GDP in the 2002–2007 period, to 2.4% in the 2010–2015 time interval, to a projected 1.4% on average for the 2016–2021 time frame. The Hong Kong Current Account surplus is expected to fall from the incredible average annual rate of 11% reflected in 2002–2007, to a projected 3.3% in the 2016–2021 time frame, according to IMF data. Similarly, the Malaysian Current Account surplus is expected to drop from an average annual rate of 12.3% of GDP shown in the 2002–2007 time interval, to 6.1% in the 2010–2015 time interval, to a projected average annual rate of 1.8% of GDP in the 2016–2021 time frame (Table 3.7 IMF Data, 2016).

Vietnam in terms of current account had a deficit of -3.4% of GDP between 2002 and 2007. A deficit of -8.7% in the recessionary years of 2008–2009. The Current Account reflected on average a surplus of 2.2% between 2010 and 2015. According to IMF projections, between 2016 and 2021 the Current Account will come into approximate balance, with a value of 0.5% of national GDP (Table 3.7 IMF Data, 2016).

The evolution and fluctuation of prices are just about the most important market signals possible. As such, the end of year inflation rates are important variables to consider when choosing to do business in another country. End of year inflation measures the average annual increase in prices measured from the month of December in a given year, against the month of December in the previous year.

Regarding the inflation rate at the end of each year in the important economies of Asia, it is important to remark at the outset that there are generally low inflation rates even though there is high economic growth in these selected countries.

Vietnam is expected to see its average annual inflation rate fall from an average of 7.5% in the 2002–2007 time frame, to a projected average annual rate of inflation of 3.2% projected for the 2016–2021 time frame, according to IMF data. Similarly, Indonesia is expected to see its average annual inflation rate fall from an average of 8.5% in the 2002–2007 time frame, to a projected average annual rate of inflation of 4.3% projected for the 2016–2021 time frame, according to IMF data (Table 3.8 IMF, 2016).

For its part, Cambodia is expected to see its average annual inflation rate fall from an average of 5.5% in the 2002–2007 time frame, to a projected average annual rate of inflation of 2.9% projected for the 2016–2021 time frame, according to IMF data.

China had an average annual inflation rate between the period of 2002–2007 of 2.7%. As expected, inflation rates dropped in the recessionary period of the crisis years of 2008–2009. Between 2008 and 2009 Chinese end of year

Table 3.8 Average Level of Inflation (actual and projected) for selected Asian Countries

Inflation, Average End of Year	*2002–2007*	*2008–2009*	*2010–2015*	*2016–2021*
Cambodia	5.5	8.9	3.2	2.9
China	2.7	1.6	2.8	2.4
Hong Kong	0.7	1.8	4.1	2.8
Indonesia	8.5	7.0	5.7	4.3
Japan	0.0	-0.5	0.6	0.9
Korea	3.1	3.5	2.0	2.0
Macao	2.9	3.4	5.3	3.0
Malaysia	2.3	2.7	2.5	3.0
Philippines	4.2	6.1	3.2	3.4
Singapore	1.4	2.5	2.5	1.8
Vietnam	7.5	13.2	7.5	3.2

Source: Table and calculations by authors using I.M.F. Data, accessed on Saturday, November 19, 2016, available in: http://www.imf.org/external/pubs/ft/weo/2016/02/weodata/weoselgr.aspx

inflation showed an average rate of 1.6%. In the period between 2010 and 2015, when the world and Chinese economy resurged, China had an average annual inflation rate of 2.8%. According to IMF projections, between 2016 and 2021 the average annual inflation rate for China will be 2.4%. This is remarkable, considering that GDP is expected to grow at an average annual rate of 6.1% (Table 3.8 IMF Data, 2016).

Japan is a country in economic stagnation, albeit at a high level of quality of life. In terms of inflation, Japan had an average between the period of 2002 and 2007 of 0%, this on account of that country's low growth rates. Price levels actually fell in the period between 2008 and 2009, when inflation reflected an average rate of –0.5. In the period between 2010 and 2015, Japan showed an average annual inflation rate of 0.6%. According to IMF projections, between 2016 and 2021 the average inflation rate for Japan will still be a scant 0.9% (Table 3.8 IMF Data, 2016).

The growth rate of exports of goods and services for certain countries in Asia are projected to remain high. This is the case of Cambodia and Vietnam. Whereas Cambodian exports of goods and services reflected an average annual growth rate of 10.7% in the 2002–2007 time frame, Vietnam reflected a growth rate of 11.3% in the same interval. Other

Table 3.9 Average Annual Growth of Export Goods for selected Asian Countries

Exports of Goods and Services, Average Annual Growth	*2002–2007*	*2008–2009*	*2010–2015*	*2016–2021*
Cambodia	10.7	-1.4	19.7	12.4
China	24.7	-0.3	9.6	2.6
Hong Kong	10.8	-3.7	4.7	2.5
Indonesia	1.7	2.4	2.6	7.5
Japan	9.4	-11.4	6.1	2.0
Korea	13.4	3.6	6.7	2.8
Malaysia	7.5	-8.9	2.3	4.3
Philippines	6.5	-3.1	8.3	5.7
Singapore	12.2	-1.5	6.1	4.3
Vietnam	11.3	4.3	15.8	13.9

Source: Table and calculations by authors using IMF Data, accessed on Saturday, November 19, 2016, available in: http://www.imf.org/external/pubs/ft/weo/2016/02/weodata/weoselgr.aspx

countries are projected to continue to show positive, healthy growth rates in their exports of goods and services, but nothing like the double digit average annual growth rates of years past (Table 3.9 IMF Data, 2016).

In terms of the average annual growth of exports of goods and services, China's exports grew at an average annual rate of 24.7% between 2002 and 2007. On account of the slowdown in the world economy after the 2008–2009 economic crisis, the average annual growth rate in Chinese exports of goods and services decelerated to 9.6% in the 2010–2015 time frame. According to IMF date, Chinese exports of goods and services are expected to grow at a much lower average annual rate of 2.6% in the 2016–2021 time frame.

Hong Kong showed an average annual rate of growth in exports of goods and services of 10.8% in the 2002–2007 time frame, compared with 13.4% for South Korea, and 12.2% for Singapore. In the 2016–2021 forecast, using IMF date, the average annual rates of growth in exports of goods and services for Hong Kong, South Korea, and Singapore are 2.5%, 2.8%, and 4.3%, respectively (Table 3.9 IMF Data, 2016).

In terms of the average annual growth of exports of goods and services, Philippines represents a value of 6.5% between 2002 and 2007, a value of

−3.1% between 2008 and 2009, a value of 8.3% between 2010 and 2015, and according to IMF projections between 2016 and 2021 it will have an average annual growth rate of 5.7% in its exports of goods and services (Table 3.9 IMF Data, 2016).

The benefit of trade is the import. The cost of trade is the export. The openness of economies to imports is an important market signal of the friendliness of a host country to market oriented principles. In this regard, the Asian economies are more export-oriented than import-oriented, but their openness to imports is increasingly evident.

In terms of the average annual growth of imports of goods, and services, China represented a value of 19.6% between 2002 and 2007, and a value of 4.8% in the recessionary years of 2008–2009. China's imports of goods and services then rebounded to an average annual growth rate of 10.4% between 2010 and 2015. According to IMF projections, between 2016 and 2021, China will have an average annual growth rate in imports of goods and services of 2.9%, a reflection of both Chinese economic slowdown, as well as a general slowdown in the world economy. As aggregate demand falls, consumption falls, as does consumption of imported goods (Table 3.10 IMF Data, 2016).

Table 3.10 Average Annual Growth for Imported Goods and Services for selected Asian Countries

Imports of Goods and Services, Average Annual Growth	*2002–2007*	*2008–2009*	*2010–2015*	*2016–2021*
Cambodia	4.7	1.2	9.0	8.0
China	19.6	4.8	10.4	2.9
Hong Kong	9.8	-3.4	5.1	2.7
Indonesia	6.4	5.2	7.2	7.6
Japan	3.9	-7.7	5.4	2.1
Korea	11.6	-1.8	6.8	3.6
Malaysia	8.4	-12.9	4.2	4.3
Philippines	1.0	-0.5	8.9	5.5
Singapore	11.4	-0.2	6.3	5.1
Vietnam	19.0	7.3	14.1	13.0

Source: Table and calculations by author using I.M.F. Data, accessed on Saturday, November 19, 2016, available in: http://www.imf.org/external/pubs/ft/weo/2016/02/weodata/weoselgr.aspx

Not all countries in Asia show a slowdown in their growth rates of imports. In terms of the average annual growth of imports of goods and services, Indonesia showed a value of 6.4% in average annual growth of imports and goods and services between 2002 and 2007, and a value of 7.2% between 2010 and 2015. According to IMF projections between 2016 and 2021, Indonesia will have an average annual growth rate of 7.6% in her imports of goods and services (Table 3.10 IMF Data, 2016).

Vietnam is another important and interesting case. In terms of the average annual growth of imports of goods and services, Vietnam represented a value of 19% between 2002 and 2007, 14.1% between 2010 and 2015, and, according to IMF projections, between 2016 and 2021 Vietnam will have an average annual growth rate of 13% in her imports of goods and services.

Cambodian imports of goods and services show an increase from the average annual rate of growth of 4.7% in the 2002–2007 time interval to the 8% projected for the 2016–2021 time frame, according to calculations made using IMF date. Philippines imports of goods and services show an increase from the average annual rate of growth of 1% in the 2002–2007 time interval to the 5.5% projected for the 2016–2021 time frame, according to calculations made using IMF date.

Asian economies grow because they invest, and they invest because they save. Almost all the main Asian economies have healthy rates of savings.

Some of the most important economies of Asia show important high rates of savings this can represent a higher growth in the long term. Although high rates of savings can represent a relative lack of consumption opportunities, that is not the case with respect to the burgeoning economies of Asia. For the 2016–2021 interval, Singapore is projected, according to IMF data, to have a savings share of GDP of 46.2%, ahead of China with 40.9% for the same time period. [South] Korea, Indonesia, Vietnam, and Malaysia follow suit with 34.2%, 33%, 28.6%, and 27.5%, respectively, for the 2016–2021 time frame (Table 3.11 IMF Data, 2016).

The important economies from Asia reflect a high percentage of investment measured against their GDP. This high percentage of investment is constant in the last years. According to the projections of the IMF the projected investment share of GDP for the 2016–2021 time frame is similar to what has been seen over the last years.

China had an investment share equivalent to 40.0% of its GDP between 2002 and 2007. This rose to 44.2% of GDP in 2008–2009, and 46.1% of GDP in the 2010–2015 time interval. According to the

Table 3.11 Savings as a Percent (%) of Gross Domestic Product (GDP)

Savings % GDP	*2002–2007*	*2008–2009*	*2010–2015*	*2016–2021*
Cambodia	18.3	13.2	11.4	15.7
China	45.4	51.2	48.6	40.9
Hong Kong	33.1	33.9	27.1	24.5
Indonesia	24.6	33.0	32.3	33.0
Japan	26.3	24.2	23.0	25.9
Korea	33.6	32.8	35.1	34.2
Malaysia	35.8	35.8	30.9	27.5
Philippines	23.5	20.5	23.5	26.1
Singapore	43.3	44.7	47.9	46.2
Vietnam	31.6	28.1	31.2	28.6

Source: Calculations by author using I.M.F. Data, accessed on Saturday, November 19, 2016, available in: http://www.imf.org/external/pubs/ft/weo/2016/02/weodata/weoselgr.aspx

projections of the IMF, investment in China will be 39.5% of GDP between 2016 and 2021 (Table 3.12 IMF Data, 2016).

Indonesia had an investment share of 27.7% of GDP between 2002 and 2007. This rose to 32.1% of GDP in 2008–2009 as GDP value fell due to the economic crisis. Investment share of GDP rose to 34% in the recovery years of 2010–2015. According to the projections of the IMF, investment share of GDP will be an estimated 35.9% in the 2016–2021 time period.

Similarly, Vietnam had an investment share of 35.0% of GDP between 2002 and 2007, which rose to 36.8% of GDP in the crisis years of 2008–2009. In the 2010–2015 time interval, investment's share of GDP in Vietnam decreased to a still relatively high 28.9% of GDP. According to the projections of the IMF, the GDP share of investment will be an estimated 28.1% of GDP, on an average annual basis, in the time interval of 2016–2021 (Table 3.12 IMF Data, 2016).

The more advanced Asian economies of Hong Kong, Japan, South Korea, and Singapore are projected by the IMF to have an investment share of GDP of 21.1%, 22.2%, 27.5%, and 26.7%, respectively, in the time frame of 2016–2021. These are high levels of investment for developed economies. The foregoing points to continued growth-fueled development for the Asian economies. The key Asian economies, although export-based, will certainly continue to demand significant levels of imports of precisely the types of raw materials and commodities that the Latin

Table 3.12 Investment as a Percent (%) of Gross Domestic Product (GDP)

Investment, % GDP	*2002–2007*	*2008–2009*	*2010–2015*	*2016–2021*
Cambodia	20.6	20.0	22.0	22.9
China	40.0	44.2	46.1	39.5
Hong Kong	22.1	21.4	23.8	21.1
Indonesia	27.7	32.1	34.0	35.9
Japan	22.6	21.3	21.0	22.2
Korea	32.1	30.7	30.4	27.5
Malaysia	23.5	20.0	24.7	25.7
Philippines	21.0	17.9	20.2	24.0
Singapore	22.2	29.1	28.3	26.7
Vietnam	35.0	36.8	28.9	28.1

Source: Table and calculations by author using I.M.F. Data, accessed on Saturday, November 19, 2016, available in: http://www.imf.org/external/pubs/ft/weo/2016/02/weodata/weoselgr.aspx

American economies generally export, albeit in the forthcoming years at lower prices than those which prevailed in the boom years preceding the global economic crisis of 2008–2009 (Table 3.12 IMF Data, 2016).

Discussion

Modern Economic History and Trade deals with the general discussion of the chronology and development of trade evolved over time to where it is today among Latin American countries and the Asian frontier. The process of globalization has been good for some and not so good for others. While some may think that globalization is a relatively new phenomenon, it has been around for over 100 years. The first wave of globalization began around 1870 seemed to initiate the first foundation factors that have promoted trade today. Removal of trade barriers, reduction of transportation prices have all contributed to trade and movement of good. This approach to international business continued in the second and third waves of globalization each adding new advances that made trade via exports and imports relatively easy around the world. Such actions created a reduction in consumer prices, increased job opportunities, and a significant introduction of technology and knowledge-based industries such as Silicon Valley business ventures. Globalization for the most part has provided a rise in incomes, better education, and a better standard of living that would not have occurred if this phenomena had not occurred.

The import substitution-industrialization (ISI) concept was introduced to attempt to make the environments in Latin America independent and able to produce most of the goods and services that it was previously importing. This public policy strategy failed because of poor administration and an absence of leadership among the countries involved. Countries were not able to effectively implement the ISI ideas with much success. It had a noble goal but did not work in Latin America. Additionally Latin American countries have tinkered with the notion of protectionism where country producers are protected from imports using the protectionist strategies. Unfortunately, this strategy has some major disadvantages that cause prices to rise and consumption to decline ultimately causing economic growth to decrease. This policy did not meet with much success either. As such, Latin America had to resort to the tried and true import/export strategy which required countries to examine what goods and services they could present for export and what goods they needed as imports.

When one reviews the economic decisions of Asian countries, one sees that trade has been the catalyst for economic success. The centerpiece of China's economic policy revolves around international trade. The ASEAN countries have demonstrated over and over the successful techniques that have lead them to become economic powers in the world economy. As such, Latin American countries and especially the Pacific Alliance can learn lessons from studying the decisions, actions, and results that Asian countries have experienced and continue to experience in trade economics.

Conclusion

Trade looked at from all dimensions seems to lead to economic success. Obviously, there needs to be a good product(s) and good service(s) to trade but by and large a country that can master the import/export game can significantly enhance the economic growth of its country and thereby providing a higher standard of living for its citizens. Trading blocs have highlighted the benefits or regional integration among countries. One can conclude that a group of countries that focus on mutual economic and social benefits for its citizens through trade will work diligently to create structures, rules and innovations that are conducive to economic success.

Globalization has provided examples of pathways for making trade a tool of economic success for countries that want to follow certain rules and meet certain obligations. The bottom line is that countries that analyzes their situations and strategically implement good well thought out trade policy can benefit significantly and create a great many opportunities and benefits for its entire society.

References

Brown, A. (2011). *The rise and fall of communism* (p. 184). New York: Harper Collins e-books. Available in: http://www.usislam.org/pdf/The-Rise-and-Fall-of-Communism.pdf.

Bulmer-Thomas, V. (2003). *The economic history of Latin America since independence*, 2d edition, (p. 15). London: Cambridge University Press. Available in: http://catdir.loc.gov/catdir/samples/cam034/2002041243.pdf.

IMF Data. (2016). http://www.imf.org/external/pubs/ft/weo/2016/02/weo data/index.aspx. Accessed October, 2016.

Mascelluti, E. (2015). The extraordinary growth of the four Asian tigers, LUISS Guido Carli, p. 42. Available in: http://tesi.eprints.luiss.it/15269/1/176201.pdf

Nitin, A. (2013). Common market of the South, Indian Council of World Affairs. Available in: http://www.icwa.in/pdfs/shp022013.pdf.

Paiva, P., & Gazel, R. (2004). *MERCOSUR economic issues: Successes, failures and unfinished business* (p. 15). Center for Latin American Studies. UC Berkeley: Center for Latin American Studies. Retrieved from: http://escholarship.org/uc/item/3zd0h0z0.

PWC. (2002). South East Asia investment opportunities, tax & other incentives, p. 15. Available in: http://www.pwc.com/th/en/publications/download/south-east-asia-web.pdf.

Radelet, S., Sachs, J., & Lee, J.-W. (1997). *Economic growth in Asia* (p. 33). Boston, Mass: Harvard Edu. Available in: http://www.cid.harvard.edu/archive/hiid/papers/ecgasia.pdf.

Trade, Growth and World Affairs, EU. (2010). Trade as a driver of prosperity, Brussels, p. 10. Available in: http://trade.ec.europa.eu/doclib/docs/2010/november/tradoc_146940.pdf.

Trade.ec.europe. (2010). http://trade.ec.europa.eu/doclib/docs/2010/novem ber/tradoc_146940.pdfP.9.

United Nations Development Programme UNDP. (2015). *The 2015 Human Development Report*, NY USA, p. 1. Available in: http://hdr.undp.org/sites/default/files/2015_human_development_report.pdf.

Walker, R., & Daniel, B.. (2007), The Chinese Road cities in transition to capitalism, p. 48. http://geography.berkeley.edu/wp-content/uploads/2016/01/Walker_86.pdf.

Werner, B. (1972). Import substitution and industrialization in Latin America: Experiences and interpretations. *Latin American Research Review*, *7*(1), 95. Available in: http://www.jstor.org/stable/2502457.

World Bank Policy Research Report. (2002). *Globalization, growth, and poverty* (p. 25). London: Oxford University Press. Available in: http://spot.colorado.edu/~maskus/teach/4413/NewWave.pdf.

WTO. (1999). 10 benefits of the WTO trading system. Available in: http://www.iatp.org/files/10_Benefits_of_the_WTO_Trading_System.htm.

Yanex, C.Ducoing, C., & Jofre, J. (2010). La industrializacion por sustitucion de importaciones y la frustracion de la modernizacion economica, Chile 1890–2000, CLADHE II, Mexico DF, Mexico.

CHAPTER 4

Chile

A Historic Overview of the Chilean Experience

Chile is a long narrow country running along the western seaboard of South America. It has a population of more than 17 million people. It borders Argentina on the east and Peru and Bolivia on the North. It has demonstrated significant resilience over the years. It has had its ups and downs politically, economically, and socially. The famous Allende and Pinochet governments have presented controversial political, social, and human rights issues. Ironically, during these administrations, the Chilean government was able to manage an economy that grew, reduced poverty, and increased Chile's chances of sustaining a democratic form of government (CIA Factbook 2016). While Chile is the smallest of the Pacific Alliance nations, it has been recognized as the best economy in Latin America with some sources saying Chile is an emerging economic power on world stage.

Roberts (1997) has stated that Chile is an example of a country that has exploited entrepreneurship and innovation to establish and promote a rapidly expanding economy. Emerging from the depths of economic depression that engulfed the country several years ago, Chile has become a showcase of economic development. Chile's citizens demanded the reforms that now attract worldwide attention. They recognized the pain and suffering caused by the old selfishly motivated regime of Salvador Allende. Officials implemented major changes in government management structures that have become models for other nations. For example,

J.E. Spillan, N. Virzi, *Business Opportunities in the Pacific Alliance*,
DOI 10.1007/978-3-319-54768-8_4

transformation of the national pension system gave workers portable accounts that only they could manage. Chile also was the first country in the world to privatize its social security system.

The remarkable shift that brought stability to Chile was the introduction of the market-oriented economy. Fueling this transformation was the harnessing of energetic, innovative thinking, and entrepreneurship. President Augusto Pinochet brought in Sergio De Castro as a consultant. De Castro was the intellectual leader of the "Chicago boys," a group of university deans and scholars who studied at the University of Chicago. These free-market-oriented thinkers brought new ideas on how Chile should conduct its national business. Privatization was one of their first goals. These policy-makers brought out Chilean society's innovative spirit, the country's greatest asset.

The strategic application of innovation and entrepreneurial policies in deregulating Chile's banking system is an example of new ideas benefiting the economy and society by bringing control back to the people. By modernizing the country's legal framework, the Chicago boys pushed private economic development as the main engine of growth. Because of the enormous effort to privatize, the role of the public sector has been reduced to an important supportive function, rather than the lead factor in decision-making. The public sector is now part of the team that sets the ground rules and maintains macroeconomics stability.

Background of Reforms and Economic Development in Chile

The Chilean economy was in a state of shambles in 1973. Roberts' research (1997) shows that President Salvador Allende, who took office in 1970, had socialized most business activity, dismantled democratic institutions, and obtained control of the main economic forces. His political maneuvering and logistical tactics brought more than 500 companies under government control. He politicized business operations and gave jobs to his supporters.

During the Allende era, economic production collapsed and the public sector imploded. Almost all resources flowed to governmental operations. Chile's development stagnated. According to Roberts (1997), the average citizen's buying power was paralyzed. By September 1973, state-run companies registered losses of more than $500 million. Allende printed money to cover public-sector debts but this aggravated the problems.

Moreover, his policies initiated dissent among the people. By late 1973, Chileans demanded that the military stop Allende's economic and societal destruction (Roberts 1997).

This was an opportunity for Gen. Augusto Pinochet to seize power in 1974. Using a strategy that employed economic development, innovation, entrepreneurship, and a free-market model as foundations, Pinochet was able to stabilize the economy and revive the basic institutions of Chilean society. Pinochet's free-market economy called for radically different organizational thinking. It required government managers to act entrepreneurially, rather than bureaucratically. This new culture was focused on making the process of government efficient, goal-oriented, and participative-management directed. It was also designed to filter into all other Chilean establishments. Unfortunately, many organizations were ill prepared to handle such a fundamental transformation. Their culture types and mechanistic processes were often focused on their internal functions.

Roberts (1997) found that Pinochet's economic agent, De Castro, opened Chilean markets by using innovative and entrepreneurial methods. This included the introduction of new financial institutions such as securities firms and mutual fund business. Free trade was another major policy turnaround. For example, tariff barriers in 1973 averaged 94%, and often reached 500%. However, by 1979, Chile had instituted a maximum tariff of only 10%. This demonstrated an open international trade strategy. McGugan (1995) points out that this was also demonstrated by changing Chile's approach to foreign direct investment. The new policy was aggressive in soliciting foreign corporations to establish business in Chile. An export promotion drive and a move to modernize the legal framework followed. These new methods were called the business philosophy of pragmatism. This was a different premise than generally found in Latin American nations (McGugan 1995).

Roberts' research (1997) indicates that from 1982 to 1984, extended economic shocks forced the Chilean peso to go off the fixed exchange rate. This monetary turbulence and uncertainty about the free-market concept called into question the wisdom of the model used to transform decision-making in Chile. Again, serious concerns waged among the Chilean people. Additional measures were taken to counter the new set of economic problems, but the remedies proved unsuccessful. This created even more concern among the Pinochet administration and the Chilean people. Resentment began to rise among not only the benefactors of government largess, but also the pedestrian on the street. A call for action spread throughout the country.

To counter this dire situation, the finance minister, Herman Buchi, came to the rescue in 1985. He further realigned the reform strategy and restructured the process by focusing on supply-side economics. He did not roll back, but rather continued the aggressive foreign direct investment promotion policy. This accomplished two objectives. First, it reinforced the privatization movement. Second, it changed the organizational culture from a mentality of central government control of all assets, toward a market-oriented approach of profit and return on investment. This new philosophy of valuing private businesses' practices as a way of increasing economies of scale and enhancing output introduced empowerment to the Chilean work force. These actions spurred more innovation and propelled the country again toward economic growth and development.

After achieving a sounder pattern of economic performance, Pinochet called for free elections and handed power to civilian rule in 1989. By this time, he had instituted extraordinary novel strategies that commanded a vibrant economy. This was also accompanied by a firmly institutionalized democratic constitution. The crucial infrastructure of banking and free market mechanisms was in place to continue Chile's transformation process under civilian authority.

In 1990, Patricio Aylwin was elected president. His administration kept up the Pinochet momentum of focusing policy toward fostering innovation and entrepreneurship. Aylwin moved away from the traditional values of central control and pursued a path of private ownership and free markets. His focus was oriented to "bottom line" results that were measurable and meaningful for the Chilean society and economy.

Major Accomplishments

Several major strategic initiatives caused the transformation of the Chilean society and economy. The following are some of the key elements that helped bring about changes in the decision-making culture at all levels in the economy:

- **Social Security System** – This major institution was completely overhauled on May 1, 1981. Its conversion helped to de-politicize Chilean society and created a system that was totally dependent on individual investments. Roberts (1997) states that workers took ownership of their savings and the savings rate increased to 26% of GDP. This was the first major effort to privatize government functions, and it gave assets back to the citizens.

- **Industry and Business Development** – According to Roberts (1997), the reform centerpiece was privatization of most sectors of the economy, a massive process started between 1974 and 1978. This allowed the people to decide what businesses they wanted to enter, as well as what economic investments they wanted to pursue. Giving people a chance to create wealth on their own was a major step in development. Aggressively pursuing investment in self-sustaining business enterprises, rather than having the government consume the entire assets, put Chile in a growth mode. This effort freed prices, forced public companies to be competitive with private ones, and reduced central government employment by 67,000.
- **Health Care** – Privatizing the health-care industry was a priority of the Pinochet government during 1974 and 1975. Roberts (1997) explains that this effort promoted new methods of financing health care and realigned the system from a focus on curative medical treatment to preventive care. It opened opportunities for innovative solutions, such as private insurance and quality care-oriented programs of health-service delivery through individual choice.
- **Trade Policy** – Chile's international business was realigned by 1979 with the introduction of a policy that vigorously encouraged trade. Reducing tariffs and promoting foreign direct investment brought about additional changes.

More recent achievements that have demonstrated the lasting effect of the reforms and continue to propel Chile to further economic success include the following: GDP grew by 4.0% in 2013, by 1.8% in 2014, and 2.1% in 2015. During 2015, the per capita GDP remained at $23,500 a level that is significant among Latin American countries (CIA Factbook 2016).

While Chile has generally good economic news other areas of challenge exist. Chile's demographic transition is becoming a major issue for its policy-makers. Because of its aging society it needs and life expectancy rate equal to that of developing countries, Chileans have to be concerned about the future of their country. The two major age categories in Chile exist in the 25–54 level and the 65 and above level. The combined population of these two age categories is over four million people. As such, Chile must keep its large working-age population productively employed, at the same time making sure that their aging population is taken care of. Chile's poverty rate is now lower than most Latin American countries. This took a lot of hard work and good policy development to achieve. One major economic issue that remains is that of severe income inequality. Chile ranks low in this category among OECD countries. One factor that contributes significantly to this inequality is the unequal access to quality education and uneven income distribution (CIA Factbook 2016).

The preceding graph provides a glimpse of the economic turbulence thatconfronted the Chilean economy over the last decade and one half. The rise and fall of its GDP has had an impact on the economic fortunes of Chile and has forced it to change some of its economic policies. The graph shows that the Great Recession had a major impact on the GDP growth. Chile grew out of the deep economic depression and rose to a growth rate close to 6%. This was a great recovery. However, as the graph also discloses, Chile's growth has declined approximately 4% to around 2% in recent years. While 2% is not a terrible rate of growth it does have an impact on the overall economy in terms of economic develop, job growth rate and standard of living.

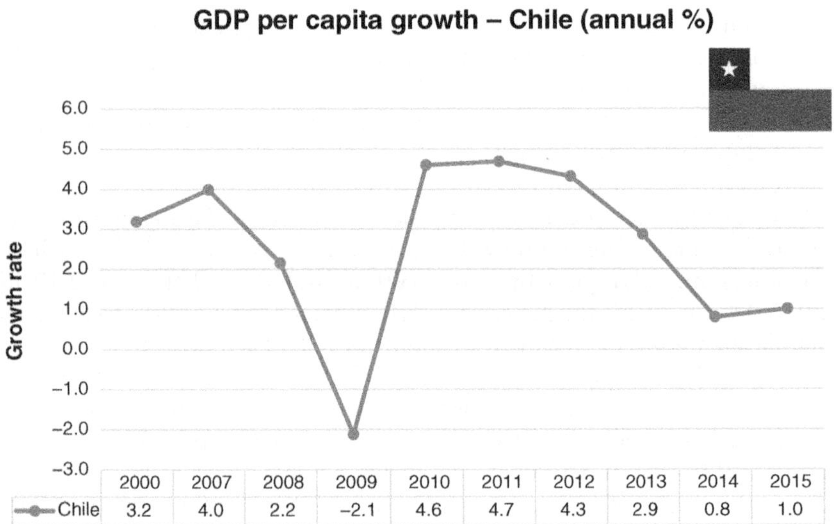

	2000	2007	2008	2009	2010	2011	2012	2013	2014	2015
Chile	3.2	4.0	2.2	−2.1	4.6	4.7	4.3	2.9	0.8	1.0

Graph 4.1 Summary of Chile's GDP performance 2000–2015

Source: Authors reconfiguration of CIA Factbook, 2016 GDP Data

The Best Managers Do Not Manage the Traditional Way

Examination of the Chilean transformation indicates that significant policy decisions had to be made. The first step was to set the goal. The change to free enterprise was not simple. Top policy-makers cannot implement this by governmental decree. They must build an appropriate infrastructure and climate to begin such a quest within a national economy. Guiterrez de Pineres (1997) indicates that this problem can also be observed on a micro-organizational level. Managers do not manage innovation and entrepreneurship. Instead, they nurture it. This cultivation process is not achieved by managing people, but rather by catalyzing them. This can be demonstrated in the international trade activities of Chile. It used export diversification and structural changes in export marketing to achieve many of its foreign-trade successes. It moved from the "traditional" to "nontraditional" way of pursuing export marketing. This approach deviated from the historical methods and offered a competitive edge in foreign trade.

For the governmental policy-maker attempting to implement the entrepreneurial processes, the challenge is often less with defining or structuring the task; rather it is in introducing new ways of thinking. This occurred when Pinochet introduced the Chicago-trained economists. Barber (1995) states that they provided a completely different way of looking at governmental operations. Their business-oriented approach to managing governmental agencies and their belief that privatization was the only means of economic salvation for Chile produced the success story that continues to thrive (Barber 1995).

Chile accomplished change by example and leadership from the very top. Pinochet introduced the concept of an innovation and entrepreneurship czar in Chile. Sergio De Castro's task was to bring together all political organizational units into play. It was believed that a business-oriented leadership approach should create a core team with the authority to implement change. This was a top-down transition for ambitious goals. At the same time, initiatives from the bottom up needed encouragement and involvement for effective implementation. Organizational change will not occur if people who have to live with the change have no part in creating it. Participative programs can be effectively harnessed in the process of implementing radical cultural change once strong leadership has set targets. A culture change, like Chile's, needs a framework to provide a context for decision-making in the new culture. For this context, Barney's model of organizational culture and performance measurement may be used (Barber, 1995).

Culture and Competitive Advantage

According to Barney (1986), an organization's culture can be a source of sustained competitive advantage if it is valuable, rare, or perfectly reproduced. The economic impact of organizations that possess such special characteristics can be substantial. Many organizations do not have these attributes and thus cannot reap a competitive advantage. They struggle to define themselves and to achieve any level of sustained economic rewards. Barney examined the economic value of culture. He found that certain organizational cultures enable firms to do and be things for their employees, customers, suppliers, and others.

Barney's (1986) studies indicate all that could be done – or not done – by organizations is based on their culture. Certain cultural characteristics encouraged activities that have shown positive financial impact on organizations. Barney built on the Peters and Waterman descriptions and developed the economic value of certain organizational cultures. He found that characteristics of excellent companies reflected strong values and beliefs in organizational cultures.

In the case of Chile, Barney's principles (1986) can be ascribed to the behavior of the new culture developed by the Chicago Boys, who introduced a market-oriented method of thinking. These values encouraged creativity and innovativeness. Privatization, free trade, and competition were all innovative ways of doing business in Chile. Implementing them required risk-taking behavior on the part of the government leadership and by the business people who participated in this change. Chile could not have attained the level of economic success that it has achieved today unless it changed its culture to market-oriented methods. Economic development, as well as sustainable economic growth, is contingent on application of ideas that promote competition and free exchange of goods at market prices.

It can be concluded that nations without appropriate organizational cultures cannot expect to attain competitive advantages. Some countries have replicated the best elements successfully. Those that do not have the proper culture often engage in activities that modify their culture to include some economically valuable attributes. Organizational culture can provide a strategic force that moves people toward sustained economic rewards. In other words, organizational culture directly relates to economic profit. The same approach can be applicable to governmental administration. Chile is just one example of a nation where this parallel approach can be studied.

Map of Chile

Source: The World Factbook – Central Intelligence Agency: Chile Map. (n.d.). Retrieved from https://www.cia.gov/library/publications/the-world-factbook/geos/ci.html

The preceding map provides a picture of Chile's topography and its geographic structure. This is important to know in order for the reader to obtain a perspective on its location and relationship to the other members of the Pacific Alliance (PA). As mentioned above, Chile is a very narrow country that borders on three other countries, Argentina, Bolivia, and Peru. Its major access to the Pacific Ocean is a huge advantage for import and export, globalization or world trade. Since all the other PA members have major coastal ports and are not long distances from each other, it is clear that the ability to trade with the PA partners is very easy and inexpensive.

Strengths and Weaknesses of Chile

The following section provides an outline of the major strengths and weaknesses that Chile presently confronts and those that will be challenges in the future:

Strengths

Chile's Economy

Its economy is presently a very attractive economy in Latin America. Its debt to GDP ratio is at 11.2% very low for a country of this size and characteristics. Unique to government financial management is the "saving" for a rainy day concept. Chile has been doing this for years and thus is prepared for any slowdown that may occur. This is generally an unheard of policy among modern governments. Chile also has a very low unemployment rate, which is around 6.2% (Kaiser 2016).

Natural Resources

Chile is classified as the largest exporter of copper in the world. It also has large deposits of other minerals such as silver, moybdentite, and lithium. This mineral wealth gives Chile a real advantage in the area of mineral exports. Copper has for a very long time been a major source of revenue for the private businesses that operate the mines and also the government that has access to the revenue that is produced by copper exports. Additionally, there is great revenue sources associated with the other minerals previously mentioned.

Property Rights

One of the unique aspects of a free market economy is the existence of property rights. At the foundation of wealth creation is a person's ability to exercise his/her property rights (De soto 2015). In the digital age one can purchase property without being physically in Chile. This is a great advantage to the business world. Additionally, foreigners are given the same property rights as Chilean citizens.

Corruption
While many of the other Latin American countries have had a great deal of corruption, which has crippled their economies, Chile has had very little corruption. It has been able to function very effectively with out corruption and because of this it has been able to attract FDI. Foreign investors are interested in secure, corruption free environments to invest in.

Culture
Provides a very welcoming tone and acceptance of foreigners. There is ease for foreigners to integrate themselves into the culture. This is critical to FDI and important part of being a member of the Pacific Alliance (Kaiser 2016).

Numerous Trade Agreements
Presently Chile maintains trade agreements with 22 nations (Kluwer 2015; Globaledge 2016). This is a large array of connections. Being able to link itself with so many countries has become a big advantage for its export activity and it's FDI. This is a major positive attribute for being a member of the Pacific Alliance.

Stable Political and Institutional Environment
One factor that investing businesses want is stability, some level of certainty. Chile has had this stability for close to two decades. The predictable business environment is important and attractive to business investors (Global edge 2016). While Chile is presently probably the most developed country in Latin America, it is still a significant distance from being a fully developed country (Lustig et al. 2012).

Already Has International Companies in Country
Several major distributions, air transport, and paper companies already operate in Chile (Globaledge 2016). These companies are finding it convenient and advantageous to operate in this country and this market. Additionally, they can access other Latin American markets from Chile.

Is a member of OECD – being part of this grouping of economically growing countries gives Chile an advantage and also a connection with a wider array of countries to do business with? Clearly it is a major asset to have as a member of the Pacific Alliance.

Weaknesses

Energy
Chile is very dependent on outside countries to furnish it with the energy it needs for home heating and for business operation. While it does have some hydroelectric plants and small oil fields, there just is not sufficient to fully neither operate the economy nor sustain a business. The economy and society is vulnerable in this area and there are no real contingency plans that could fully respond to problems that may emerge in this area. High prices of energy are a major negative within Chile's regular and business communities (Globaledge 2016).

Economy Is Small
It is vulnerable to external shocks. Even though it has been saving for a rainy day with its cash reserves, the question becomes is it sufficient for the duration of an extended economic shock

Dependence on Copper
While Chile has other minerals and natural resources, it has primarily exploited the copper mining environment. This arena has produced a lot of revenue for Chile.

However, what happens if this natural resource is somehow compromised or not in demand?

What is the backup for this popular mineral?

Exposure to Climatic and Earthquake Risks
Historically Chile has been in a hazardous position from an earthquake position. It has not been hit recently but within the last decade a major earthquake hit Chile and did significant damage to residential and commercial areas. The infrastructure of the some of the major transportation networks was severely damaged. Clearly this is an issue that business and investor populations take note of and add to their list of concerns about doing business in Chile. The business disruption concept is always on business investors' minds.

Why Chile is a good Pacific Alliance Partner

The existence of continuous economic development and competitive business environment has been pointing in a very positive direction. The stability that Chile offers has become the showcase for Latin America. For a long period of time Chile has demonstrated strong economic growth, good business practices, and an ability to attract investors from around the world. With a growing 17 million population, Chile has been focused on transforming its economy into a magnet for business development. With trade agreements with 22 countries, Chile's partnership with the PA bloc provides a win/win situation for all the partners involved with this Alliance.

Discussion

The overwhelming belief is that Chile is the strongest country economically and politically among all the Latin American countries. It has been the showcase for economic development in Latin America. While Chile has not fully achieved "developed nation status" it has, for over two decades, demonstrated a progressive economic and progressive agenda. Chile did at one time was a very politically turbulent country. Even during the turbulent times, Chile's economy seems to be able to function successfully. The consultation of the Chicago Boys regarding how an economy should operate planted the foundation upon which the solid economy exists today. Today in 2016 Chile continues to make progress in sustaining its national reputation as a country to do business with and a place to invest in. The fact it Chile has trade linkages with 22 countries is a tremendous boost to the economy. It clearly allows Chile to be considered, without question a main member of the Pacific Alliance. With the framework established all Chile's leaders have to do is continue managing the nation with an open mind and carefully thought out decisions.

Conclusions

Chile has had an interesting recent 50 years evolving as a modern economy and society. The reign of General Augusto Pinochet created an environment of fear and ugliness for a lengthy period of time. His approach to governing was not very friendly nor beneficial for the Chilean society. It created major divisions and resentment that brought his government end. The paradox of the Pinochet era was that he introduced major economic and business reforms that have made Chile the showcase of Latin America. Pinochet brought the Chicago Boys to Chile. This was a group of economists who recommended many market-oriented reforms that completely transformed the way business was transacted. This groups' suggestions became the catalyst for change and economic growth. Since the institutionalization of these reforms Chile has demonstrated over and over again how powerful market oriented methods can be in promoting economic development and individual prosperity. Today, in 2017 these reforms continue to give the Chilean citizens many positive economic opportunities.

The succeeding Chilean presidents have sustained the market oriented reforms and have demonstrated that such structures in the Chilean society have been by and large beneficial. All of these reforms have contributed to Chile's ability to do business around the world in a more efficient and effective way.

Because of its many ports along the Pacific Ocean, Chile has become very experienced with import and export activities among its sister Latin American countries and with global partners in other areas of the world. With the implementation of strong market-oriented policies and an appreciation of the inter face with democratic form of government Chile has grown, developed, and become a major economic power in Latin America.

Since the implementation of the market reforms, Chile has had some ups and downs but nothing that has had a major negative impact on the society. The political process has allowed the market oriented activities to continue with only limited modifications. Managing an economy is always a difficult process but with the market oriented tools that exist in Chile it has made the process much more realistic and goal oriented. Economic and social goals have been achieved using this market-oriented process.

While all of this is good news Chile has had to think about how to sustain its growth and stability. So far Chile has had no major social controversies which would retard the economic growth that it has experienced. Minor issues exist but have not impacted the entire society. Chile has to worry about its one source exporting activity. It needs to diversify its exports. Presently its major industry is copper mining. Creating more industries that have sustainability and are not vulnerable to the turbulence in world economies is necessary. Additionally, Chile has to think about a better way to procure natural gas. Presently it imports all of its natural gas. This approach has vulnerabilities and could lead to problems in distribution among its citizens. More work needs to be done in negotiating with Bolivia for economically procuring natural gas from Bolivia.

Chile has lots of potential and has developed the instruments suitable for achieving many positive social, political, and economic goals.

Chile's path to success has been based on realistic economic development. It has often been cluttered with pitfalls and treacherous conditions that seemed to present complex barriers each step of the way. The Chilean strategy for reforms succeeded because the leaders enabled individuals to make their own choices regarding matters of vital importance. The initiatives toward privatization, innovation, and entrepreneurship energized the Chilean society. Citizens were empowered with new ideas and options to develop their entrepreneurial capabilities. This approach gave the people and the policy-makers the freedom to think innovatively to promote individual growth, development, and wealth. This strategy was successful in part because an entrepreneurial culture was established from the top. The Chilean people were receptive to such a new model of decision-making. Chile's administration under Pinochet found that introducing privatization and worker involvement elevated its reputation and paved the way for acceptance of its innovative policies, effectively revitalizing the nation's economy.

References

Barber, W. J. (1995). Chile con Chicago: a review essay. *Journal of Economic Literature, 33*(4), 1941–1950.

Barney, J. (1986). Organizational culture: Can it be a source of sustained competitive advantage? *The Academy of Management Review, II*(3), 656–666.

CIA Factbook. (2016). https://www.cia.gov/library/publications/the-world-factbook/geos/ci.html?. Accessed on 11 Oct 2016.

De Soto, H. (2015). Where does the end of Poverty Begin? A discussion with Hernando De Soto. Convergences 2015, http://www.convergences.org/wp-content/uploads/2014/11/Where-does-the-end-of-povertybegin.pdf

Global Edge. (2016). Chile: Risk assessment. http://globaledge.msu.edu/countries/chile/risk.

Guiterrez de Pineres, S., & Ferrantino, M. (1997). Export diversification and structural dynamics in the growth process: The case of Chile, *The Journal of Development Economics, 52*(2) 352.

Kaiser, D. (2016). Chile's strengths and weaknesses. In Casey Research International Man, http://www.internationalman.com/articles/chile-s-strengths-and-weaknesses.

Kluwer, W. (2015). What the Pacific Alliance Trade Gloc Means for Investors. https://ct.wolterskluwer.com/resource-center/articles/what-the-pacific-alliance-trade-bloc-means-for-investors. New York: CT Corporation. Accessed on 13 July 2016.

Lustig, N. et.al. (2012). The impact of taxes and social spending on inequality and proverty in Argentina, Bolivia, Brazil, Medico and Peru, CEQ working paper No. 3, August 2012, Tulane University.

McGugan, I. (1995). A boom heard around the world. *Canadian Business, 68*(1), 58–66.

Roberts, P. C., & Araujo, K. L. (1997). *The capitalist revolution in Latin America*. New York: Oxford University Press.

CHAPTER 5

Peru

Overview and Contribution

Latin American businesses were some of the first full partners in the globalization process. Companies competing in this region responded not only to new trends in technology, but also to the influence of fundamental changes that keep Latin America a dynamic business environment (Robles et al. 2003). The globalization of markets has offered great challenges and opportunities for domestic and international marketers. One of the important trends is that specific customers in international markets are selecting a wider range of foreign branded products than ever before. (Robles et al. 2003). This situation has caused marketers to show a growing interest in understanding the factors related to consumers' evaluation and selection of imported products. The variety of imported goods available for sale in developing countries is quite large. Peru is no different than any other developing nation in its desire to obtain popular products to sell in its markets. Peru's participation in the globalization process has helped its economy grow as a worldwide trading partner. Peru can now be seen to be entering a more stable phase in its history. After several years of inconsistent economic performance, the Peruvian economy continues to one of the fastest growing economies in Latin America. While the economy has slowed somewhat in the last three years, it has maintained an average annual growth of 6.3% since 2002. Public investment has grown and has become increasingly important over time. The free market ideas were adopted in the 1990 and have been promoted ever since.

J.E. Spillan, N. Virzi, *Business Opportunities in the Pacific Alliance*,
DOI 10.1007/978-3-319-54768-8_5

Today President Ollanta Humala continues to push the ideas that drive the market driven ideas. Efforts to address and encourage private spending and reduce poverty are a major goal of the Peruvian government. The Peruvian government has attempted to integrate itself into the global economy with its trade agreements. The United States-Peru Trade Promotion agreement (PTPA), which was enacted in 2009, was a significant step forward in promoting Peruvian exports to outside Latin American markets. Additionally, Peru has preferential trade agreements with 49 countries. There are still some cumbersome rules and regulations that exist in Peru's bureaucracy that are a constraint to doing business in Peru. Some businesses have indicated that they have found it difficult to resolve commercial disputes or enforcing arbitration awards. Despite its growth, the current account deficit has widened. The relatively weak mining production and lower commodity prices have contributed to this problem. The FDI inflows have helped to cover most of the debt. As such the overall balance of payment risk is relatively modest (Loman 2014). Peru primarily exports primary products, which makes the economy vulnerable to commodity price stocks. With this in mind, the economy needs more diversification to allow for more economic and social development over the long run (Loman 2014).

Peruvian consumers are interested in and desire foreign products, but they also recognize the need to purchase their own goods to sustain their economy (CIA Factbook 2009). Economic survey, (2003–4). With Peruvian consumers actively involved in the consumption of foreign goods, it is important that marketers understand their perception of these goods in relation to goods produced in Peru. One way to do this is through an understanding of consumer ethnocentrism. Consumer ethnocentrism (CE) is a means of differentiating consumer groups who prefer domestic goods to imported goods. The more significance a person places on a product that is made in his/her country, the greater will be his/her ethnocentric tendency. For such a person, a product's country-of-origin serves as a signal that may trigger consumer ethnocentric tendencies (Huddleson et al. 2001).

The rapid and widespread changes that are occurring in global markets are also moving consumers toward an increasing personalization in their product purchase decision-making. This new consumer focus can be explained more by changes in lifestyles than by socio-demographic and economic factors. Consumer lifestyles have become a determining factor in selecting market segments (Gonzalez and Bello 2002).

One way that marketers and retailers can understand these market transformations is through the collection of technically reliable information on the foreign markets segment and consumer ethnocentric characteristics. This knowledge will give marketers an opportunity to provide superior customer service by meeting the ever-changing needs of their customers (Du Preez and Zietsman 2007). As such, understanding Peruvian consumer ethnocentric perceptions of foreign products, market segmentation, and consumer lifestyles are the main focus of this paper. The objectives of this research are to:

- describe and understand the market segments that exist in the Peruvian population;
- analyze the relationship between ethnocentrism and the socio-demographic characteristics of the Peruvian people;
- highlight the implications for marketers who are interested in the Peruvian market.

Peru: A Developing Nation

Peru is South America's third largest country. It has a diverse geography divided into three distinct regions. The most notable region is the central high sierra of the Andes. The second region is the lowland costal region, which extends to the northern Atacama Desert. The third region is the dense forest that surrounds the headwaters of the Amazon beneath the slopes of the Andes.

Today, Lima, the capital has come to represent all that went wrong with Peruvian development. One city now concentrates most of country's services and other resources, but they are grossly inadequate to sustain its more than 8 million inhabitants.

A striking feature of contemporary Peruvian society is the massive scale of the informal economy. The decay of the national economy has led to an abundance of traditional market street trade and bartering at market stalls as an integral part of daily life. Ambulantes (street vendors) can be found on every corner selling a huge variety of goods (www.peru-travel-adventure).

Despite decades of political upheaval and social unrest, Peru can now be seen to be entering a more stable phase in its history. An increasing level of governmental consistency and growing economic strength has led to growing confidence from within. Of its 23 million people, 7 million live in the capital city of Lima. The Peruvian population is mainly mixed with an important native minority living mainly in the Andean south and the Amazon (peru.gotolatin.com).

Peru has a dual economy. There is a relatively modern sector on the coastal plains and a subsistence sector in the mountains of the interior, which is isolated by poor transportation and communication. Services account for nearly 60% of the GDP, which include telecommunication, and financial sectors representing 40% even with this active reliable sector, the country still has a long way to go toward the modernization and competitiveness of its service sectors. Industry, which represents around 35% of GDP. This sector has experienced a process of modernization, which has translated into increased employment in the country's primary industrial areas. Manufacturing industry is fairly diverse, with food, fishmeal, metals, steel, textiles, and petroleum refining being the largest sectors (Focus Economics 2016).

The workforce is largely a land of peasant farmers and underemployed shantytown dwellers. Unemployment has hovered around 8–9% annually. The service sector employs 50% of the economically active population in Lima. This figure conceals the fact that most of those included

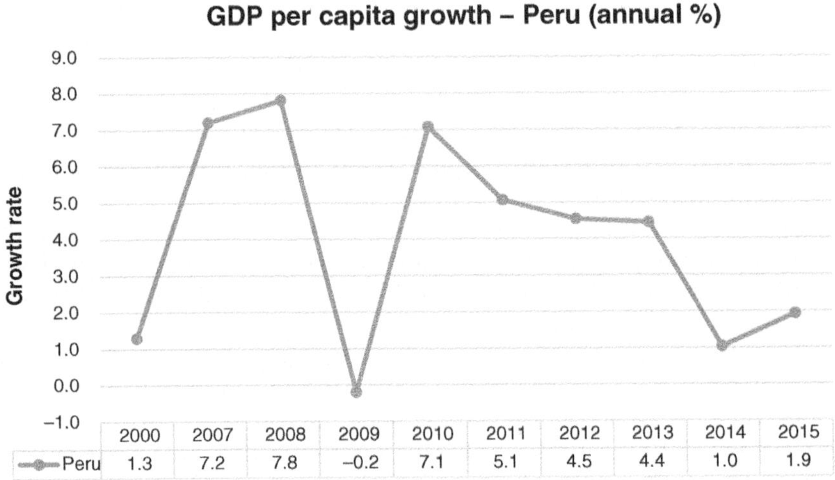

Graph 5.1 Gross Domestic Product (GDP) Per Capita Growth annual Rate of Change in Percentage

Source: Banco Central de Reserve del Peru – BCRP/Ministry of Economy and Finance – MEF/International Monetary Fund, 2015.

Map of Peru

Source: The World Factbook – Central Intelligence Agency: Peru Map. (n.d.). Retrieved from https://www.cia.gov/library/publications/the-world-factbook/geos/pe.html).

in this figure eke out a precarious existence selling low-value consumer items in the informal economy or driving unlicensed taxis (economist.com). Primary products represent the bulk of Peru's export earnings with mining and fisheries production the two major export categories (economist.com 2010).

Graph 5.1 is similar to the other PA partners. The ups and downs of the GDP for Peru indicates that the economic environment has been challenging and it created situations that required more drastic economic policy implementation that impacted the continual increase in GDP growth. The future seems positive for Peru. We will have to observe its new President's approach to continuing the economic growth that has been developing over the last two years.

The preceding map shows the geography of Peru. One of Peru's unique characteristics is the fact that it borders five countries two (Colombia and Chile) of which are members of the PA. Additionally, Peru is able to transact business easily with one of the largest economies in the world Brazil. This can contribute significantly to its trade activities. Additionally, having easy proximity with other four countries just enhances its import/export activities. One feature of Peru that is a negative is its weak infrastructure. Outside of Lima, Peru it is many times difficult to travel because of road conditions and lack of transportation and storage facilities. Be it as it may, Peru with its strong seaports and its economically growing economy has much to offer the Pacific Alliance well into the future.

Strengths and Weaknesses of Peru

The following section provides an outline of the major strengths and weaknesses that Peru presently confronts and those that will be challenges in the future:

Strengths

Peru Has a Strong Fiscal Condition and Generally Good Economic Management

The public debt is low with a financial surplus available for emergencies or other critically needed policy implementation. The "Fiscal Responsibility and Transparency Law that was enacted in Peru have made this possible.

Economic Growth Continues

Based on good fiscal management and because of investment that has continued to grow Peru has been able to sustain its structural growth.

Low Public Debt and Balanced Budget
this is important for Peru to grow and the ability to sustain its development. It provides a solid fiscal foundation. It gives Peru the opportunity to think about the future and make some improvement into other major challenges that face the country.

Banks Are Independent and Have Solid Fiscal Foundations
One of the hallmarks of a fiscally responsible country is the existence of a well-developed and independent banking system.

Peru has been able to create this entity. It is one of the institutional requisites for movement toward sustained economic development.

Tourist Attractiveness
Peru is a very beautiful country with lots of history, culture, and excitement. One can see the old and the modern for Cuzco to Lima. What a contrast. This asset can attract many people, which will enhance Peru's exposure to the world, coincidently attract business investors, and continue to improve Peru's development (Loman 2014).

Weaknesses

Dependence on commodities. Peru has lots of natural resources but in terms of its exports it relies on its commodities to send to foreign markets. Unfortunately the commodities market is an entity that has lots of ups and downs. This unpredictability can create a question in terms of revenue flows. This has an impact on public debt and future development.

Regional Disparities
While Peru has been showing great fiscal results in terms of macroeconomics, when one travels the country he/she can observe very severe poverty and large geographic areas (i.e. Andean and Amazon) that are undeveloped and underdeveloped. To change the economic, social, and structural arrangements to this area would be extremely expensive and terribly time consuming. It is a huge issue that Peru will have to deal with for a very long time. Future financial planning must seriously consider this major challenge.

Infrastructure Deficiencies
As with the issue of poverty. Infrastructure has many deficiencies. There are three major areas that need significant improvements. First is the

educational system. It has deficits that need to be removed before progress can be made. For Peru to become a more fully developed country emphasis on education at all levels must be addressed. Again this is primarily a regional issue but throughout the country educations is not up to par. Secondly, is health care. In the major city of Lima one can find high level of care for those who can pay for it. However, for those who do not have the resources the regular basic health care is just that basic not well developed. Many poor families in the Altiplano, in the Andes and the Amazon region of Peru do not have quality health care. Finally, roads and transport infrastructure. While the major cities have some good roads, those outside of the cities are not in great condition. This situation has a major impact on the supply chain networks of Peru.

Coca cultivation and cocaine production – while this is just another industry in Peru, to the outside world it is a major scourge. Production, transport, and distribution of this product are frown upon in most of the Western world. How to stop it and how to deal with its production has become a major public policy dilemma.

Large Informal Market

This segment of the economy will remain significant for a long time. While it is slowly fading away it is estimated that it will exists until at least 2050 (Post 2016). Generally, the activities of the informal sector are not incorporated into the country's GDP. In Peru approximately 60% of the jobs exist in the informal sector. Generally the jobs that exist in this sector of the economy are low paid with questionable job security. This sector provides jobs that alleviate some of the poverty. The informal sector has both positive and negative contributions to the economy. Depending on the state of the economy one can assess the contribution this sector makes to the overall economy. Even with decreasing national unemployment rates and moderate increases in levels of income, the informal economy – comprised of unprotected jobs and unregulated enterprises – remains an important source of employment for the majority of the population. This is really negative for training (Linares 2010).

Why is Peru a Good Pacific Alliance Partner?

Peru has many areas that investors are interested in and consumers want the goods that these sectors produce. These areas include such products as fishmeal and oil, zinc, plastics, chemical products, alcoholic beverages and fabrics and woven goods. For the consumer, they are interested in and want to buy fabrics and woven goods, plastics, and alcoholic beverages. Other important products Peru can produce are perfumes and cosmetics, cereals and pasta, and ceramic products. All of these goods make Peru an important area to consider for investment and business development.

The years 2002 to 2013, constituted a period of time when the Peruvian economy experienced a phase of fast and strong growth. All through this period, the average annual growth rate was 6.1%. Consequently, in a comparatively short period of time, the per capita purchasing power of Peruvians nearly doubled and poverty declined by approximately 30 percentage points.

Based on new estimates, at this rate of GDP growth not enough jobs would be created to absorb the new entrants in the labor force. Moreover, with weak growth it will be much more difficult to continue reducing poverty. Therefore, Peru should recover greater economic dynamism so its income indicators continue to improve (Juan Ruiz, BBVA Peru/Mexico, June 2016).

From this foundation of respect for the rule of law, Peru becomes an obvious investment opportunity for national and international private sectors. In addition, it makes it possible to strengthen the role of institutions.

Peru is in search of investment both domestic and foreign in all sectors of the economy to achieve this goal it requires some major economic and political measures to establish coherent policy that eliminates barriers that foreign investors may be faced. A consequence of this policy making has caused Peru to be considered one of the countries with the most open investment regimes in the world. Peru has adopted a legal framework that does not require prior authorization for foreign investment. As such, foreign investments are allowed, without restrictions, to invest in a huge majority of economic activities. Those activities with restrictions are very specific, such as air transport, maritime transport, and public and private security, and the manufacture of weapons of war. Moreover the laws necessary to protect the economic stability of investors, and reduce government interference in economic activities were established (Pacific Alliance 2015–2016).

The Pacific Alliance's regionalism helps the partners share their resources, talents, and opportunities. It has a strong fishing, petroleum, textile, mining, and food processing industrial environment. With its growing 31 million citizens, Peru is demonstrating an ability to positively address the opportunities globalization offers. Peru makes a good partner because it has a fast-growing economy and it can provide businesses both internationally and domestically a good environment to do business.

Pacific Alliance's Benefit to Peru

It is evident that The Pacific Alliance important result in benefits to Peru. First among the benefits is that it helps strengthen and expand Peru's two decades and more promise to free trade and an open economy. This process began in 1991. Some of the important milestones during this journey include the negotiation of a free trade agreement (FTA) with the United States in 2008–09 and an FTA with China three years later. In reality, around 95% of our total trade is carried out under FTAs.

Another major gain from the alliance is a key forum for mutual support. Since the four countries share a common approach to the development of their economies, the alliance gives them a powerful way of sharing advice, skills, and insights on how to tackle shared or similar problems. An illustration of this is the infrastructure investment deficit, maybe experienced most intensely by three out of the alliance's four members; Peru, Colombia, and Mexico. The essence this notion is that acting together the four countries may be able to attract greater foreign investment inflows into infrastructure projects than if they were to act separately.

A third benefit for Peru is that the Pacific Alliance has proven to be an efficient promotional and marketing tool. Within the framework of the Alliance it has been possible to significantly raise Peru's profile with investors and global financial markets (Regional agreement 2015).

Based on information Velarde-Alvarez Magali Silva, Minister of Foreign Trade and Tourism and President of PromPeru, has presented, Peru's most likely areas for investment and development are non-ferrous metal manufactures, mining, chemicals, plastic and rubber products, and foodstuffs. Peru is mainly a transformer in the case of plastic tableware, fruit juices, wooden furniture, detergents, and jeans and denim garments (Carlos Camacho, mastercardbiz, Carribbean 2016).

Five areas of the Peruvian economy are the primary drivers of investment and development. These areas are listed below:

- Agroindustry: Cheese; ingredients and inputs for the food industry; sugarcoated confectionaries (without cacao); beef.
- Services: Real estate or property management; software and IT; head hunting.
- Manufacturing: electrical materials and devices; special packaging; personal care; cosmetics; pharmaceuticals; construction materials.

- Apparel: Underwear and control-top intimate wear; synthetic cloth; costume jewelry, accessories common metals (Carlos Camacho, mastercardbiz, Carribbean 2016).

Discussion

One of the main reasons for including Peru in the Pacific Alliance relates to its economic strength and its demonstrated trading capabilities. Over the last 15 years Peru has made a name for itself in Latin America. It has had a stable political environment, a solid economic performance and the necessary growth that attracts people's attention. Recently there were new national elections in Peru. How the results will impact Peru is not yet known. The newly elected president Pedro P. Kuczynski is a former prime minister and a former World Bank Executive. It would seem that he has significant experience to understand the public policy issues and the challenges facing Peru. He will be inheriting a relatively strong economy yet those weaknesses described above still exist and will continually present issues that need to be resolved. There is no equal distribution of wealth in Peru. As mentioned the Andean and Amazon regions still have significant economic and social issues. Understanding the country, the culture and the history will give President Kuczynski the perspective he needs to be successful. Hopefully he can continue the economic roll and give Peru the opportunities it needs.

Conclusion

Peru has had and interesting last decade of business and economic activity. Being a country that also has a major Pacific Ocean coast line it has the advantage of having many ports of entry and many opportunities to trade with global partners. Such capabilities put Peru in a great position for economic development if it chooses to use trade as a mechanism to pursue this avenue of economic development. In reality, Peru's economic power comes from three major areas: (a) the region around Lima, (b) the region along the coast north and south and (c) the northern inland area near Trujillo and Piura and Chimbote. These are the primary economic areas that are now producing many of Peru's economic success. Communities around the Cuzco and Puno area high in the Andes are much, much less economically developed. Peru had some major social and economic issues in the past when the Sendero Lumina was active during the Fujimore administration. Since then political and social stability has essentially been consistent during the last few years. Presidents Garcia and Ollanta promoted economic development and introduced a variety of new ideas some that were successful and others that were not as successful. The new President Pedro Kuczynski, who was inaugurated in June of 2016, may introduce other ideas that could be novel but it is speculated that he will become a traditionalist and focus on tried and tested approaches to economic advancement. Peru has great potential if it could marshal the correct resources together and find a path or paths to successful implementation of its plans. Infrastructure issues are a major concern for Peru's economic development Right now one could speculate that no major deviations from the past approaches are on the horizons.

Peru is a good choice for inclusion in the Pacific Alliance. Since export and free trade are a major part of globalization and market integration is the essence of the Pacific Alliance Peru comes to the table with a host of positive assets. It will be a strong partner and furnish good support for the other three members. One element of uncertainty exists however. Will the newly elected president Pedro P. Kuczynski be as excited as former president Ollanta Humala is about the Pacific Alliance? Foreign policy was not a big issue in the campaign. However, given Peru's rising position as a Pacific Rim nation, it should be an important component of President Kaczynski's first one hundred days. Peru has been a natural leader of the Pacific Alliance; an economic bloc focused on integration, and will host the Asia-Pacific Economic Cooperation (APEC), a regional economic forum (Spotlight 2016).

References

Camacho, C. (2016). C&A GROUP SAS. Published with permission granted to MasterCard and RGX See more at: http://www.mastercardbiz.com/caribbean/2016/03/21/business-opportunities-with-the-pacific-alliance/#sthash.Q1sTdNZK.dpuf. Master Card Biz Caribbean.

CIA Factbook. (2009). http://www.cia.gov/library/publications/download/download/2009

Du Preez, R., Visser, E. M., & Zietsman, L. (2007). Profiling male apparel consumer's lifestyle, shopping orientation, patronage behavior and shopping mall behavior, managing dynamics. *Journal is Managing Dynamics*, *16*(1), 2–19.

Economist. (2010, September 11). Societies on the move. *The Economist*, Vol. 396, issue 8699, pp. SS12–SS16. London.

Focus Economics. (2016). http://www.focus-economics.com/countries/peru. Accessed on 5 Nov 2016.

Gonzalez, A., & Bello, L. (2002). The construct "lifestyle" in market segmentation: The behavior of tourist consumers. *European Journal of Marketing*, *36*(1), 51–85.

Huddleston, P., Linda, K., & Leslie, S. (2001). Consumer ethnocentrism, product and polish consumers' perceptions of quality. *International Journal of Retail and Distribution Management*, *29*(5), 236–246. http://dx.doi.org/10.1108/09590550110390896.

Linares, L. A. (2010). Informal economy budget analysis in Peru and metropolitan lima WIEGO Working Paper 13, WIEGO Women in Informal Employment Globalizing and Organizing, pp. 1–40.

Loman, H. (2014) Country Report, Rabobank Economic Research. http://economics.rabobank.com/publications/2014/october/country.

Pacific Alliance Business and Investment Guide. (2015/2016). el Dorado Investments, February 2015, http://www.ey.com/Publication/vwLUAssets/Gu%ADa_de_la_Alianza_Pac%C3%ADfico_2015_2016/$FILE/EY_g uia_alianza_pacifico_2015_2016_ingles.pdf.

Post, C. (2016). Peru's Informal economy to persist for decades: report Peru Reports. http://perureports.com/2016/05/10/perus-informal-economy-persist-decades-report/.

Regional agreement key to Peru trade strategy, Oxford Business Group. (2015). http://www.oxfordbusinessgroup.com/analysis/specifics-pacific-new-regional-agreement-spearheads-peru's-trade-strategy.

Robles, F., Wiess, N., & Torres-Baumgarten, G. (2003). *Business in emerging Latin America*. NewYork-London: Routledge – Taylor &Francis.

Ruiz, Juan, BBVA Peru Mexico. (2016). https://info.bbva.com/en/news/economy/top-investment-banks-fight-retain-talent-heres-theyre/.

Spotlight. (2016). What are top four issues President-elect Kaczynski must address in his first one hundred days in office?. http://publications.atlanticcouncil.org/spotlight-peru/.

CHAPTER 6

Colombia

Can a Sound Economy Thrive Amid Political Turmoil?

Colombia is an interesting country in that it has many different features that make it, in many ways, unlike the characteristics that exist among the other Latin American countries. For example it is the only South American country with a Caribbean and a Pacific coastline. Moreover, it has a five-country frontier with Panama, Venezuela, Brazil, Peru, and Ecuador. Its capital is Borgata located in the center of the country. Colombia is the third largest economy in Latin America. Over the last decade it has demonstrated an ability to reverse downward trends and increased its ability to endure external turbulence both economically and politically (CIAfactbook 2016).

Relatively speaking, Colombia has a large population with approximately 48 million citizens. It is second to Mexico in population levels as a member of the Pacific Alliance. Some of the reasons why the population has not grown as fast as other countries are due to the limited or insignificant immigration. Major hesitation toward immigrating to Colombia has resulted due to the long-held reputation as a violent and dangerous country to live in. This is primarily caused by the history of drug trafficking and guerrilla activity that has been prevalent in Colombia over the last two and a half decades (Encyclopedia.com 2016). Recently, however, the Revolutionary Armed Forces of Colombia (FARC) came to a tentative peace agreement. With this news it is hopeful that the two sides can begin to make Colombia much stronger.

J.E. Spillan, N. Virzi, *Business Opportunities in the Pacific Alliance*,
DOI 10.1007/978-3-319-54768-8_6

Colombia is an exporting country. Among its more powerful exports are oil and energy products. Oil exports comprise in excess of 50% of its annual exports. It also exports large amounts of coffee and cut flowers. Overall we can say that Colombia's economic fundamentals are sound. Generally, the macroeconomic stability and openness to worldwide trade has been robust. The government has instituted reforms that have improved the regulatory structure and has centered its attention on strengthening the private sector. By and large the public debt is under control and has allowed an open market and public finance transparency.

As these economic policies have been implemented and produced success, the rate of inflation has decreased along with the level of poverty. Reducing both of these items can help reduce the level of inequality that has existed in Colombia. There has been major improvement in the structure and operation of the Colombian society and economy. Because of conscientious diplomacy, hard work, and compromise the country has been transformed into a different place than it was 15 years ago. President Alvaro Uribe was instrumental in getting rid of the major rebel insurgents. President Juan Manuel Santos has continued the efforts effectively by moving the peace movement forward toward total completion. All of this diligence has allowed the middle class to grow and as stated above allowed the poverty level to progressively decline. Additionally the entrepreneurial spirit has returned. With a well-educated workforce a strong business class now is able to manifest itself and realize many of its valued expectations. This progress and transformation (stability and certainty) has allowed Colombia become 34th in the World Bank's "Doing Business" index. This is a major change from 53 that was recorded in 2013 (World Bank 2016). This rating is even more significant than Brazil, Mexico, Belgium and Italy.

Graph 6.1 provides a view of Colombia's GDP vacillation over a ten-year period of time.

Graph 2 presents the ebbs and flows of Colombia's GDP line in percentage rate of change in about a twelve-year period of time. Colombia has had some good times and not-so-good times. One can see that the major downturn occurred almost exactly when the Great Recession transpired. One can also see that while Colombia did recover it did not maintain a major recovery but has stayed in the 4.5% GDP range for the last couple of years. It looks like the last couple of years have demonstrated that some good macroeconomic policies have been producing results in terms of growth and development in Colombia.

Free trade has been aggressively pursued. Companies that make Kia, Hyundai, and other automobiles have become a common sight on the

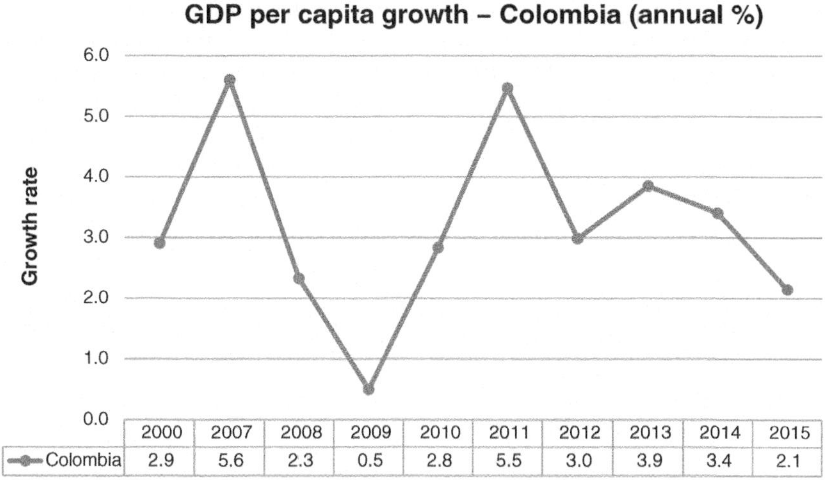

	2000	2007	2008	2009	2010	2011	2012	2013	2014	2015
Colombia	2.9	5.6	2.3	0.5	2.8	5.5	3.0	3.9	3.4	2.1

Graph 6.1 GDP Per Capita Growth Colombia (annual %)

Source: Adapted from Banco de La Republica de Colombia, January 2015 estimated

streets of Colombia. Additionally, companies like Exito, Bancolombia, and EPM utility company have become mainstays in Colombia's business environment. This foreign direct investment (FDI) has accelerated the economic engines and promoted economic growth. Trade has been an engine for economic development and a path for future development.

While Colombia is a safer place the introduction of new businesses and business development has manifested a real vulnerability in Colombia's infrastructure and ability to move goods. One of the outcomes of this determined trade effort is the lack of a solid and reliable infrastructure. It has become one of the major obstacles to pervasive economic development (Chan 2015). Presently, air transport and river transport are the major effective means of transportation. The river transportation has become the major mover of freight and cargo. Air transport has been a major transporter of people. In fact, the air transportation in Colombia is excellent. The service is well developed and a critical means of movement of people in Colombia. With the public budget extremely limited, a public private partnership or the PPP model has emerged as a possible solution to this development issue. The designs for a suitable infrastructure are already available. The Colombians are ahead of the game in this endeavor. They have recognized that resolving the infrastructure and peace issues are the two major obstacles to making Colombia a major business in the global arena. Pursuing this path of development requires cooperation among several partners: (a) Colombian government, (b) private sector businesses, (c) FARC – peace committee, and (d) global partners who are willing to invest in Colombia (Chan 2015). Once all of these partners can focus on the same goals then the development of a progressive, forward-moving business

The Map of Colombia

Source: The World Factbook – Central Intelligence Agency: Colombia Map. (n.d.). Retrieved from https://www.cia.gov/library/publications/the-world-factbook/geos/co.html

environment can be established and attract more stable and permanent businesses. The factors of endowment, the will, and the capabilities are all available. Leadership and dedication to goal attainment are the key elements that need to be addressed in Colombia. Colombia's greatest assets are its people. They are generally willing to move forward. They are tired of instability and war. They want Colombia to participate in the Global business environment because they have recognized that when Colombia is recognized in world business then the economics of Colombia are enhanced and the individual lives of the Colombian people are improved. It is a win/win situation (Chan 2015).

The preceding map shows exactly where Colombia is located among other Latin American Countries. Excellent access to the Panama Canal is a factor of endowment that promotes the strong exporting business of Columbia, which has great seaports. Additionally, one can see that Colombia has almost immediate access to five other country boarders, which increases the opportunities for trade and business development. Finally, Colombia is close to Central America and the United States; both areas are additional locations where great business opportunities reside.

Colombia's Strengths and Weaknesses

The following section provides an outline of the major strengths and weaknesses that Colombia presently confronts and those that will be challenges in the future.

Strengths

Access to Two Oceans
This is a major asset. Having two major bodies of water that can provide ports of entry for goods from all over the world is a huge advantage. It opens up many opportunities. It does require significant attention with regard to maintenance of ports, equipment, and access. The ports are not fully useful unless they have the infrastructure to dispatch and receive goods from worldwide markets.

Large Population
Colombia has a population that is hovering around 50 million people. That is a lot of citizens and a huge market for goods and services. It also provides a large resource for labor needs. This human resource provides

the necessary factor of production that can help Colombia make goods and provide services. A large population helps the consumption function and provides consumers of products and services, hence initiating and promoting the multiplier effect in the economy. This has a major impact on the country's GDP and economic growth.

Plentiful Factors of Endowment (Natural Resources)
The existence of these resources furnishes the raw materials for production of finished goods for domestic and global markets. The minerals and other raw materials from the extractive industries can be exported to neighboring and distant global markets. The demand for minerals in global markets seems to be unending; hence, Colombia can exploit this need worldwide.

Tourism Opportunities
Now that the peace has been restored Colombia with its enormous beauty throughout the country can begin to exploit these assets to the maximum. The tourism industry incredibly potential. Each day new choices for touristic ventures arise. As the industry organizes and begins to return to the active state it was before the instability, additional opportunities will arise and fortify the touristic industries capabilities.

Economic Policy That Makes Sense
Colombia's politicians appear to have figured out that the best economic policy is the free market and the ability to promote solid macroeconomic policy and economic development. In cooperation with the business sector (Private Partners) Colombia's politicians have created an economy that is durable, stable, growing and is on a path that will help the country achieve many of its development goals (CoFace 2016).

Stable Institutions
One of the hallmarks of a stable economy is the existence of stable institutions. When citizens know that the government institutions, NGOs like hospitals, and care-taking organizations provide consistent and reliable service delivery then people and businesses have confidence in their ability to increase the quality of living for the country's citizenry. Stable institutions generally produce stable societies. With stable institutions it is much easier to attract and sustain businesses. They want to stay and do business because the environment has a level of predictability. When there is uncertainty businesses shy away from taking risks and do not want to enter into entrepreneurial activities.

Reliable and Sturdy Banking System

One of the main characteristics of a sound economy and stable environment for doing business is a reliable and sturdy banking system. History has demonstrated that when there is fear of instability in the financial segment of the society then many people become nervous. We have seen that in the 2009 financial calamity that engulfed the world and the recent financial problems in Greece. A sound banking system is at the core of a stable society and as such it can promote robust economic activity and continuous business development (CoFace 2016).

Weaknesses

Susceptible to Raw Material Prices

As raw material prices change so do the prices of many other goods. That activity has an impact on the marketability of products. Trying to make sure that there are stable prices among raw material suppliers is important. Acquiring market intelligence about which suppliers provide the best pricing schedule is a fundamental requirement for businesses and policy makers.

Predisposition to the American Economic Cycle

Since Colombia exports a lot of goods to the United States its economic stability has a linkage to the American economic cycle. How goes the US economy so goes the Colombian economic cycle. This dependence on the large American market makes Colombia vulnerable and produces some unwanted uncertainties (Coface 2016).

Infrastructure Deficiencies

As mentioned earlier in this chapter, road and port infrastructure have major deficiencies that have had and are presently having a major impact on business development. Road transportation is especially prominent in the discussion. Lack of good solid roads to transport goods is a major problem for businesses. While Colombia has borders on two major seas, some of its ports are not up to speed and are not capable of accepting some of the major vessels that are vital for importing and exporting goods to the country. Major attention the infrastructure is needed immediately. The issue is how to pay for it and finance the magnitude of the infrastructure need.

Country Security Questions Related to Drug Trafficking
Colombia has a long history of drug trafficking. The city of Medellin was the home base of Pablo Escobar. For a long time Colombia had a reputation as the drug capital of South America. This status had a major negative impact on the economic stability of the country and the overall safety of the citizens of the country. Since the death of Mr. Escobar, there has been a significant reduction in violence. Coincidently there has been a major reduction in violence due to the long civil war that has been occurring in Colombia. Both of these incidents/circumstances created a huge problem for businesses, government, and citizens. Over the last decade the reduction in violence and war activity both from the civil war and from the drug-related scourge has allowed Colombia to take a more productive path toward significant stability. It has become a place of choice for FDI among Latin American countries.

Lack of Sufficient and World-Class Educational and Health-Care Services
Everyone knows that a strong economy depends on a well-trained workforce. The main factor in achieving a well-trained workforce is having a strong and appropriate educational system. Colombia has not been able to achieve world-class education that is competitive with all of its global partners. While positive progress has been made more rigorous implementation of education structures, content, curriculum, and development is critical to the economy's advancement (CoFace 2016).

Health-care service delivery depends on where a person resides in Colombia, Borgata, or Medellin is major cities, which have a full array of medical services. A person who lives in the rural areas may not find immediate access to high-quality medical/health services. Since the roads are not well developed in remote areas it is sometimes difficult for people to get the level of health care that would be normally available to population. This is a negative that needs to be addressed. It requires resources that have not been immediately available in Colombia.

Existence of Informal Sector
This is the part of the Colombian economy that is neither taxed nor monitored by any government department. Generally, the activities of the informal sector are not incorporated into the country's GDP. In Colombia approximately 60% of the jobs exist in the informal sector. Generally the jobs that exist in this sector of the economy are low paid with questionable job security. This sector provides jobs that alleviate

some of the poverty. The informal sector has both positive and negative contributions to the economy. Depending on the state of the economy one can assess the contribution this sector makes to the overall economy.

Corruption in Political Institutions Like Judiciary, Legislature, and Executive Office

These entities are slow in transacting business. Major delays are inevitable. Many times they do not meet the essential needs of the population. They are easily changed by a majority of the voters' dissatisfaction. Unfortunately, these political bodies are subject to various forms of corruption. Economies with large amounts of corruption, like Colombia, are not able to function properly because the corruption become a constraint and does not allow the economy to operate freely. Corruption weakens country institutions and has a major negative impact on the country's economy and its population.

Structural unemployment, inequality, and poverty

The demands of the twenty-first century have forced economies like Colombia to change ways. Technology and globalization have forced Colombia policy makers and business people to transform their approaches to economic development. These changes require different skills sets, some of which many Colombians do not have nor will ever be able to acquire. As such, people employed in some agricultural or labor positions may not be able to obtain jobs that have been lost because their industry has evaporated. The indroduction of modern advanced equipment has eliminated many of the manual labor jobs that were historically very plentiful in the agricultural industry (Coface 2016).

Why Colombia is a Good Pacific Alliance Partner

Over the last decade, Colombia has become one of the most attractive destinations for investments in Latin America. This circumstance is primarily due to its institutional stability and, its interconnectedness with the world. Additionally, Colombia has made commitments to economic development that are driving investment, and its obvious strategic location in Latin America all makes for an important attraction for potential investors. Colombia also has an innovation strategy and its competitive legal framework that gives companies confidence that they can invest in Colombia and generate a good return on their investment. Colombia's regulatory framework is focused on appeal to foreign investment. This is attractive to investors because it is a mechanism to protect international investments and reduce unnecessary barriers to business development. Currently, Colombia has Free Trade Agreements with Mexico, the United States, Chile, Canada, the European Union, Switzerland and Liechtenstein, Venezuela, the Republic of El Salvador, Honduras, Guatemala, Cuba, and Nicaragua. Besides this Colombia has trade agreements with the Andean Community of Nations and Caribbean community (Caricom) (Pacific Alliance 2015–2016).

For a long period of time Colombia was written off as a possible partner for any organization. The turbulence that played out across the country for more than a decade dissuaded potential business people from even thinking about Colombia as an investment destination. Fortunately changes in governments and changes in attitudes provided an environment that produced public and private policies that promoted business development and investment. This new philosophy or the introduction of new policies have created different approaches to economic growth which emphasize doing business in global markets and with world trade makers. With a large and growing population of 48 million people Colombia provides a large domestic and international market. Now that almost total stability has come to the country, there are an abundance of business investment opportunities for those interested in making money.

Maria Claudia Lacouture Pinedo, President of ProColombia, Colombia, posits that there are about 24 valuable groups with Pacific Alliance trade partners. These relationships or connections have both short- and long-haul capabilities for investment and economic development. These connections are outlined below:

- Colombia – Chile: agroindustry, cosmetics, containers, and packaging
- Colombia – Peru: colorants and dressmaking
- Colombia – Mexico: autoparts, metal mechanics, and mobile telephones (Carlos Camacho, mastercardbiz, Caribbean 2016)

Specifically, in terms of economic sector possibilities for attracting investment, the following constitute the most likely and most favorable given the infrastructure and nature of Colombias present country situation. The most obvious and readily available are the following:

- **Manufacturing:** equipment; autoparts; instruments, and devices; cosmetics and personal care; containers and packaging; construction materials; metal mechanics; promotional material.
- **Agroindustry:** agriculture; agroindustry; flowers and live plants; aquaculture and fisheries; meat; dairy products.

- **Textiles:** jewelry; footwear and inputs; apparel; leather and leather goods; textiles and inputs for apparel.
- **Services:** digital animation; video games and audiovisual; mobile applications; oil-related services; business process outsourcing (BPO); software graphic (Carlos Camacho, mastercardbiz, Carribbean, 2016).

Discussion

Colombia has come a long way since its devastating problems of guerrilla warfare during the 1990s and thereafter. Additionally, the scourge of the drug trafficking cartels' omnipresence cast Colombia in a very bad light in the world. Finally, in 2016 Colombia has become a country of major interest. Globalization has provided major opportunities and has given the Colombians a new path that can be economically rewarding and provide a higher quality of life than has been the historic experience. People and businesses now want to go to Colombia to visit, tour, and transact business. The government has changed with positive policies and a progressive agenda. The abundant human and natural resources position Colombia as a major contender in world economics. We all know when a country has a good, thriving, and stable economy where opportunities exist then citizens can adequately care for themselves, their families, and their society as a whole. Stability economically and politically are the critical factors that the government, the NGOs, and the people must positively monitor all the activity to make sure the path and direction are aligned to make Colombia a respected, and progressive nation of opportunity and economic progress.

Conclusion

Colombia's history has been scarred with major negatives and failures. The narco traffic activity that became the hallmark of Colombia internationally did a lot of damage for a long time. New ideas, new policies, and new leadership over the last two decades have begun to turn the society and the economy around. Great things have been happening in Colombia and presently it has begun to achieve a good reputation as a good place to do business. This is a huge positive step forward and a major achievement for its leaders and citizens.

Business development has begun in earnest and economic statistics have been showing major positive performance over the last few years. This is great news for the Colombian citizens. It now establishes a future foundation for more growth, more opportunities. Colombia has some of the same factors of endowment as Peru, good coastline with substantive ports on the Pacific Ocean, and lots of underdeveloped land in the internal parts of Colombia. While Bogotá and Medellin are the primary economic hubs little by little the economic success is beginning to move across Colombia to more remote areas.

A major issue that is an obstacle to development is Colombia's infrastructure. Supply Chain process is slower because of the major obstacles in transportation.

Recently the final signing of the FARC agreement signals major progress. After more than 50 years of fighting, the society is finally at peace. Hopefully this will be a major catalyst for more reforms, more economic growth, and more rigorous implementation of the market-oriented approaches that have benefited many Colombians.

We have demonstrated with the foregoing discussion that Colombia is a prime candidate for the Pacific Alliance. The past and continued progress that this country has made is commendable and remarkable. It has been a major transformation. Yes, there is a variety of weakness especially the infrastructure and the issue of corruption. The infrastructure is easier to correct or resolve than the corruption. Hopefully, as the economy gets stronger and stronger, resources can be devoted to the amelioration of the infrastructure and the development of a supply chain arrangement so that the FDI activity will begin to accelerate. Getting goods to market is a critical element of economic development. Attention to the infrastructure needs to be a priority for policy makers.

The issue of corruption is a different problem. Removing it from society is almost impossible but minimizing its existence so that no one is disadvantaged is a possible approach. No matter what a government or private entity does corruption will emerge is some shape or form?

Colombia is positioned to become an economic powerhouse. Its entry into the Pacific Alliance is a step toward this goal. Being part of a strong alliance can only strengthen Colombia as a nation and a global competitor. We have seen Colombia come a long way and now it can continue to become a standout in world business.

References

Chan, S. P. (2015). Colombia: from failed state to Latin American powerhouse, http://www.telegraph.co.uk/finance/globalbusiness/11441732/Colombia-from-failed-state-to-Latin-American-powerhouse.html, pp. 1–8.

CIA factbook. (2016). https://www.cia.gov/library/publications/the-world-factbook/fields/2116.html.

Coface. (2016). Major Macro Economic indicators, http://www.coface.com/Economic-Studies-and-Country-Risk/Colombia.

C&A GROUP SAS, Carlos Camacho. (2016). Business opportunities with the pacific alliance. Published with permission granted to MasterCard and RGX See more at: http://www.mastercardbiz.com/caribbean/2016/03/21/business-opportunities-with-the-pacific-alliance/#sthash.Q1sTdNZK.dpuf.

Encyclopedia.com. (2016). http://www.encyclopedia.com/places

World Bank Group –IBRD-IDA. (2016). http://www.doingbusiness.org/rankings.

CHAPTER 7

Mexico

Overview

Mexico is a very large country with over 100 million inhabitants. It is a country of contrasts. There are two perspectives of Mexico. On one hand one can see affluence and natural magnificence of its physical countryside while on the other hand one sees huge socioeconomic disparity with poverty and urban plight scattered all over the country. The obvious picture, throughout the countryside, especially in the rural areas, is underdeveloped villages and towns with traditional building and housing structures of yesteryear. Even the fast-paced highly developed Mexico City has shantytowns surrounding the entire city. Clearly one could say put together a story of the tale of two countries, one of opulence and modernization and the other of backwardness and obsolescence.

Mexico is geographically located on the southern border of the USA and the northern borders of Belize and Guatemala. Since Mexico has access to the Caribbean and the Pacific Ocean, it is strategically positioned to easily transport goods to the USA especially the cities of New Orleans, Houston, Miami, and Tamps. On average it is only 600 miles from these destinations (Gordon and Williams 2002).

Economics and Trade

Mexico has a large labor force consisting of over 55 million workers. The primary employees work in the service industry composing about 62.4% of the workforce. The unemployment rate is approximately 4.9%, and the

J.E. Spillan, N. Virzi, *Business Opportunities in the Pacific Alliance*,
DOI 10.1007/978-3-319-54768-8_7

Mexican economy had a GDP growth of 2.3% in 2015, a rate better than the two prior years (Global Edge 2016). Mexico is a major manufacturing center for electronics. This circumstance, historically, has allowed Mexico to make its name and continues to be noted for the concept of *Maquiladoras. Maquiladoras* are Mexican corporations or subsidiaries that can import raw materials and equipment temporarily and duty-free to Mexico for the purpose of assembling the raw materials into component parts or final products. *Maquiladoras* were given certain customs privileges under the NAFTA agreement, which allow Mexico to import and export materials much, much easier than was historically possible. One of the major benefits of a free trade agreement (Gordon and Williams 2002). These business organizations were generally located on the northern border of Mexico again having easy access to the largest market in the world good old USA. Over time some of the *Maquiladoras* have moved south and provided employment to people in the Yucatan area of the country. These *Maquiladoras* provided employment for many Mexicans and also provided cheap labor for foreign companies that wanted to invest in Mexico. As the *Maquiladoras* enterprises move into the Yucatan area, Mexico became well positioned to do business with many partners around the world (Gordon and Williams 2002).

It has 44 trading agreements and transacts trade with more than 50 countries around the world. A major step forward has been Mexico's infrastructure enhancements to promote trade, renovations, and improvements in the telecommunication environment that have allowed for major connections with trading partners and others around the world (Mexico Economy 2016). The biggest challenge is getting rid of drug cartels. President Pena Nieto has launched a major crackdown on organized crime and corruption. This policy has, however, been received with major pushback, conflict, violence, and retaliation. It is an extremely difficult problem to resolve, but a start has been made (Mexico Economy 2016).

Another bright spot in business development for Mexico was the 1993 signing of the North American Free Trade Agreement (NAFTA). This has dramatically assisted the Mexican businesses with development, profitability, and expansion. Exporting to two huge economies, i.e., the US and Canada, has provided Mexico with huge export opportunities and thus assisted in giving it a good reputation for doing business in other parts of the world. Mexico has trade agreements with over 50 countries. As mentioned earlier, its major trading partners are the US and Canada.

Over the last 10 years or so, China has become an additional reliable and large trading partner. Mexico exports primarily motor vehicles, motor vehicle parts, electrical machinery, and industrial machinery (Mexico Economy 2016).

To explain the investment in Mexico two major theories address the reality of why investment has occurred in Mexico. First is the theory of localization which states that foreign direct investment (FDI) moves based on the specific advantages a country possesses and the geographical location it possesses. The factors of endowment (mainly natural resources) and the factors of production (land, labor, capital, and entrepreneurship) are critical success factors that attract and sustain business development (Osorio and Delgado 2014). Additionally, the theory of international production states that a company's decision to invest or set up operation in a country is motivated by comparing a company's parent country's resources and factors of production with those of the target country. If the resources are better in the target country, it is a no-brainer and the investing company will invest in the target country (Osorio and Delgado 2014). Finally, the theory of trade and resource endowment states that FDI is focused on countries where low wages and resource endowments are abundant and provide expanded opportunities for a business to invest (Osorio and Delgado 2014). All of these theories point to the main theme of resources that are less expensive, more abundant, and easy to access. This is a very real profile of Mexico. Mexico has all of these elements and is able to operationalize them rather quickly.

Other items that are critical to FDI are stable government institutions and economies of agglomeration (Osorio and Delgado 2014). Business investors want to avoid complex bribery and government bureaucracy obstacles.

By and large, Mexico has been able to reduce or eliminate many of the barriers to investment. This is why it has been able over the last two decades to attract so many investors.

With all of its negatives and positives, Mexico has, over time, has become an acknowledged and respected country in Latin America. Its wealth, its large population, and its horrific stories about drug cartel activity and corruption make Mexico a very interesting country to study, visit, and understand.

Its involvement in the NAFTA created a path for it to gain economic force and increase its influence in world trade and markets.

The decline in trade barriers has been the hallmark of globalization and the free flow of goods, services, and capital. FDI has grown or increased faster than trade and global production.

Over the last two years challenging external factors like lower oil prices, and the general slowing of the world economy and emerging economies worldwide has caused concern in Mexico's economic circles (World Bank 2016). These challenges can be addressed with prudent public policy regarding monetary, fiscal, and financial policy. In the medium term there needs to be structural reforms that will center on more substantive economic issues that are part of this fiscal and monetary arrangement (World Bank 2016).

Mexico demonstrated a changing GDP environment and a significant reduction in GDP during the period of the great depression which began in 2008 and 2009. The Mexican economy was functioning way below the norm and not making life easy of anyone.

Mexico is considered one of the most entrepreneurial countries in the world; roughly 25% of the Mexican workforce is self-employed compared to 11% in the United States. According to estimates of the Organization for Economic Cooperation and Development (OECD), Mexico ranks at

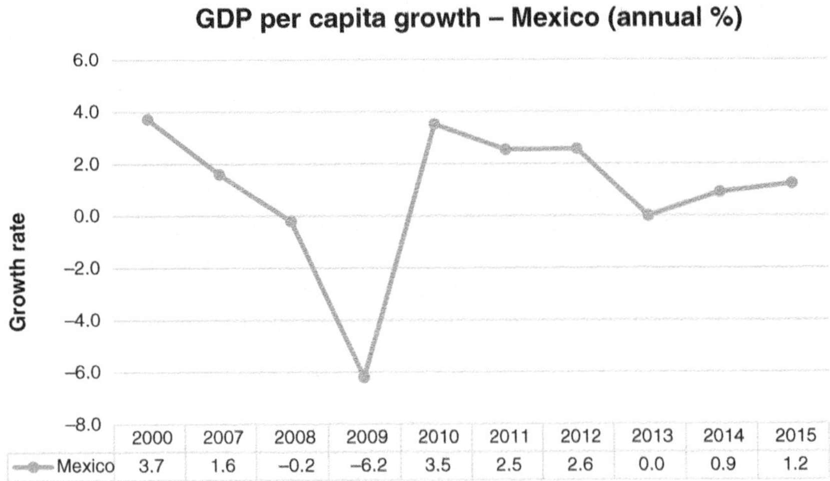

Graph 7.1 GDP Per Capita Growth Mexico (annual %)

Source: Banxico/Oxford Economics, 2015

the top of the list of all the OECD country members. The Global Entrepreneurship Monitor also ranks Mexico among the most entrepreneurial countries in a list of 41 countries. Family-owned businesses have a significant role in the private sector in Mexico, and children of Mexican entrepreneurs show a preference for entrepreneurship as a career option (Van Auken et al. 2006).

However, despite the role that entrepreneurship plays for the Mexican economy, studies on the topic of entrepreneurship in Mexico are scarce, and studies that specifically address factors that influence university students' inclinations to pursue entrepreneurship as a career path in Mexico were not found. Nevertheless, there are studies that provide insight into factors that influence Mexicans to become entrepreneurs. Sloka et al. (2014) conducted a study in which motivations to start a business in Latvia, Canada, the United States, and Mexico were explored. The findings of the study indicate that in Mexico there are four complex factors that influence entrepreneurship: income, independence, personal motivation, and family security. Additionally, the findings indicate that the most important factors influencing business success were the following: good client service, honesty reputation, charisma and friendliness with clients, and good management abilities. Among the less important factors were previous entrepreneurship experience, geographical location, political support, and interest.

Radojevich-Kelly (2012) conducted a study to explore small business and entrepreneurship in Mexico. The author cited the NAFTA as a driver for entrepreneurship in Mexico. However, due to the lack of entrepreneurship skills and education, many Mexican entrepreneurs have found themselves in a position of disadvantage compared to Canadian and US entrepreneurs. Kelesidou (2013) suggested that Mexicans must study entrepreneurship and become familiar with the different methods to fund start-ups in order to gain confidence and take advantage of the opportunities associated with NAFTA.

The given map is a comprehensive view of the geographic layout of Mexico and its surroundings. Mexico has a large landmass, which border the United States to the North and Central America to the south. Mexico has lots of access to the sea with ports on the east with Gulf of Mexico and on the west with the North Pacific Ocean. Such ports access is great for trade allowing imports and exports to flow freely to both sides of the country. Its easy access to the United States and its membership in the NAFTA provides another means for trade and business development. Geography is important and Mexico has an important geography.

Map of Mexico

Source: The World Factbook – Central Intelligence Agency: Mexico Map. (n.d.). Retrieved from https://www.cia.gov/library/publications/the-world-factbook/geos/mx.html

The aforementioned discussion presents a substantive overview of contemporary Mexico, as it has existed in the last two decades a brief perspective on the path to the future. The subsequent discussion presents the strengths and weakness confronting Mexico. It is important to understand these two directions in order to explain Mexico's participation in the newly formed Pacific Alliance (PA) trade pact.

Strengths

External Debt

Mexico's external debt it equal to about 23% of its GDP. This is a relatively good status and indicates that it is able to manage its external debt transactions and has the flexibility to meet its external obligations (van der Molen 2013).

Competitiveness in the World

Because Mexico has a multitude of resources and economic agglomerations, it offers an attractive environment for efficient and effective operation of business. Since China's labor cost has been rising, Mexico's cheap labor has been attracting FDI. This is good news for Mexico because it provides jobs and labor opportunities for its economy. Opening new factories is great recognition of the power of Mexico's business environment. Since Mexico has an abundance of skilled workers it indicates that it can continue to attract FDI in the future (van der Molen 2013).

Global Manufacturing and Logistics Center

Mexico is recognized for its competitiveness due to its major factors of endowment and availability of the factors of production. Since supply chain management is a critical part of any business and an activity that can service a great many businesses both domestically and internationally, Mexico can use this center as leverage for more business development, expanded export marketing. Additionally, with the modernization of its infrastructure, Mexico is solidifying its competitiveness and attracting more FDI to its cities and states.

Mexico is a Global Champ in Trade Agreements.

Since it transacts business with over 50 countries and has approximately 12 trade agreements across 44 countries. This allows it to provide goods and services to approximately around 12 billion consumers. Clearly this is a very strong trade position that can enhance the economic growth and development of Mexico.

Open Legal Framework

Mexico's legal framework is conducive to international business. It is highlighted with attributes such as transparency, certainty, and safety. These are important characteristics that help Mexico attract and retain business development (Olander 2015).

Weaknesses

Complicated Security Situation

The last decade has really raised serious questions about the safety of doing business in Mexico. Violence in the northern cities and the incident where 43 students were missing then found to have been tortured and killed have increased the questions about the ability of the government to maintain security and peace in the country. Presently there has not been a major report of security breaches, but history has been deadly for many of the people in Mexico.

Pervasive Corruption

Unfortunately this phenomenon exists at all layers of society. It is one of the negative attributes that businesses review in their decision making for investing in foreign countries.

High Dependence on Oil Revenues

Since the prices of oil have significantly dropped such dependence has created a shortfall of revenue which Mexico depended on. Because there is a narrow tax base where 60% of the workforce is not registered in the tax payment system, this creates shortages of revenues that cause funding problems for many public programs that can promote business development (van der Molen 2013).

Why Mexico is a Good PA Partner

Since Latin America, for the most part, has been growing at a relatively fast pace over the last decade, other countries have become interested in doing business with Latin American partners. Mexico has a powerful economy rich in business diversity and talent, yet not sufficiently connected with the Latin American southern countries to have any quid pro quo impact. Mexico has a huge population with 122 million inhabitants. This is gigantic compared to the other three partners in the Alliance. It has a lot to offer as a market for goods but also an improved infrastructure, in many parts of the country, that can move goods quickly and efficiently. For the most part, the transport system has significantly improved and offers good transport capabilities for the Mexican businesses. Additionally, Mexico has a modern telecommunication system that is in the commercial parts of Mexico a state-of-the-art arrangement. This asset is critical for the conduct of domestic and international business, especially for the import and export business that Mexico engages in (Wolters Kluwer 2015).

Mexico for the most part has good educational system that can produce the talent businesses can use to sustain and expand their business ventures both domestically and internationally.

Why is Mexico a Good PA Partner?

Mexico works hard to attract foreign investment that will bring it long-term sustained growth. In order to reach this level of trade over the past few years, the Mexican government introduced several structural reforms affecting the energy, education, labor, financial, and the political sectors that are focused on having the right condition in Mexico, which would foster investment and economic growth. Besides Mexico's structural reforms that have appeal to investors the free trade treaties that Mexico has signed with approximately 43 other countries have given Mexican companies a competitive advantage. FDI is a fundamental incentive factor for economic development because it has the potential to create jobs, increase personal savings, and raise capital for businesses. It also drives competition in the market, stimulates transfers of new technologies, and boosts exports. Altogether these features have a positive effect on Mexico's productive and competitive business environment. Mexico has situated itself as an important manufacturing hub that supplies the North American market. This arrangement has led to large foreign investment in various sectors, such as the automotive and end aerospace sectors (Carlos Camacho, mastercardbiz, Caribbean 2016).

Based on information from Francisco N. González Díaz, Director General of ProMéxico, the most promising sectors for production chains are: aerospace, automotive, electronic, pharmaceutical, medical devices, and more sophisticated services including software and business consulting services. Mexico has four major sectors that have become the lifeblood of it economy. These sectors include the following:

- **Manufacturing:** cosmetics and personal care products; hotel equipment; designer kitchen and dining products; high-end furniture; backpacks
- **Agroindustry:** confectioneries; tropical fruits; processed fruit and vegetables; rum and coffee liquor; gourmet products; products for diabetes
- **Apparel:** Jeans; women's intimate wear (private label); bathing suits; footwear leather goods
- **Services:** corporate and holiday tourism; printing and publishing; software & ICT (Carlos Camacho, mastercardbiz Caribbean 2016)

Discussion

Mexico has been considered a strong partner in many international business transactions. It is a country that has enormous resources both natural and human. It has a growing population and it offers many positive reasons for businesses to invest in Mexico. We have seen over the years that Mexico has been the place to go for cheap labor, and many North American companies have taken advantage of the resources and skilled workforce that exist in Mexico. Mexico is a strong partner in the PA trade pact because it can manufacture goods, and it has the expertise in export marketing and management. With its geography, Mexico is strategically positioned to maximize its interaction with world partners and customers. It large efficient seaports give it the transport capability to reach anywhere in the world with just about any product it produces. Being a global logistics center provides Mexico a means of processing goods efficiently and effectively in domestic and international markets. All of these positive attributes have established a business structure, which is attractive to business investment and FDI opportunities. Government efforts to reform and modernize the Mexican infrastructure for more business accommodation is a great step in the right direction and a major effort to attract and sustain present businesses and develop others. Unfortunately Mexico has some major negative attributes. Two items are clearly deal breakers. The first is the complicated security issues. The last five years has demonstrated a culture of ugly, violent, and unnecessary attacks on innocent people for just living, working, and being where they are. This is very tumultuous and scary. People become fearful and this fear leads to a lot of negative reactions.

The second negative attribute is that of the pervasive bribery. While it has been going on for years, and years, it has been recognized that it is a real negative factor in attracting business to Mexico. This issue has been around for a long time. It seems to be part of the culture and every political candidate promises to eradicate it from the society but it still remains. Unfortunately, the intertwining of the general corruption with the drug cartels has made some parts of Mexico lethal and places no one wants to go. The present President Pena Nieto has promised reforms to eliminate or curtail corruption. How this will play out in the future is any ones guess. Be it as it may, Mexico has all of the right assets to be a strong and solid player in the PA. Its worldwide connections enhance its capabilities but also it has the goods and services that it can share with its PA partners. Working together they all can benefit from the interchange of goods, services, and resources.

Conclusion

Of all the partners in the PA, Mexico represents the most economically powerful. It has demonstrated its capabilities over and over.

Like all other members Mexico has a strong coastline which is important for imports and exports and has been used for a long time as a mechanism of international trade for Mexico. Because Mexico has such a huge expanded network of trade partners, it brings lots of experience and other resources to the PA.

While Mexico is strong and offers a great deal to the PA, it still has major struggles that can be a major distraction to the economic development of Mexico.

Such issues as narco trafficking through Mexico and on its borders has people, companies and the entire society freightened. The last decade has exhibited extremely violent episodes among traffickers and people in route to its destinations. Such violence has frightened companies and raised concerns about placing businesses in this area of the world. Additionally, the continual corruption accusations and incidents that have been discovered in Mexico´s government. This has weakened the emphasis on economic development and raised questions as to who benefits from business developments and trade in Mexico.

Mexico is a strong partner for the PA. Its ability to produce goods through its manufacturing sector and its highly educated population with lots of skilled workers provides a resource pool that can be exchanged with other partners and mutually help each other in their economic development. While there have been many trade groups in Latin America, this one seems to be anchored in solid leadership and pragmatic business principles. Mexico is clearly the economic powerhouse of the entire group. It can be the catalyst for a synergistic relationship that can benefit all the other countries that are involved.

References

C&A GROUP SAS, Carlos Camacho. (2016). Business opportunities with the pacific alliance. Published with permission granted to MasterCard and RGX Mastercardbiz Caribbean http://www.mastercardbiz.com http://www.mastercardbiz.com/caribbean/2016/03/21/business-opportunities-with-the-pacific-alliance/#sthash.Q1sTdNZK.dpuf Master Card Biz Caribbean. /caribbean/2016/03/21/business-opportunities-with-the-pacific-alliance/.

Gordon, G. & Williams, T. (2002). Doing business in Mexico: A practical guide, (Best Business Books- The Haworth Press, New York).

Global Edge. (2016). http://globaledge.msu.edu/countries/mexico/economy. Accessed on 7/22/16.

Kelesidou, F. (2013). Innovative Mexican entrepreneurs to watch. The Motley Fool. https://www.fool.com/investing/general/2013/12/19/innovative-mexican-entrepreneurs-to-watch.aspx.

Kluwer, Wolters. (2015). https://ct.wolterskluwer.com/sites/default/files/What_Pacific_Alliance_Means_For_Investors_0.pdf.

Mexico Economy, 2016 - Flannery, Nathaniel Parish. (2016). Will Mexico's economy finally start to grow in 2016? Forbes. http://www.forbes.com/sites/nathanielparishflannery/2016/02/29/will-mexicos-economy-finallys tart-to-grow-in-2016/#aef29bd5cc4d.

Olander, H.. (2015).Economy heading in right direction-but institutional reforms still needed. EKN,–Creating Confidence in Your Exports.

Osorio, J. Botello, C. & Delgado, M. D. (2014). Public policy as a determinant for attracting foreign direct investment in Mexico since 2000-2013. *International Journal of Business and Economic Development*, *2*(1), 78–89.

Radojevich-Kelly, N., & Hoffman, D. L (2012). Analysis of accelerator companies: An exploratory case study of their programs, processes, and early results. *Small Business Institute Journal*, *8*(2), 54–70.

Sloka, B., Kantane,I., Avotins, V., & Jermolajeva, E. (2014). Analysis of entrepreneur's motivation to start business (comparative studies in Latvia in comparison with Canada, USA, Mexico). *European Integration Studies*, (8), 152–158.

Van Auken, H., Stephens, P., Fry, F. L., & Silva, J. (2006). Role model influences on entrepreneurial intentions: A comparison between USA and Mexico. *The International Entrepreneurship and Management Journal*, *2*(3), 325–336.

van der Molen, M. (2013). Country report Mexico, RaboResearch-Economic Research, http://economics.rabobank.com/publications/2013/june/coun try-report-mexico/.

World Bank. (2016). Overview of Mexico, http://www.worldbank.org/en/coun try/mexico/overview, accessed on 7/22/16.

CHAPTER 8

Central America: The Logical Next Step

Introduction and Background

Central America is one of the regions in the world with the most economical potential due to its geographic location. This part of the world easily connects the Pacific and Atlantic Oceans and all the economies that depend on them.

Of the seven countries that make Central America, six have exit to both oceans: Guatemala, El Salvador, Honduras, Nicaragua, Costa Rica, and Panama. In 2016 these six countries had a population of approximately 47.01 million people, a production $241.67 billion, and a GDP per capita of $5,140.63. Much of Central America's production is based on services, 64.47%; another 26.94% is from industry; and only 8.59% are agriculture-based products (Table 8.1a World Bank and IMF Data, 2016).

The region scores 4.20 in the Global Competitiveness ranking. With a score in the middle of the table, the pillars of health and education and macroeconomy are the more solid. Innovation and institutions are still weak and there is a lot of work that can be done (Table 8.1b World Bank, and IMF Data, 2016).

Based on the ranking of these six countries, Central America would be in the 78th rank of the Doing Business Index. Getting Credit (17.73) and electricity (48.05) is not too complicated in general terms. But staring a business (100.63) or solving an insolvency (120.38) can get pretty difficult. This varies from country to country. The region has a score in customs

J.E. Spillan, N. Virzi, *Business Opportunities in the Pacific Alliance*,
DOI 10.1007/978-3-319-54768-8_8

burdens of 3.66 out of 7 and it takes approximately 16 days to start a business (Table 8.1c World Bank and IMF Data, 2016).

The Index of Economic Freedom scores the isthmus countries with 63.66 out of 100 with low government spending, and a solid fiscal and trade freedom. On the other hand, weak institutions make freedom from corruption and problems with property something that should be taken into account (Table 8.1d World Bank and IMF Data, 2016).

Table 8.1a Level of Gross Domestic Product (GDP) for Central American Region

GDP	*Central America*
GDP, billions $	$241.67
Population, millions	47.01
GDP per capita, $	$5,140.63

	Central America
Agriculture, % GDP	8.59
Industry, % GDP	26.94
Services, % GDP	64.47
Agriculture, % growth	2.16
Industry, % growth	3.75
Services, % growth	4.44
Exports, % GDP	35.41
Imports, % GDP	44.59
Exports, % growth	1.80
Imports, % growth	3.66
Trade in services, % GDP	18.95
Travel services, % service imports	20.55
Logistics (5 best)	2.80
Days to start a business	16.01
Start-up costs, % GNI per capita	23.10
Customs burdens (7 best)	3.66

Table 8.1b Global Competitiveness Rankings According to Specific Areas

Global Competitiveness Index rank	*Central America*
GCI Global Score	4.20
GCI Pillar 1 Institutions	3.62
GCI Pillar 2 Infrastructure	4.06
GCI Pillar Macroeconomy	4.98
GCI Pillar 4 Health and Education	5.57
GCI Pillar 5 Higher Education and Training	4.04
GCI Pillar 6 Goods Market Efficiency	4.36
GCI Pillar 7 Labor Market Efficiency	4.01
GCI Pillar 8 Financial Markets	4.63
GCI Pillar 9 Technological Readiness	3.93
GCI Pillar 10 Market Size	3.41
GCI Pillar 11 Business Sophistication	4.11
GCI Pillar 12 Innovation	3.25

Table 8.1c Doing Business in Region Ranking

Doing Business, rank	*Central America*
Ease of Doing Business Rank	78.21
Starting a Business	100.63
Dealing with Construction Permits	91.61
Getting Electricity	48.05
Registering Property	76.40
Getting Credit	17.73
Protecting Minority Investors	140.35
Paying Taxes	111.60
Trading Across Borders	71.37
Enforcing Contracts	142.28
Resolving Insolvency	120.38

Table 8.1d Index of Economic Freedom

Index of Economic Freedom	*Central America*
2016 Score	63.66
Property Rights	31.39
Freedom from Corruption	38.66
Fiscal Freedom	80.77
Gov't Spending	85.66
Business Freedom	65.49
Labor Freedom	48.49
Monetary Freedom	77.87
Trade Freedom	82.52
Investment Freedom	69.19
Financial Freedom	56.60

Source: Author's calculation from World Bank Data 2016

Table 8.1e Index of Globalization

Various Indicators	*Central America*
Index of Globalization 2013	61.75
Index of Economic Globalization	65.93
Index of Political Globalization	69.82
Index of Social Globalization	51.86
Human Development Index	0.70
Travel and Tourism Index	3.91
Corruption Perceptions Index	38.27

Source: Author's calculations from World Bank and IMF, Data 2016

The region is fairly globalized and scores 61.75 out of 100 in the Globalization Index. In the Human Development Index, of the United Nations Development Program, it scores 0.7 out of 1. The Travel and Tourism Index, that measures the efficiency of this industry, gives a score of 3.91 out of 7. Corruption is a problem in the Central America as shown in the Corruption Perception Index in 2015, with a score of 38.27 out of 100 (Table 8.1e World Bank and IMF Data, 2016).

Central America is essentially progressing for its entrance into the Pacific Alliance (PA). Costa Rica and Panama have met the basic prerequisites for entering the trading bloc. Other Central American countries like El Salvador, Honduras, and Nicaragua each continue to progress at various stages of negotiations with an individual member of the PA or the entire Alliance, i.e., Colombia invited Guatemala to integrate into the bloc. Nicaragua already has an agreement with Colombia and a free trade agreement with Mexico. One can see that active negotiations and arrangements are in process for a real expansion of the PA, which include many of the Central American countries. This arrangement can only strengthen the Alliance by offering more import and export outlets and a broader range of goods and services that these countries offer. It creates the making of a huge boom for the Latin American business community and an opportunity for countries around the world to take part in economic opportunities that the enlarged PA will offer (Central Law 2016).

Costa Rica Leads the Way: A Comparison of the Economies of Central America

The following sections contain brief but substantive presentations of the current economic and demographic statistics that are relevant to each country's entry into the PA. Reviewing each of these profiles gives the reader a better perspective on the readiness of each country to enter the PA.

Guatemala

Government

Type: Unitary Presidential Republic
President: Jimmy Morales
Vice President: Jafeth Cabrera

Economy

The "eternal spring" country is the biggest economy in Central America. With a population of approximately 16.67 million, a GDP of $68.14 billion, and a GDP per capita of $4,086.96 the Central American country presents interesting characteristics.

Its GDP comprise of 11.12 % of agriculture, 28.06% of industry, and 60% of services. The competitiveness of the economy is scored 3.34, with strengths in the handle of macroeconomy by the Central Bank of Guatemala. Despite this, weak institutions are still a problem in the competitiveness of the country (Table 8.2a and b World Bank Data, 2016).

The Doing Business Rank positions Guatemala in the 81st. Electricity is becoming less of a problem every day (21), but protecting minority investors (174) and dealing with construction permits (106) is an obstacle for doing business. The Economic Freedom Index shows

Table 8.2a Gross Domestic Product (GDP) for Guatemala

GDP	*Guatemala*
GDP, billions $	$68.14
Population, millions	16.67
GDP per capita, $	$4,086.96

	Guatemala
Agriculture, % GDP	11.13
Industry, % GDP	28.06
Services, % GDP	60.81
Agriculture, % growth	3.25
Industry, % growth	3.74
Services, % growth	4.35
Exports, % GDP	21.29
Imports, % GDP	30.04
Exports, % growth	4.04
Imports, % growth	8.90
Trade in services, % GDP	9.15
Travel services, % service imports	24.60
Logistics (5 best)	2.68
Days to start a business	18.50
Start-up costs, % GNI per capita	25.00
Customs burdens (7 best)	3.48

Table 8.2b Global Competitiveness Index Rank for Guatemala

Global Competitiveness Index rank	*Guatemala*
GCI Pillar 1 Institutions	3.34
GCI Pillar 2 Infrastructure	3.82
GCI Pillar Macroeconomy	4.93
GCI Pillar 4 Health and Education	4.98
GCI Pillar 5 Higher Education and Training	3.61
GCI Pillar 6 Goods Market Efficiency	4.56
GCI Pillar 7 Labor Market Efficiency	3.92
GCI Pillar 8 Financial Markets	4.88
GCI Pillar 9 Technological Readiness	3.37
GCI Pillar 10 Market Size	3.68
GCI Pillar 11 Business Sophistication	4.19
GCI Pillar 12 Innovation	3.23
GCI Global Score	4.08

that weak enforcement of property rights and not being free from corruption threatened economic freedom of the citizens. On the other hand, the government spending is low and the trade freedom is high with low interference from the government. The customs burdens score can be better, 3.48, and open a new business is a slow process of 18.5 days (Table 8.2c and d World Bank Data, 2016).

Guatemala is a very interesting country in the Globalization Index. It scores 59.28 out of 100 in the total score, but the subindex of political globalization shows that the country is highly politically globalized (83.82). Many international institutions are very active in Guatemala, and the country has signed many international treaties in human rights issues and climate change. The economy is fairly globalized (58.30), and it has a very conservative society with many groups of its population isolated from the globalized world (42.23). The efficiency of the tourism sector is scored with 3.51 out of 7 by the Travel and Tourism Index. Since the end of a thirty-six-year long armed conflict in 1996, Guatemala has made advances in Human Development indicators, with a current score of 0.63 (Table 8.2c and d World Bank Data, 2016).

Table 8.2c Doing Business rank for Guatemala

Doing Business, rank	*Guatemala*
Ease of Doing Business Rank	81
Starting a Business	101
Dealing with Construction Permits	106
Getting Electricity	21
Registering Property	75
Getting Credit	15
Protecting Minority Investors	174
Paying Taxes	50
Trading Across Borders	78
Enforcing Contracts	173
Resolving Insolvency	153

Table 8.2d Index of Economic Freedom for Guatemala

Index of Economic Freedom	*Guatemala*
2016 Score	61.81
Property Rights	20
Freedom from Corruption	32
Fiscal Freedom	79.09
Gov't Spending	94.3
Business Freedom	62.5
Labor Freedom	50.9
Monetary Freedom	77.9
Trade Freedom	86.4
Investment Freedom	65
Financial Freedom	50

In 2015 the citizenship pressed for the resignation of the former President of the Republic Otto Perez Molina. In a series of social demonstrations, the Congress of the Republic was pressured to remove the President's immunity, event that lead to his resignation. This event eroded even more the perception of the corruption in the country with a score of 28 out 100 in 2015.

Table 8.2e Index of Globalization for Guatemala

Various Indicators	*Guatemala*
Index of Globalization 2013	59.28
Index of Economic Globalization	58.30
Index of Political Globalization	83.82
Index of Social Globalization	42.23
Human Development Index	0.63
Travel and Tourism Index	3.51
Corruption Perceptions Index	28.00

Source: Author's calculation from World Bank Data, 2016

El Salvador

Government

Type: Unitary Presidential Constitutional Republic
President: Salvador Sánchez Cerén

Economy

Despite being the smallest country in size on the region, El Salvador presents some aspects that make it stand out among its neighbors. It has a population of $6.4 million people, produces $27.33 billion, and its GDP per capita is of $4,267.87. Most of the production is based on services, representing 61.85%, followed by the industry with 26.87%, and finally the agriculture represents 11.28% (Table 8.3a World Bank Data, 2016).

El Salvador scores 3.81 out of 7 in the Global Competitiveness Index. It stands in the pillars of financial markets (4.03), the health and education (5.37), and macroeconomy (4.22). El Salvador is ranked 86 in the Doing Business rank. Getting credit (15) and trading across borders (46) is relatively easy. But dealing with construction permits (156) and paying taxes (162) are problems that hinder investments. It would take approximately 16 days to start a new business and the custom burdens are scored 3.48 out of 7 (Table 8.3b & c World Bank Data, 2016).

Table 8.3a Gross Domestic Product (GDP) for El Salvador

GDP	*El Salvador*
GDP, billions $	$27.33
Population, millions	6.40
GDP per capita, $	$4,267.87

	El Salvador
Agriculture, % GDP	11.28
Industry, % GDP	26.87
Services, % GDP	61.85
Agriculture, % growth	0.78
Industry, % growth	3.16
Services, % growth	2.49
Exports, % GDP	25.96
Imports, % GDP	42.03
Exports, % growth	2.40
Imports, % growth	3.15
Trade in services, % GDP	14.99
Travel services, % service imports	19.04
Logistics (5 best)	3.16
Days to start a business	16.50
Start-up costs, % GNI per capita	42.70
Customs burdens (7 best)	3.48

The Economic Freedom Index gives 65.12 out 100 to El Salvador. The country has a strong trade (83.4) and monetary freedom (83.4), but property rights and freedom from corruption are still a threat to the economic liberty (Table 8.3 d – World Bank Data, 2016).

Similar to its neighbors, El Salvador is fairly globalized with a score of 61.72. But the Salvadorian society is far from being at the same level with a social globalization score of 49.27. On the other hand, the political globalization is high with a score of 79.65.

Table 8.3b Global Competitiveness Index for El Salvador

Global Competitiveness Index rank	*El Salvador*
GCI Global Score	3.81
GCI Pillar 1 Institutions	2.99
GCI Pillar 2 Infrastructure	4.03
GCI Pillar Macroeconomy	4.22
GCI Pillar 4 Health and Education	5.37
GCI Pillar 5 Higher Education and Training	3.57
GCI Pillar 6 Goods Market Efficiency	4.03
GCI Pillar 7 Labor Market Efficiency	3.57
GCI Pillar 8 Financial Markets	4.27
GCI Pillar 9 Technological Readiness	3.40
GCI Pillar 10 Market Size	3.18
GCI Pillar 11 Business Sophistication	3.69
GCI Pillar 12 Innovation	2.63

Table 8.3c Doing Business rank for El Salvador

Doing Business, rank	*El Salvador*
Ease of Doing Business Rank	86
Starting a Business	125
Dealing with Construction Permits	156
Getting Electricity	107
Registering Property	71
Getting Credit	15
Protecting Minority Investors	155
Paying Taxes	162
Trading Across Borders	46
Enforcing Contracts	109
Resolving Insolvency	79

The Central American country also had a long and difficult civil war that lasted more than 12 years and ended in 1992. More recent problems are gang violence and finding ways to provide a better standard of living

Table 8.3d Index of Economic Freedom for El Salvador

Index of Economic Freedom	*El Salvador*
2016 Score	65.12
Property Rights	35
Freedom from Corruption	39
Fiscal Freedom	79.1
Gov't Spending	85.3
Business Freedom	56
Labor Freedom	52.6
Monetary Freedom	83.4
Trade Freedom	85.8
Investment Freedom	75
Financial Freedom	60

Table 8.3e Index of Globalization for El Salvador

Various Indicators	*El Salvador*
Index of Globalization 2013	61.72
Index of Economic Globalization	61.01
Index of Political Globalization	79.65
Index of Social Globalization	49.27
Human Development Index	0.67
Travel and Tourism Index	4.41
Corruption Perceptions Index	39.00

Source: Author's calculation from World Bank Data, 2016

to the Salvadorian society with a Human Development score of 0.67. The efficiency of the tourism industry is the highest of the region with a score of 4.41 out of 7 in the Travel and Tourism Index. The Corruption Perceptions Index scores 39 out of 100 to El Salvador (Table 8.3e World Bank Data, 2016).

Honduras

Government

Type: Unitary presidential Constitutional Republic
President: Juan Orlando Hernández
Vice President: Ricardo Álvarez Arias

Economy

With Guatemala and El Salvador, Honduras is the third country of the *Central America's Northern Triangle* region. The country has a population of 8.61 million; its GDP is of $20.63 billion with a GDP per capita of $2,397.47. Most of this production consists in services with 59.49% of the total GDP, 26.65% is industry production, and 13.87% is produced by the agricultural sector (Table 8.4a World Bank Data, 2016).

Table 8.4a Gross Domestic Product (GDP) for Honduras

GDP	*Honduras*
GDP, billions $	$20.63
Population, millions	8.61
GDP per capita, $	$2,397.47

	Honduras
Agriculture, % GDP	13.87
Industry, % GDP	26.65
Services, % GDP	59.49
Agriculture, % growth	3.26
Industry, % growth	3.21
Services, % growth	2.93
Exports, % GDP	45.08
Imports, % GDP	64.00

(*continued*)

(continued)

	Honduras
Exports, % growth	1.54
Imports, % growth	4.95
Trade in services, % GDP	22.19
Travel services, % service imports	22.56
Logistics (5 best)	2.47
Days to start a business	14.00
Start-up costs, % GNI per capita	38.70
Customs burdens (7 best)	3.53

Table 8.4b Global Competitiveness Index for Honduras

Global Competitiveness Index rank	*Honduras*
GCI Global Score	3.98
GCI Pillar 1 Institutions	3.34
GCI Pillar 2 Infrastructure	3.28
GCI Pillar Macroeconomy	4.95
GCI Pillar 4 Health and Education	5.56
GCI Pillar 5 Higher Education and Training	3.63
GCI Pillar 6 Goods Market Efficiency	4.12
GCI Pillar 7 Labor Market Efficiency	3.64
GCI Pillar 8 Financial Markets	4.54
GCI Pillar 9 Technological Readiness	3.12
GCI Pillar 10 Market Size	3.06
GCI Pillar 11 Business Sophistication	3.85
GCI Pillar 12 Innovation	3.09

The Central American country scores 3.98 out of 7 in the Global Competitiveness rank. The pillars of health and education (5.56), goods market efficiency (4.12), and financial markets (4.54) are the more solid. The innovation (3.09) and market size (3.06) are poorly scored. It takes 14 days to open a business and the customs burdens are scored 3.53 out of 7 (Table 8.4b World Bank Data, 2016).

Honduras is ranked 110 in the Doing Business rank with good access to credit (7), but with difficulties enforcing contracts (150), starting business (150), and paying taxes (155). The country scores 57.74 in the Economic Freedom Index. Fiscal, monetary, and trade freedom are high, but, as its neighbors, property rights, labor freedom, and corruption are obstacles for a better economic freedom (Table 8.4c & d World Bank Data, 2016).

In the Index of Globalization Honduras scores 59.99, with a very high score in political globalization of 71.83. The Human Development Index is medium with a score of 0.61 out of 1. The Travel and Tourism Index, published by the World Economic Forum, scores the country with a 3.41 out of 7. Corruption is a big concern for the Hondurans; in the Corruption Perception Index the country scores 31 out of 100 (Table 8.4e World Bank Data, 2016).

Nicaragua

Government

Type: Unitary Presidential Constitutional Republic
President: Daniel Ortega
Vice President: Omar Halleslevens

Table 8.4c Doing Business As for Honduras

Doing Business, rank	*Honduras*
Ease of Doing Business Rank	110
Starting a Business	150
Dealing with Construction Permits	87
Getting Electricity	143
Registering Property	88
Getting Credit	7
Protecting Minority Investors	134
Paying Taxes	155
Trading Across Borders	136
Enforcing Contracts	150
Resolving Insolvency	139

Table 8.4d Index of Economic Freedom for Honduras

Index of Economic Freedom	*Honduras*
2016 Score	57.74
Property Rights	30
Freedom from Corruption	29
Fiscal Freedom	84.2
Gov't Spending	72
Business Freedom	58
Labor Freedom	31
Monetary Freedom	74.8
Trade Freedom	78.4
Investment Freedom	60
Financial Freedom	60

Table 8.4e Index of Globalization for Honduras

Various Indicators	*Honduras*
Index of Globalization 2013	59.99
Index of Economic Globalization	68.37
Index of Political Globalization	71.83
Index of Social Globalization	43.34
Human Development Index	0.61
Travel and Tourism Index	3.41
Corruption Perceptions Index	31.00

Source: Author's calculation from World Bank Data, 2016

Economy

The country of the revolutionary Augusto Cesar Sandino is the most stagnated. It has a population of 6.34 million that produces approximately $12.9 billion a year, making a GDP per capita of $2,034.63. 54.33% of the production is services, 26.86% are industry products, and 18.81% is agriculture (Table 8.5a World Bank Data, 2016).

Table 8.5a Gross Domestic Product (GDP) for Nicaragua

GDP	*Nicaragua*
GDP, billions $	$12.90
Population, millions	6.34
GDP per capita, $	$2,034.63

	Nicaragua
Agriculture, % GDP	18.81
Industry, % GDP	26.86
Services, % GDP	54.33
Agriculture, % growth	2.84
Industry, % growth	2.47
Services, % growth	5.21
Exports, % GDP	37.52
Imports, % GDP	55.46
Exports, % growth	-2.02
Imports, % growth	11.60
Trade in services, % GDP	18.79
Travel services, % service imports	16.29
Logistics (5 best)	2.58
Days to start a business	13.00
Start-up costs, % GNI per capita	72.20
Customs burdens (7 best)	2.43

Nicaragua scores 3.81 in the Global Competitiveness Index. The market size is very small (2.89) and the innovation is a problem (2.42). The pillars of health (5.51) and education and macroeconomy (4.95) are well rated in this index. The Doing Business ranks the country 125 in the world, with the trade across borders, enforcing contracts and getting electricity being the best variables. Paying taxes and dealing with construction permits are a big problem for doing business. You can open a business in 13 days, but take in account that the burden of customs procedure is a major problem (2.43) (Table 8.5b & c World Bank Data, 2016).

Table 8.5b Global Competitiveness Index for Nicaragua

Global Competitiveness Index rank	*Nicaragua*
GCI Global Score	3.81
GCI Pillar 1 Institutions	3.19
GCI Pillar 2 Infrastructure	3.19
GCI Pillar Macroeconomy	4.95
GCI Pillar 4 Health and Education	5.51
GCI Pillar 5 Higher Education and Training	3.15
GCI Pillar 6 Goods Market Efficiency	3.77
GCI Pillar 7 Labor Market Efficiency	3.75
GCI Pillar 8 Financial Markets	3.31
GCI Pillar 9 Technological Readiness	2.81
GCI Pillar 10 Market Size	2.89
GCI Pillar 11 Business Sophistication	3.12
GCI Pillar 12 Innovation	2.42

Table 8.5c Doing Business Rank for Nicaragua

Doing Business, rank	*Nicaragua*
Ease of Doing Business Rank	125
Starting a Business	123
Dealing with Construction Permits	168
Getting Electricity	94
Registering Property	147
Getting Credit	97
Protecting Minority Investors	150
Paying Taxes	165
Trading Across Borders	81
Enforcing Contracts	94
Resolving Insolvency	103

The Economic Freedom Index scores Nicaragua with 58.59 out of 100. The leftist Sandinista government represents threat to property rights (10) and is considered corrupt (28). Despite this, trade (86.2) and fiscal freedom

Table 8.5d Index of Economic Freedom for Nicaragua

Index of Economic Freedom	*Nicaragua*
2016 Score	58.59
Property Rights	10
Freedom from Corruption	28
Fiscal Freedom	78
Gov't Spending	82.8
Business Freedom	61.2
Labor Freedom	55.7
Monetary Freedom	69
Trade Freedom	86.2
Investment Freedom	65
Financial Freedom	50

Table 8.5e Index of Globalization for Nicaragua

Various Indicators	*Nicaragua*
Index of Globalization 2013	53.88
Index of Economic Globalization	60.10
Index of Political Globalization	57.66
Index of Social Globalization	45.21
Human Development Index	0.63
Travel and Tourism Index	3.37
Corruption Perceptions Index	27.00

Source: Author's calculation from World Bank, Data 2016

(78) are high. Nicaragua is the less globalized country scoring 53.88 in the Index of Globalization of 2013 (Table 8.5d World Bank Data, 2016).

The Human Development Index of Nicaragua is 0.63. The tourism industry is comparable with that of its neighbors with a score in the Travel and Tourism Index of 3.37 out of 7. The State is considered corrupt according to the Corruption Perception Index that scores Nicaragua with a 27 out of 100 (Table 8.5e World Bank Data, 2016).

Costa Rica

Government

Type: Unitary Presidential Constitutional Republic
President: Luis Guillermo Solís
1st Vice President: Helio Fallas Venegas
2nd Vice President: Ana Helena Chacón Echeverría

Economy

Costa Rica is one of the most stable countries in Central America. With stronger political institutions than its neighbors, it presents a window of opportunity for development. This institutional development is product of a series of reforms in the years of 1948–1949 that profoundly changed the political system in the country. They abolished the armed forces, institutionalized the civil career, and created new public services.

The population of Costa Rica is $4.9 million, its GDP is $56.91, and the GDP per capita is $11,613.61. The production consists of 5.61% agriculture, 24.97% industry, and 69.42% services. Costa Rica's economy is fairly competitive; it scores 4.41 in the Global Competitiveness Index. Good health, higher education, and technological readiness are some of its competitive strengths. The innovation could improve for achieving a more competitive economy. Starting a business is very slow, it takes 28 days and the customs burdens are scored 3.8 out of 7 (Table 8.6a , b World Bank Data, 2016).

In the Doing Business rank Costa Rica is in the spot 58. Getting credit (7) and electricity (23) is very easy. But like other countries in the region protecting minority investors (166), enforcing contracts (124), and starting a business (121) are problems for business (Table 8.6c World Bank Data, 2016).

Table 8.6a Gross Domestic Product (GDP) for Costa Rica

GDP	*Costa Rica*
GDP, billions $	$56.91
Population, millions	4.90
GDP per capita, $	$11,613.61

	Costa Rica
Agriculture, % GDP	5.61
Industry, % GDP	24.97
Services, % GDP	69.42
Agriculture, % growth	3.73
Industry, % growth	2.38
Services, % growth	4.09
Exports, % GDP	35.06
Imports, % GDP	37.24
Exports, % growth	-1.66
Imports, % growth	-3.96
Trade in Services, % GDP	20.47
Travel services, % service imports	19.02
Logistics (5 best)	2.86
Days to start a business	24.00
Start-up costs, % GNI per capita	11.10
Customs burdens (7 best)	3.80

Table 8.6b Global Competitive Index for Costa Rica

Global Competitiveness Index rank	*Costa Rica*
GCI Global Score	4.41
GCI Pillar 1 Institutions	4.09
GCI Pillar 2 Infrastructure	4.05
GCI Pillar Macroeconomy	4.44
GCI Pillar 4 Health and Education	6.21
GCI Pillar 5 Higher Education and Training	5.07
GCI Pillar 6 Goods Market Efficiency	4.23
GCI Pillar 7 Labor Market Efficiency	4.26
GCI Pillar 8 Financial Markets	4.37
GCI Pillar 9 Technological Readiness	4.77
GCI Pillar 10 Market Size	3.35
GCI Pillar 11 Business Sophistication	4.30
GCI Pillar 12 Innovation	3.55

Table 8.6c Doing Business Rank for Costa Rica

Doing Business, rank	*Costa Rica*
Ease of Doing Business Rank	58.00
Starting a Business	121.00
Dealing with Construction Permits	49.00
Getting Electricity	23.00
Registering Property	53.00
Getting Credit	7.00
Protecting Minority Investors	166.00
Paying Taxes	80.00
Trading Across Borders	67.00
Enforcing Contracts	124.00
Resolving Insolvency	87.00

Table 8.6d Index of Economic Freedom for Costa Rica

Index of Economic Freedom	*Costa Rica*
2016 Score	67.37
Property Rights	50
Freedom from Corruption	54
Fiscal Freedom	79.4
Gov't Spending	88.7
Business Freedom	68.6
Labor Freedom	53.8
Monetary Freedom	77.6
Trade Freedom	81.6
Investment Freedom	70
Financial Freedom	50

The Economic Freedom Index, of the Heritage Foundation, scores Costa Rica 67.37 out of 100. Trade (81.6) and fiscal (79.4) freedom are good, but the indicators of property rights (50) and freedom from corruption (54) can be improved (Table 8.6d World Bank Data, 2016).

Table 8.6e Index of Globalization for Costa Rica

Various Indicators	*Costa Rica*
Index of Globalization 2013	62.19
Index of Economic Globalization	63.49
Index of Political Globalization	59.45
Index of Social Globalization	62.95
Human Development Index	0.77
Travel and Tourism Index	4.10
Corruption Perceptions Index	55.00

Source: Author's calculation from World Bank, Data 2016

Costa Rica has a score of 62.19 out of 100 in the Index of Globalization. It has the second highest Human Development Index, 0.77. The tourism sector is well scored with 4.1 out of 7 in the Travel and Tourism Index. Costa Rica's government is perceived as the less corrupt by its citizens in the region, with a score of 55 out of 100 in the Corruption Perceptions Index (Table 8.6e World Bank Data, 2016).

Panama

Government

Type: Unitary Presidential Constitutional Republic
President: Juan Carlos Varela
Vice President: Isabel Saint Malo

Economy

Panama is the most competitive country in the region. It has an excellent geographical location for commerce with the interoceanic canal recently extended and ready to receive bigger boats from around the world.

The population of 4.09 million is highly productive, with a production of $55.76 billion a year and a GDP per capita of $13,643.90. Most of this production comes from services, 69.37%; industry constitutes the 27.74% and agriculture 2.89% (Table 8.7a World Bank Data, 2016).

Table 8.7a Gross Domestic Product (GDP) for Panama

GDP	*Panama*
GDP, billions $	$55.76
Population, millions	4.09
GDP per capita, $	$13,643.90

	Panama
Agriculture, % GDP	2.89
Industry, % GDP	27.74
Services, % GDP	69.37
Agriculture, % growth	-0.66
Industry, % growth	5.93
Services, % growth	6.23
Exports, % GDP	53.57
Imports, % GDP	61.41
Exports, % growth	3.30
Imports, % growth	2.96
Trade in services, % GDP	30.18
Travel services, % service imports	18.15
Logistics (5 best)	2.87
Days to start a business	6.00
Start-up costs, % GNI per capita	6.30
Customs burdens (7 best)	4.15

Panama has developed good institutions and facilities to be competitive. It has a score of 4.51 out of 7 in the Global Competitiveness Index. The infrastructure, macroeconomy, financial markets, health and education, and business sophistication are well positioned. The Doing Business Index places Panama in the 69th spot. Getting credit (19), trading across borders (54), and starting a business (44) are pretty easy compared with other countries in the region. Starting a business takes 6 days, the fastest in Central America. The customs burdens are scored 4.15 out of 7 (Table 8.7b & c World Bank Data, 2016).

Table 8.7b Global Competitive Index Rank for Panama

Global Competitiveness Index rank	*Panama*
GCI Global Score	4.51
GCI Pillar 1 Institutions	3.97
GCI Pillar 2 Infrastructure	4.85
GCI Pillar Macroeconomy	5.99
GCI Pillar 4 Health and Education	5.78
GCI Pillar 5 Higher Education and Training	4.10
GCI Pillar 6 Goods Market Efficiency	4.64
GCI Pillar 7 Labor Market Efficiency	4.27
GCI Pillar 8 Financial Markets	5.12
GCI Pillar 9 Technological Readiness	4.55
GCI Pillar 10 Market Size	3.49
GCI Pillar 11 Business Sophistication	4.34
GCI Pillar 12 Innovation	3.53

Table 8.7c Doing Business Rank for Panama

Doing Business, rank	*Panama*
Ease of Doing Business Rank	69
Starting a Business	44
Dealing with Construction Permits	70
Getting Electricity	32
Registering Property	84
Getting Credit	19
Protecting Minority Investors	66
Paying Taxes	166
Trading Across Borders	54
Enforcing Contracts	148
Resolving Insolvency	132

The Economic Freedom Index scores Panama with 64.8 out of 100. Monetary (78.6), trade (77.8), and fiscal (84.4) freedom are considered high. But like the rest of the region, property rights (30) and corruption

(37) are not as good as they should. Panama scores 66.87 out of 100 in the Globalization Index and is the most economically globalized country in Central America with a score of 80.87. It has a high Human Development Index of 0.78. In the Travel and Tourism Index Panama scores 4.28, also the best of the region. The government is perceived as corrupt with a score of 39 out of 100 in the Corruption Perceptions Index (Table 8.7d & e World Bank Data, 2016).

Table 8.7d Index of Economic Freedom for Panama

Index of Economic Freedom	*Panama*
2016 Score	64.8
Property Rights	30
Freedom from Corruption	37
Fiscal Freedom	84.4
Gov't Spending	77.9
Business Freedom	74.4
Labor Freedom	42.9
Monetary Freedom	78.6
Trade Freedom	77.8
Investment Freedom	75
Financial Freedom	70

Table 8.7e Index of Globalization for Panama

Various Indicators	*Panama*
Index of Globalization 2013	66.87
Index of Economic Globalization	80.87
Index of Political Globalization	61.24
Index of Social Globalization	57.70
Human Development Index	0.78
Travel and Tourism Index	4.28
Corruption Perceptions Index	**39.00**

Source: Author's calculation from World Bank, Data, 2016

Competing for Canals: Guatemala and Nicaragua

Mid-year 2016 the world witnessed the opening of the newly renovated Panama Canal. The renewed structure reopened for business after an investment of nearly $5 billion over budget. For a long time this structure has been the lifeblood of trade from east to west and west to east. It has generated billions of dollars in revenues and given shipping companies easy access to both sides of the world. Officials anticipate that the new infrastructure will allow for doubling of cargo travel to Atlantic and Pacific Oceans.

This canal is a magnificent public transportation mechanism that will enhance the capabilities of the PA, especially for Colombia, Mexico, and Panama as well as the rest of Central American countries. The existence of this large structure provides enormous supply chain capabilities and can improve the trading activities among all of the countries in the region and around the world. It is a major transport system that will accelerate the movement of goods and make trade transactions much easier to manage.

This canal generates lots of revenue and controls enormous amounts of trade from across the globe (Choi 2016).

While the excitement from the newly renovated Panama Canal continues, farther North we find Nicaragua involved in a major project to construct a canal across its country's geography. It has been announced that Nicaragua has entered into an agreement to construct a canal across its country side. It is one of the most ambitious and polemical construction projects of all time. A company from Hong Kong has obtained the land rights to build a canal across Nicaragua. Since Nicaragua is an extremely poor country the prospects of having such a canal that would generate tens of millions of dollars are extremely appealing to a great many people.

The concept of this new canal being built has raised the eyebrows of conservationists and some economic developers. Some protests have emerged that argue that massive environmental damage will be the consequence of the construction of this canal. Additionally, huge dislocation of large numbers of people will cause lots of human suffering. Finally, substantial amounts of excavation of land and its surroundings will be required. All of this has an estimated cost of between $60–70 billion (Game Changer 2015).

If a new canal is constructed in Nicaragua, it will be a huge change for Central America and a giant change for global shipping. Without question a new canal in Nicaragua will present real competition for the Panama Canal that will have to be dealt with by Panama and the operators of the Panama

Canal. Time will tell but the strategists are already hard at work trying to figure out effective competitive strategies to meet the existence of a new canal. This is an unprecedented situation that really is a game changer. Trade will be forever transformed when another canal is in operation. Hopefully the PA, Latin America, and the whole world will benefit.

Discussion

Central America's entrance into the PA regional trading bloc demonstrates that the PA is an outward looking entity that wants to be as inclusive as possible yet as competitive as possible in world markets. Having Central American countries become part of the PA has good points and bad points. On the positive side the Alliance is expanded and hence the opportunities for trading more goods and services are immense. Additionally, because the PA can trade in labor and capital, it is possible to initiate more economic development projects because more businesses and entrepreneurs will have more access to money and labor. This can create a multiplier effect and in the long run contribute to everyone's benefit. Having more goods and services available creates lots of competition and as a result lower prices. This is welcomed news to the consumer.

On the other side, the ability of the PA administrative councils to manage and coordinate the activities of the PA with such a large number of countries raises major questions.

The whole thing could become an administrative nightmare and eventually be a colossal problem because the challenges of managing the trading bloc become so enormous.

On paper and on face it looks exciting and full of opportunities. Time will tell whether the entire concept will be successful. Lessons from the European Union should be studied carefully.

The issue of the competing canals is intriguing. Never has such an arrangement existed and, at this point, no one knows what will happen. Lots of speculation will be advanced with all kinds of theories that explain what the impact will be and how people, trades, and other country officials will really respond to it.

Competition is good in business. However, competition between two major canals has never really been observed or tested. Time will tell and surely it will be interesting to see the results.

Conclusion

The PA has stirred up a lot of interest and concern among the business people and officials in Latin America and the world. Many questions arise. What will it be? How will it affect the economic development of Latin American countries? Will it end up like all the rest of the mediocre trading blocs in Latin America? Will it be the silver bullet that catalyzes the entrepreneurs of the region with increased trade, more productivity, and a better standard of living? Few of these questions have been answered. Not much real trade experience in substance has been transacted between and among the PA partners. As such, it is still in its infancy with a lot of growing and maturation yet to come. Its success will depend on its leadership and the commitment it receives from its individual country governments and citizens. Again time will tell the story. Let's hope it is a positive and successful story.

References

Central Law. (2016). http://www.central-law.com/en/news/item/422-central-america-will-enter-soon-the-pacific-alliance.

Choi, D. (2016). Take a look at the Panama Canal's historic transformation, Business Insider, June 29, 2016. http://www.businessinsider.com/transformation-of-panama-canal-2016-6/#construction-of-the-canal-begins-1.

Game Changer. (2015). http://www1.cbn.com/cbnnews/world/2015/April/Nicaragua-Canal-A-Game-Changer-in-Central-America.

World Bank. (2016). http://databank.worldbank.org/data/reports.aspx?source=world-development-indicators.

CHAPTER 9

Looking to the Future

Introduction and Background

At this point we can recap the aims and achievements of the nascent Pacific Alliance and its implications for the business and economic world for the decades to come. As was outlined in Chapter 1, the original four members of the Pacific Alliance share similar economic and political histories, cultures, and ideas. This makes their integration all the more a logical next step, not just in economic matters, but also potentially in political matters as well, as long as these keep in the spirit of the original intents and purposes of the Pacific Alliance, freer trade.

The potentially huge advantages of greater political integration among the countries of Latin America notwithstanding, it nonetheless remains true that the main purpose of the Pacific Alliance is to form a trading bloc that will permit the exploitation of comparative advantages and economic and commercial opportunities. The Pacific Alliance is based on the principles of free market and trade. In its essence, the Pacific Alliance seeks economic and commercial integration, growth, competitiveness, and the free movement of goods, services, resources, and people. The ultimate objective of the Pacific Alliance is the creation of an economic bloc that can not only trade with but, ultimately, compete and outcompete the big economic powers such as Asia, Europe, and the United States.

The Pacific Alliance is a trade project that should be welcomed with open arms by businesspeople all over the world. Inasmuch as the European countries are continuing to plunge into generational decay,

J.E. Spillan, N. Virzi, *Business Opportunities in the Pacific Alliance*,
DOI 10.1007/978-3-319-54768-8_9

politically and economically, the US economy struggles to recover from an eight–year-long anemic "recovery" since the financial crash of 2008–2009, and the Chinese economy decelerates to a more normal rate of growth in the 6–7% range, the world will need a more dynamic, proactive Latin American economy to help motor through economic and commercial growth in the years to come.

Though the Asian economies will adjust to the Chinese deceleration, this region of the world will no doubt continue to provide the impetus of world economic growth in the years to come. By switching to more frankly market-oriented principles of business and free trade, the Pacific Alliance economies will be better able to adjust, adapt, and exploit the opportunities presented by a growing Asian economy. In a shrinking, modern world, Asia and the Latin American countries with a Pacific Coast are, effectively, neighbors. The original member countries of the Pacific Alliance all share borders in the Pacific Ocean. This geographic fact alone makes dealing with the Pacific Alliance an attractive option to the Asian economies because of the importance of the Pacific Ocean as a trade route, and vice versa.

As we affirmed at the beginning of this book, the Pacific Alliance represents the future of business and commercial leadership in Latin America, representing approximately 37% of the gross domestic product (GDP) for the region of Latin America and the Caribbean. This alone is a reason enough to take the Pacific Alliance seriously, as have over 40 observer countries, to date. The observer countries do not just include countries from Central America, such as Guatemala, Honduras, El Salvador, and the Dominican Republic; they include even France, Italy, and Japan. Were the Pacific Alliance countries to fully practice economic integration, they would become eighth largest economic "country" in the world. That would be some economic feat. It is no wonder then that so many countries, from all regions in the world, have their eyes on the Pacific Alliance. It is quite an enticing prospect for an Asian company to set up shop in Central America, with eyes on penetrating and servicing the American market, or for a multinational to attend to the Asian market from any one of a growing number of lower-cost, productive Latin American nations.

As was covered in the chapter on the economic history of Latin America, previous trade blocs in the region have been inward looking and protectionist. In contrast, the Pacific Alliance is outward looking and open to trade. This change in focus, this "pivot to Asia" is all-important. Rather than continuing to focus on the stalled economies of the Atlantic and Europe, the Pacific Alliance looks to leverage the economic potential of emerging Asia. In this sense, a healthy synergetic relationship arises between the Pacific Alliance countries of Latin America and the growing economic powerhouse that the Asian economic region is becoming.

The United States plays a role in the Pacific Alliance in no small part because the United States has always been a beacon of free trade around the world. On July 18, 2013, the United States joined the Pacific Alliance as an observer country. This is only natural, given the fact that the United States has strong commercial ties with each member nation, and the fact that the United States remains the number one destination market for the export products of the largest economies of the world. Blazing the way toward freer commerce with more dynamic economies, Latin American leaders like Chile, Colombia, Peru, Mexico, and even some Central American countries, like Costa Rica, are blazing the trail for the penetration of the Asian markets. When contemplating Asia, one must consider the elephant in the room, China. Although the Chinese economy is slated to overtake the US economy in sheer size, China is a long way from supplanting the economic and political leadership of the United States on a global scale. Therefore, the causes of capitalism and commerce will continue to thrive in the Asian region, which benefits even, if not especially, China herself.

The best-case scenario is that China will someday progress beyond being the main supplier of cheap, low-quality goods the world over to a fully developed market economy with a liberal political regime. If this happens, the instincts behind the Pacific Alliance will pay off handsomely. There is cause for this hope. After all, as China grows economically, her middle class inevitably also grows, and middle classes in the end always demand open and transparent governments. Seen in this light, the potential for real economic and political and social progress in Asia is huge. First-mover benefits also promise to be huge. The economic and commercial business pioneers of the Pacific Alliance are these first movers. As we stated at the outset, the Pacific Pumas are betting on the Asian Tigers.

The goal of the Pacific Alliance is to become an economic bloc that can outcompete Asian countries for trade with not only the United States, but Asian countries as well, by providing lower-priced and better-quality goods. On economic terms, this seems to be a straightforward proposition. On political terms, not so much. Latin America is going through some rough spots. Venezuela is in socialist shambles, with enormous fiscal deficits and on the cusp of a hyperinflationary crisis. A president has been toppled in Brazil (Dilma Rousseff) as well as in Guatemala (Otto Perez Molina), while a former president (Antonio Saca) has been recently arrested on corruption charges in El Salvador. The region as a whole is expected to be in recession for the year of 2016. Nonetheless, the hope is that the Pacific Alliance can provide some out-of-the-box leadership in the coming years, to shake the doldrums and complacency out of the regional economy. The hope is that the ordered free trade example provided by the Pacific Alliance countries as a whole is emulated throughout the region. Hopefully, free trading nations, which tend to be less corrupted, will become a contagion in the region.

The Pacific Alliance, by itself, would represent a huge economy, among the ten largest economic powerhouses of the world, if taken as a whole. This is not farfetched. The Pacific Alliance aims for deeper regional economic integration among its member nations. To create a true economic and commercial union is its aim, and it has taken credible commitments to achieve the same. The ultimate aim is to facilitate the freer circulation of goods, services, capital, and also people as well.

The Pacific Alliance appears to be a sustainable trade group because of its sheer size alone. However, its economic and commercial fortunes in large part will continue to depend on what happens *outside* of the Pacific Alliance, inasmuch as Pacific Alliance members still trade relatively little with one another (George 2014). In short, the Pacific Alliance will enjoy tailwinds if the phenomena of increasing trade liberalization and globalization proceed apace into the future. Just the opposite, however, will occur if trade liberalization and globalization run afoul of voter sentiment, as it appears to have done in 2016, with respect to the Brexit vote in the United Kingdom, a referendum on whether or not the United Kingdom should leave the European Union (EU). Another example of voters expressing opinions contrary to the liberal world order is to be had in the election in November, 2016 of Donald Trump as the next President of the United States, a country with observer status to the Pacific Alliance. Inasmuch as these are the two countries, which have done the most to propagate the benefits of free trade in the world, the issue of the voter backlash to trade liberalization and globalization will be extensively treated in this chapter.

Is Globalization and Freer Trade Here to Stay?

The world today trades seemingly as never before. The commitment to free trade and the liberal world order as a whole has peaked and waned over the years, but scenarios foreseeing the demise of freer trade endeavors such as the Pacific Alliance are relatively scarce. In the following pages, we look at the evolution of economic growth and trade among the regions of Latin America and the Caribbean and Emerging and Developing Asia.

Graph 9.1 shows how the economic crash of 2009 negatively impacted the region of Latin America and the Caribbean, affecting even more drastically the trade volume of goods and services in the world. Latin American GDP growth is expected to subperform relative to world GDP growth in the next five years, from 2017 to 2021.

The GDP of the world as a whole grew at an annual average rate of 3.4% in the time period between 1985 and 1996. The region of Latin American and the Caribbean as whole grew at an average annual rate of 2.9%. In other words, Latin American growth was just 85% of what world economic growth was in the same time period, 1985–1996. Latin America grew substantially less than the world due, in great part, to the adjustment pains the region had to undergo on account of the civil wars against

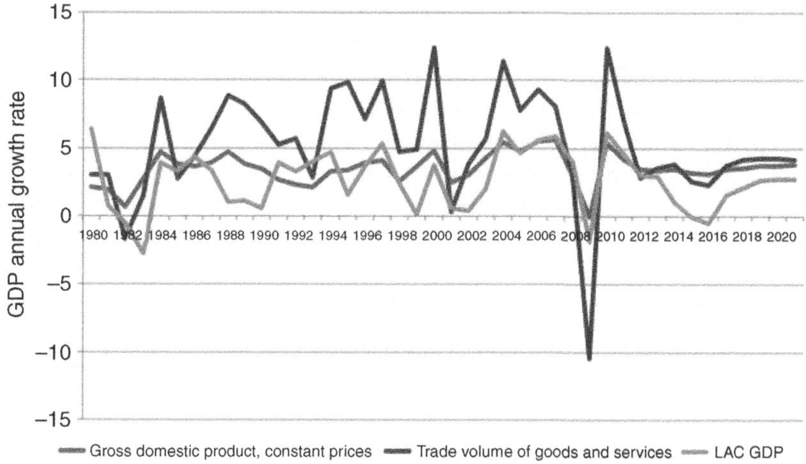

Graph 9.1 Growth in Trade and Real GDP in the World 1980–2021

Source: Calculations by authors based on International Monetary Fund data, 2016

Marxist guerrillas. For decades, from the 1960s to the 1980s, and in some cases, the 1990s, terrorism against businesses and civil society reigned.[1] Marxist terrorism had the effect of thwarting political progress, frustrating the national economies, and blunting national investment, and, in the end, scaring off any meaningful foreign direct investment for decades. Needless to say, this left strong, negative lag effects on the Latin American economies.

On top of the negative effects of decades of Marxist terrorism directed against the private sectors and civil society, the structural adjustments made necessary in fiscal, monetary, and trade policy by decades of state-led growth and import-substitution-industrialization programs, effectively bankrupted the states in Latin America. This is a chief reason why the 1980s has been called by Latin Americanists "the Lost Decade" (Spillan et al. 2014).

While the world as a whole grew at a 4.1% average annual rate in the 1997–2008 time period, Latin American grew at an average annual rate of 3.4%. Again, Latin American growth was only approximately 83% of what world economic growth was in the same time period, this time 1998–2008. This lag is certainly attributable to the mistakes of the past, more so than the more market-friendly policies of the present at that time. Strong lag effects were felt even in the 1990s as Latin America emerged from the adjustments to the damages caused to the real economy and the investment climate by the decades-long Marxist terror campaign. Investment, after all, is future-oriented. Investment gaps of the past affected then current economic performance in the Latin American region.

Even going forward, in the time period 2011–2021,[2] it is expected that the world GDP will grow at an average annual rate of 3.5% per year, compared to an average annual rate of 2.1% for Latin America. In this case, GDP growth for the region of Latin America and the Caribbean is expected to be just approximately 58% of world real GDP growth. This is attributable, astonishingly, to the policy setbacks suffered by the principal economies of the region. It is simply astonishing, in light of the lessons of economic history as to the benefits of fiscal and monetary policy discipline and free trade commercial policies, that resource-rich countries such as Venezuela and Brazil are suffering such embarrassing, humiliating setbacks on their paths to development. Venezuela, in fact, has become an economic tragedy, a moral lesson for developing economies everywhere. The poor performance of two of the richest economies in the region of Latin America and the Caribbean are a drag on the economic statistics for the region going into the future.

The region of Latin America and the Caribbean is very dependent on the health of trade in the world. The region does better when the world economy is thriving and trade spreads. This is the entire basis, after all, of the Pacific Alliance.

Graph 9.2 shows how economic growth and the volume of exports and imports of goods and services move almost in unison since the year 2000.

Graph 9.3 shows the close relationship between the World Trade volume of goods and services and the volume of exports and imports of goods and services for the region of Latin America and the Caribbean. It is evident that there is more volatility in the imports of goods and services for the region of Latin America and the Caribbean. The expectation is that in the time period between 2017 and 2021 all three variables will converge around an average annual growth rate of just under 5%.

For the world, the trade volume of goods and services grew at an average annual rate of 6.5% in the time period between 1985 and 1996, with the average annual rate of growth in the volume of imports (6.5%) slightly exceeding the rate of growth in the volume of exports (6.4%, on average). The average annual rate of growth for the trade volume of goods and services rose to 6.8% in the time period 1997–2008, again with the

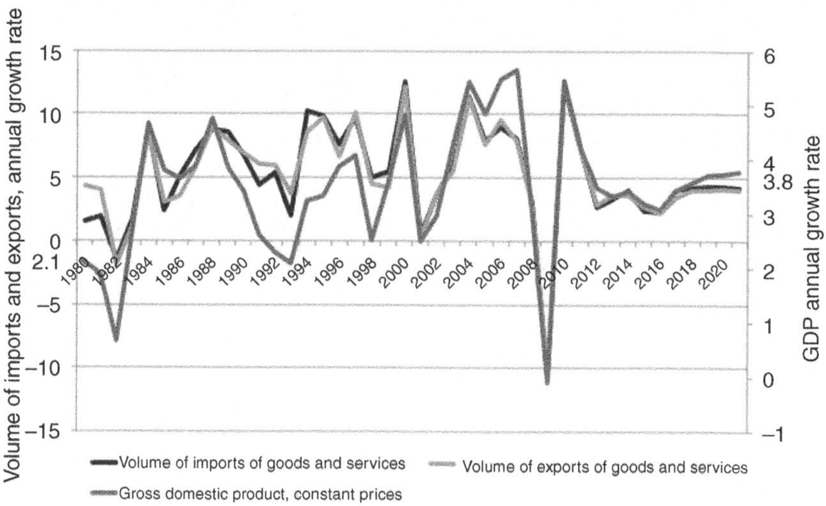

Graph 9.2 Growth in Exports and Imports and Real GDP in the World 1980–2021

Source: Calculations by authors based on International Monetary Fund data, 2016

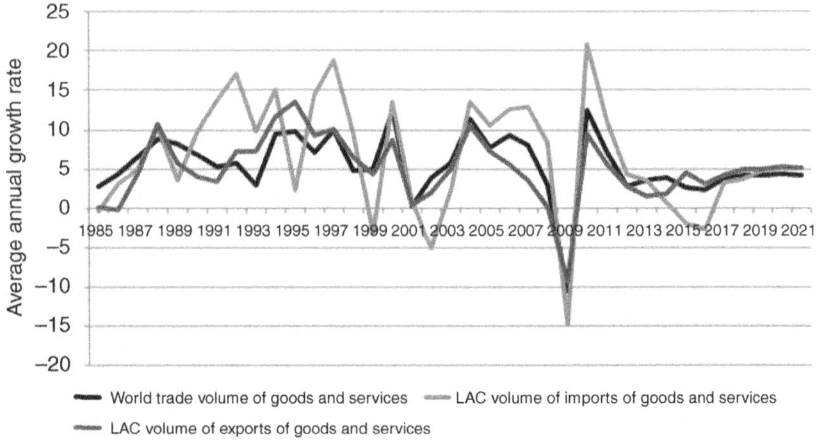

Graph 9.3 World Trade Volume and Exports and Imports of Latin America and the Caribbean 1980–2021

Source: Calculations by authors based on International Monetary Fund data, 2016

growth rate in the volume of imports of goods and services (6.9%) exceeding that of the volume of exports of goods and services (6.7%). For the time period between 2011 and 2021, the forecasts are expected to be in the range of 3.9% average annual rate of growth in the trade volume of goods and services for the world.[3]

During the time period of 1985–1996, when the average annual rate of growth in the volume of exports in the world was 6.4%, the average annual rate of growth in the volume of exports for Latin America was also 6.4%. During the time period of 1997–2008, when the average annual rate of growth in the volume of exports in the world was 6.7%, the average annual rate of growth in the volume of exports for Latin America was only 5.3%. However, it must be borne in mind that this time period includes the boom years just before the economic crash of 2009. During this time, the terms of trade for Latin American exports were soaring.[4] For the time period between 2011 and 2021, it is expected that the average annual rate of growth for exports from the region of Latin America and the Caribbean outperform slightly the average annual rate of growth for exports from the region of Emerging and Developing Asia (4% versus 3.8%).

During the time period of 1985–1996, when the average annual rate of growth in the volume of imports in the world was 6.5%, the average annual rate of growth in the volume of imports for Latin America was much higher, at 8.6%. This reflected weaknesses in the industrial sectors of the region of Latin America and the Caribbean, a region which also had to import many of its manufacturing inputs and final consumer goods in those days. During the time period of 1997–2008, when the average annual rate of growth in the volume of imports in the world was 6.9%, the average annual rate of growth in the volume of imports for Latin America was again much higher, at 7.9%. For the time period between 2011 and 2021, it is expected that the average annual rate of growth for imports of the region of Emerging and Developing Asia exceed by one half of a percentage point the average annual rate of growth for imports for the region of Latin America and the Caribbean outperform (3.9% versus 3.4%).

Graph 9.4 shows how, especially since the year 2000, the terms of trade between region of Latin America and the Caribbean has an inverse relationship to the evolution of the terms of trade for the region of Emerging and Developing Asia. From 2018 forward, it is expected that the terms of trade for the two regions evolve in a similar fashion, hovering around zero, with a slight advantage for the region of Latin America and the Caribbean.

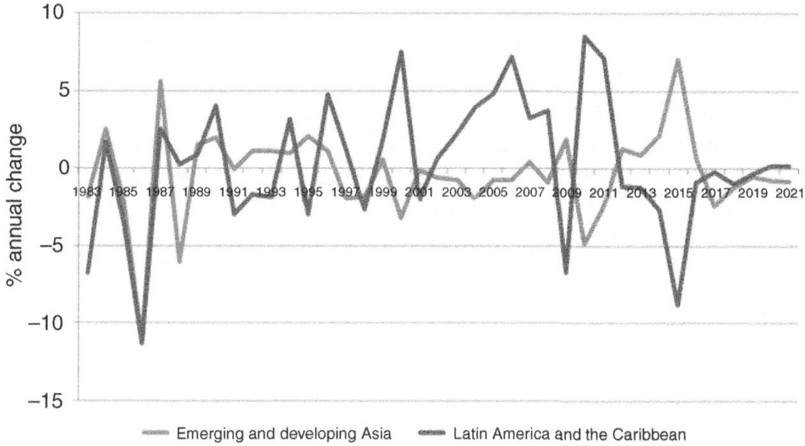

Graph 9.4 Evolution of the Terms of Trade Latin America and the Caribbean vs. Emerging and Developing Asia 1983–2021

Source: Graph by authors based on International Monetary Fund data, 2016

Brexit

Threats appear on the horizon to the cause of greater globalization and free trade. This has become manifest on account of important, recent elections in the United Kingdom and the United States. Two cases in point are those of the case of the Brexit vote in the EU and the election of Donald Trump as the President-elect of the United States in the elections of November 2016. Both votes represented a voter rejection of the globalist ideals which the Pacific Alliance embodies. Without a wide consensus on the benefits of free trade, the sustainability and potential for growth going forward of self-propagating free trade pacts, such as the Pacific Alliance, will face a tougher going. Thus, a serious treatment of these issues is in order.

In the campaign for Brexit, at issue was whether the United Kingdom should remain in the EU (the Remain camp), or exit the EU (the Brexit camp). The debate came about due to tensions between ordinary Britons who feared loss of their safety and national culture due to the sudden influx of Muslim refugees from the Middle East.[5] The forced acceptance of Muslim refugees was by imposition by EU elites of open borders upon all member countries of the EU. The expansion of this concept, originally intended to apply only within the countries of Europe, to include Muslim refugees from the Middle East, was something not contemplated in the decades of negotiations which led to the gradual changes that permitted the created the EU in the first place.

The Brexit side faced seemingly insurmountable odds. The Remain in the EU side was backed by big business, the political and economic elites, the media, academia, the population with greater levels of education, and the younger generation. The Brexit camp depended almost exclusively on older British subjects who were worried about the loss of sovereignty. When the Brexit camp won, it was a stunning rebuke for the cause of globalization and free trade. What the British people said, effectively, was that the tremendous benefits of being a part of the EU were outweighed by the costs to their national sovereignty. That this could be the assessment of the people of the United Kingdom, a country which is second only to the United States in being the cause of the spread of liberal ideas of trade and democracy in the world, is a serious rebuke to the ideas of free trade and the notion that globalization is always good. Other countries contemplating projects similar to the EU, such as the Pacific Alliance members, would do well to heed the lessons of the Brexit vote and what caused this historic rejection of what seemed to be the natural evolution of liberal history.

The reasons for the rejection of the globalist viewpoint are varied. A key factor in the vote against globalization and free trade as represented in the vote for Brexit was the opposition of older voters. Older voters are the ones that remember life under the EU and life before it. These voters rejected the EU and its promises. However much one exalts the youth vote in favor of the EU, the fact is that they have no comparative referent, whereas the older voters do have such a comparative referent. The fact that the benefits of the EU, the world's premiere integrationist project, could not be sold to voters of another European country, who could compare the before and after scenarios of life outside and under the EU, was and is potentially devastating for the cause of globalization.

Immigration concerns, reflective of a larger concern for the preservation of national culture, certainly played a role. Inasmuch as the UK does not have a constitution, its parliament can do whatever it wants. The problem perceived is that its parliament ceded its sovereign authority to the European Parliament, which no British citizen recognizes as a legitimate entity, empowered to determine British immigration policy (BBC, Mundo 2016a). Basically, a significant portion of the British populace was uncomfortable with the massive inflows of new immigrants from the most terror-conflicted zones of the Middle East that the EU was imposing on the UK, without prior consultation of the people. Were this disastrous decision not made, it is likely that the Brexit issue would have never come up to a popular referendum, much less won.

For the designers of free trade pacts in the future, the first thing to bear in mind is that the Brexit decision was not mainly an economic decision, but rather a political one. To Britons, it seems that the supranational elites of the EU viewed with greater favor foreigners over citizens, foreign dissidents over homegrown citizens and subjects. As a case in point, after all, was the fact that more than half of the 300,000 new migrants are from outside of the EU (BBC Mundo 2016b). What began as a debate for intra-European trade and immigration facilitation rapidly degenerated into a debate over the supposed rights of Third World people to come to the developed world, where many come to advocate illiberal ideas, in detriment to the liberal culture of the Western countries that accepted them, as refugees, migrants, etc. As colossal an error as this was for the EU elites to commit, it was also one that would have been astonishingly easy to avoid. Thus, the discredit one can assign to economic globalization per se in the whole Brexit mess is less than one would at first expect.

Although it is important to put the Brexit rejection of globalism into context, it is no small thing that the UK decided to leave the EU. The real danger is in the imitation effects which may follow. This decision has contributed to the rise of similar movements against free trade and economic integration throughout Europe. Brexit won, despite all warnings from political, economic, and intellectual elites against the adverse economic effects for the UK of its leaving the EU. The institutions that came out against Brexit were not just national ones, but also international ones. The International Monetary Fund (IMF) is a case in point. The IMF warned that if the UK left the EU that the UK economy would stall, there would be massive increase in unemployment and that the British pound would plummet in credibility and value. The Bank of England predicted an economic recession would result from Brexit, while the Office of the Exchequer predicted that the UK would have to implement severe austerity policies based on reduced public spending combined with higher taxes. The President of the United States Barack Hussein Obama intervened to warn the people of the UK on the dangers and costs of Brexit, and the benefits of remaining in the political and economic union of the EU. EU leaders practically argued that a vote for Brexit was a vote for the end of the world. It was not enough.

The fact that none of the doomsday scenarios have come true throws even more egg on the faces of the representatives of the institutions that promote globalization in the world. In this respect, it is important, and positive, that the impetus for the Pacific Alliance comes not from these international bodies, such as the International Monetary Fund, the Economic Commission for Latin American and the Caribbean of the United Nations, or the World Bank, but rather from the national governments of the Latin American countries involved and with a direct stake in the economic and political outcomes of their endeavor.

In large part, the vote for Brexit was a vote to reject the political and economic establishment, which happens to promote globalization. That the Brexit vote represented a rejection of elites is sustained by the fact that the British believed more in Nigel Farage, the leader of the Independence Party of the UK, than in David Cameron, the Prime Minister of the United Kingdom. It bears remembering that David Cameron won two general elections and two referendums in the last decade, a clear indication that the vote for Brexit was a vote in spite of what the political elites said. The elites simply did not convince the majority of the British populace that the benefits of remaining in the EU outweighed its evidently increasing costs. Perhaps the rejection of the EU by the voting populace in the UK was more of a rejection of the management of certain sensitive subjects, such as immigration and welfare for new immigrants, than of free trade in and of itself (BBC, Mundo 2016b).

What began as an economic union rapidly progressed into a political union, in which the citizen voters were never fully consulted on the changes to their societies that these "trade" pacts represented. This is what led to the success of Brexit and the apparent rejection of globalization. However, in the case of the Pacific Alliance, things should, and could, be different. In the first place, all of the countries of Latin America share a common cultural heritage, mainly Spanish, but in Brazil, also Portuguese. The fact is that a Latin American integrationist project, along the lines of the EU, should, in theory, proceed with much less difficulty than was the case with the EU. What gets in the way are rival political and business interests, but not cultural and social issues, as was the case with Brexit. The difference is important, in that the divergence in political and business interests can be substantially resolved by an economic approach to negotiations (i.e., splitting the difference), whereas social, cultural issues cannot be, and are thus more prone to lead to either/or situations and heightened political tensions. Thankfully, the Pacific Alliance does not face the same divisive issues as were present in the Brexit vote and its rejection of globalization.

Trump and Globalization: The Implications for the Pacific Alliance and Free Trade in General

In addition to the Brexit vote in rejection of the EU, the other seeming deathblow to globalization was the election to the Presidency of the United States of the man named Donald Trump. After all, the United States is the beacon of free trade around the world, and an observer and a potential member someday of the Pacific Alliance. Donald Trump is a man who campaigned against free trade treaties and uncontrolled immigration. As Andres Oppenheimer has argued, taken Trump's campaign promises literally, to build a wall to control illegal immigration, a 35% import tax on Mexican car imports and the deportation of 11 million illegal immigrants in the United States would not only hurt the cause of globalization and free trade, but the US economy as a whole, and the American consumer, in particular (Oppenheimer 2016 [1]).

Certainly, by any objective measure, this would have to represent a serious threat to the cause of free trade and globalization in the world.

This is particularly so on account of the fact that it has been the United States which has done the most to advance the cause of liberal commerce in the world. It is judicious to consider the issue here.

Trump won the presidential election in the United States because he promised the working class respite against the trials and tribulations attendant to the cause of free trade deals (Montaner 2016). As was elucidated in the section on Public Choice economics in Chapter 2 of this book, there are always winners and losers to public policy, even good ones. Here, it bears remembering that, although free trade benefits countries in the aggregate, there are always winners and losers to freeing up trade. Trump spoke to the losing classes in free trade deals, mainly the manufacturing classes in the United States, no longer competitive against cheaper labor in the Third World. Trump successfully postulated that the American working class finds itself on the losing end of free trade deals, which outsource American livelihoods abroad. The foregoing puts into question whether the impetus toward freer trade and greater globalization will continue, in light of a presumptive withdrawal of American leadership.

Before tackling head-on the implications of the Trump election victory and the seeming validation of anti-illegal immigration, antitrade policies, and what they mean for globalization, we must first establish and understand what we mean by globalization. It must be remembered that globalization has three components: economic globalization, political globalization, and social globalization. In addition to three indices measuring these dimensions, the KOF Index of Globalization[6] calculates an overall index of globalization and subindices referring to the following:

- actual economic flows
- economic restrictions
- data on information flows
- data on personal contact
- data on cultural proximity.[7]

The KOF Index of Globalization defines globalization to be the process of creating networks of connections among actors at multicontinental distances, mediated through a variety of flows including people, information and ideas, capital, and goods.[8] KOF conceptualizes globalization as a multifaceted process that erodes national boundaries, integrates national economies, and cultures, thus producing complex relations of mutual interdependence.

Broadly speaking, economic globalization has two dimensions: actual economic flows as measures of globalization and proxies for restrictions to trade and capital. For economic flows, data on imports, exports, flows of foreign direct investment, and income payments to foreign nationals are included. For economic restrictions, hidden import barriers, mean tariff rates, taxes on international trade, and capital controls are taken into account. It is this type of globalization which will likely continue, even after Brexit and the election of Donald Trump. The opposition to globalization represented in the Brexit vote, and even in the Trump election, had more to do with political and social issues.

The KOF Index of Globalization also takes into account other dimensions, such as political globalization and social globalization. Political globalization measures such things as the number of embassies and high commissions in a country and, the number of international organizations to which a given country belongs to, as well as the number of UN peace missions a country has participated in, the number of treaties signed between two or more states since 1945. The KOF Index of Globalization segments social globalization into three categories: personal contacts, information flows, and cultural proximity.[9] Personal contacts is meant to capture direct interaction among people living in different countries, measuring telecom traffic, tourism, and the stock of foreigners among a given country's population. Information flows are meant to measure the potential flow of ideas and images. Cultural proximity takes into account the degree to which beliefs and values move across national borders. Implicit in the cultural proximity concept is the notion that there is and should be a convergence to Western, i.e., American, norms, because the United States is the trend-setter for much of the sociocultural realm around the world.[10]

It is perhaps in the cultural, if not the political, realm where the election of Donald Trump as President of the United States might seem to be the death knell for globalization. If globalization implies a certain convergence to the American norms, to American values, and principles, and the United States itself is seen to jettison its traditional support for free trade, then the global impetus for ever-more liberal trade treaties seems certainly to be coming to an end. Were this to be true, it would certainly put an upper limit to the possibilities of expansion of the Pacific Alliance, keeping in mind that the United States has an immense Pacific Ocean coastline itself.

Trump's election victory can be said to be more against social globalization than economic globalization. For the practical intents and purposes of free trade treaties, these can be confined to the regulated movement of goods, services, capital, and people, without introducing sudden, jarring challenges in the realm of social globalization, as happened in the EU, with the case of the sudden opening up of the borders to immigrants from terrorist havens. In contrast to the elitist way this was conducted in the EU, treaties such as the Pacific Alliance treat specific economic issues, and these are identified in long, protracted negotiations where consensus is built. If care is taken not to overdo the effects of social globalization, it is not outside the realm of possibility that the United States, even under a President Trump, might want to become part of the Pacific Alliance.

Candidate Donald Trump lambasted bad trade deals, that is for sure, and not just for their flaws in the areas of social globalization. Trump opposed the 12-country Trans-Pacific Partnership, a free trade endeavor quite similar to the Pacific Alliance in spirit and letter (Oppenheimer 2016 [2]). However, Trump has not criticized free trade in and by itself so much as he has criticized *bad* trade deals. The Trump critique of trade deals is not so much the trade part as the "deal" part; in effect, they weren't good deals for the United States, according to Donald Trump. While this is small comfort for those who believe any trade deal is better than no trade deal, it is wise to keep perspective on the opposition of the new President of the United States to trade deals. In short, the United States is unlikely to abandon its traditional support for free market economics under a President Donald Trump, and may even possibly join the Pacific Alliance, under the proper conditions, such as limiting its extension to economic globalization.

Graph 9.5 shows how the members of the Pacific Alliance all improved on their scores on the Index of Globalization, which takes into account the economic, social, and political dimensions of globalization, in the years between 1970 and 2013. Whereas Colombia and Peru barely scored above 30 out of 100 in 1970, they both improved to 60 or better by 2013. Mexico, too, improved, from about 40 to over 60 in the same time period. Chile improved from about 45 to over 70. For Chile and Peru, the rate of improvement has slowed down noticeably in the last few years, while Mexico and Colombia show the opposite. It bears remembering the close political and economic ties Mexico and Colombia have with the United States, in particular.

Graph 9.6 shows only the dimension of economic globalization for the Pacific Alliance countries. Colombia improves from a score just above the mid-20s in 1970 to a score just under 60, a 30-point improvement! Mexico improves from a score around 38 in 1970 to over 60 in 2013, more than a

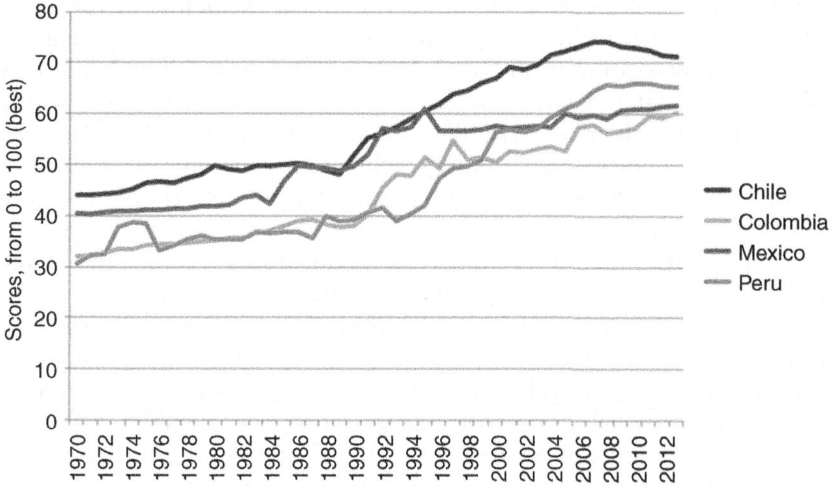

Graph 9.5 Index of Globalization in the Pacific Alliance countries 1970–2013

Source: Calculations by authors based on International Monetary Fund data, 2016

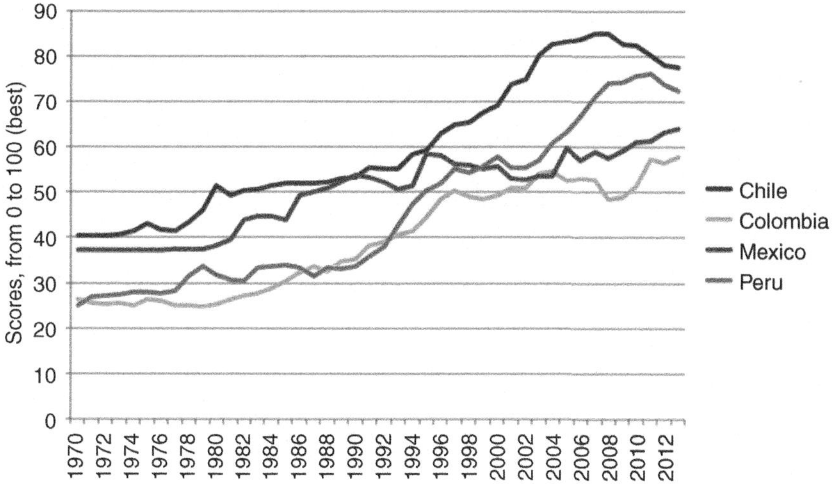

Graph 9.6 Economic Globalization in the Pacific Alliance countries 1970–2013

Source: Calculations by authors based on International Monetary Fund data, 2016

20-point improvement. Chile improves almost 40 points in the same time frame. Peru makes the greatest, most dramatic improvement, of over 45 points, going from about 25 in 1970 to over 70 in 2013. It is noteworthy that the score for economic globalization for both Chile and Peru falls off in the last few years, while Mexico and Colombia continue to improve. It is noteworthy how economic globalization takes off, especially in Chile and Peru, after roughly the year of the fall of the Berlin Wall in 1989.

Graph 9.7 shows the evolution of social globalization among the Pacific Alliance countries in the 1971–2013 time frame. Peru improves over 20 points, as do Mexico and Chile. Colombia is the only country not to make a 20-point improvement in the time period. It is noteworthy how much the later scores on social globalization for the Pacific Alliance countries lag the economic globalization scores in the later years. While in 2013, the social globalization scores range in the 42–52 interval, the corresponding range for economic globalization among the Pacific Alliance countries is 58–78.

Graph 9.8 illustrates an important detail right off. It is noteworthy how much better all of the Pacific Alliance countries start off in the political

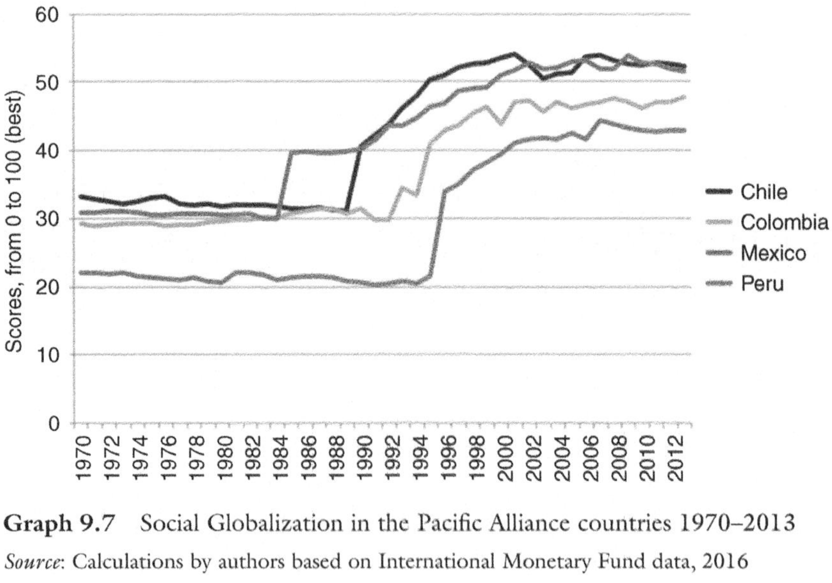

Graph 9.7 Social Globalization in the Pacific Alliance countries 1970–2013

Source: Calculations by authors based on International Monetary Fund data, 2016

globalization dimension in 1970. Whereas in the economic globalization dimension the countries in 1970 had scores in the range of 25–40, the range for political globalization in 1970 among the Pacific Alliance countries is about 43–63. As of 2013, although all countries perform better than 70, in the range of 71–88, Mexico is the country that improved the least, starting off at just under 60 and finishing off at just over 70. Colombia improves markedly from below 45 to 80. Chile starts off best at just under 65 and almost nears 90 by 2013. Peru improves the most, from 50 to over 85.

Contrary to the popular belief, the Asian countries are not necessarily more globalized than the countries of Latin America, at least when compared to the Pacific Alliance countries. It is noteworthy that China and Vietnam both score exceptionally bad in 1970, both under 20 out of a possible score of 100. Cambodia and South Korea barely score better, in the mid-20s, in 1970. Korea shows the most steady, consistent rate of improvement, going from the mid-20s in 1970 to the mid-60s in 2013. China improves dramatically, going from under 20 in 1970 to over 60 in 2013. Cambodia started off better than Vietnam, with a score of about 23 in 1970, compared to under 20 for Vietnam; however, as Vietnam

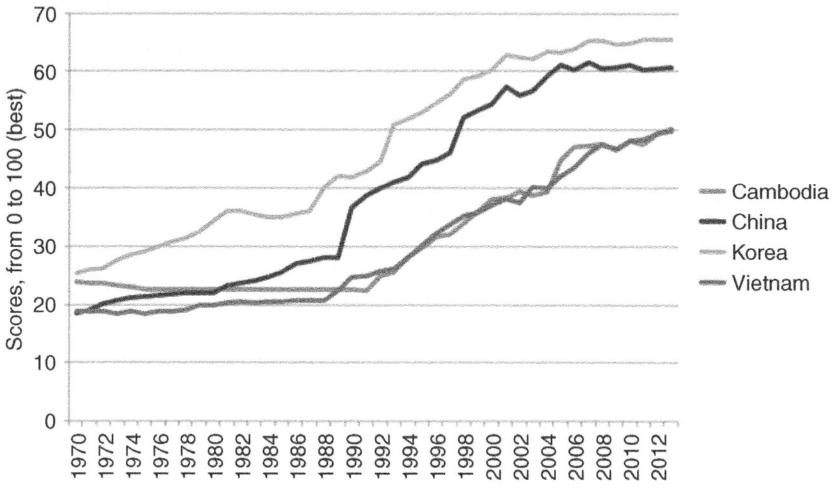

Graph 9.8 KOF Index of Globalization in key Asian countries 1970–2013

Source: Calculations by authors based on International Monetary Fund data, 2016

remained relatively flat in the first two decades, Cambodia actually regressed. All four countries show a marked improvement on their general scores of globalization after the end of the Cold War. This is a testament to the power of the example of the victory of the American-led liberal world order in the propagation of the freer movement of goods, services, ideas, and people across the globe.

Graph 9.9 shows remarkably little economic globalization took sway in Cambodia and Vietnam until the end of the Cold War. Korea improved from a score of 30 in 1970 to about 40 by 1990. China's score on economic globalization takes off with the implementation of capitalist reforms at the end of the 1970s. All four countries selected show marked improvement in their economic globalization scores after the end of the Cold War. China ends up improving from a score of 25 in 1970 to 50 in 2013. Vietnam shows the most improvement, going from the worst position in economic globalization in 1970 to the best score in 2013, out of the key Asian countries selected.

Graph 9.10 shows the evolution of social globalization in key Asian countries for the 1970–2013 time interval. China shows remarkable

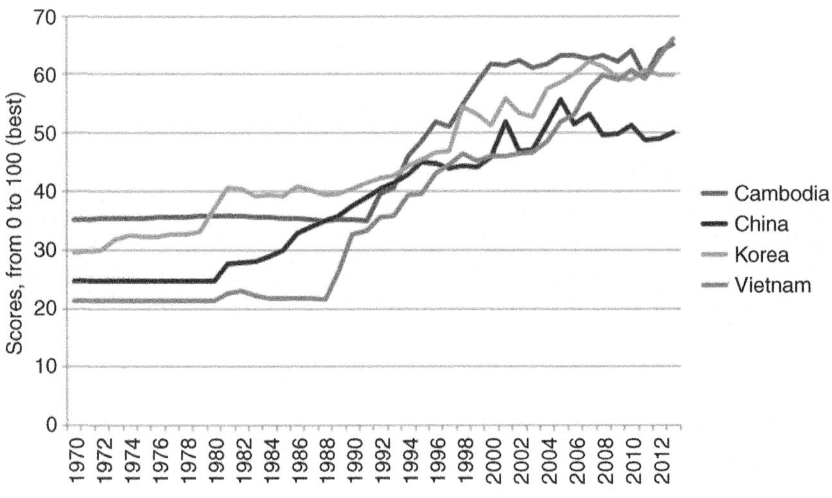

Graph 9.9 Economic Globalization in key Asian countries 1970–2013

Source: Calculations by authors based on International Monetary Fund data, 2016

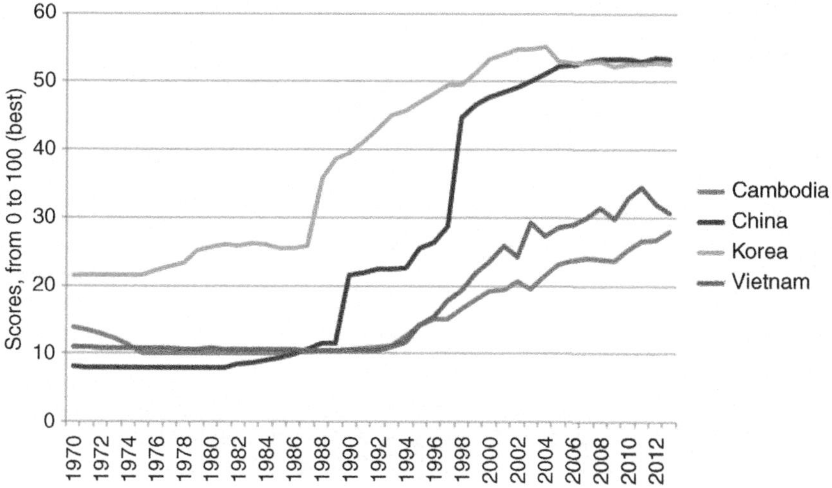

Graph 9.10 Social Globalization in key Asian countries 1970–2013

Source: Calculations by authors based on International Monetary Fund data, 2016

improvement, going from under a score of 10 in 1970 to over 50 in 2013, besting even the last score of South Korea, which started off with a poor, but much better, score of around 21 in 1970. Once again, the most dramatic improvements for all the countries involved occurs after the end of the Cold War.

Graph 9.11 shows that on the dimension of political globalization, China and Korea vastly outperform Vietnam and Cambodia, although the tendency is toward improvement in all four selected countries since the end of the Cold War. Cambodia, China, Korea, and Vietnam all start, interestingly enough, with scores located at about the mid-20s (out of a top score of 100). While Vietnam improves from about 28 to about 55, Cambodia goes from about 24 in 1970 to just over 60 in 2013. Remarkably, China and Korea start off with a similar score as that of Vietnam in 1970, but China surpasses 85, while Korea surpasses 90 as of 2013. The increasing trade by Cambodia and Vietnam with the rest of the world, particularly Westernized countries, accounts for much of the observed improvement in political globalization.

Graph 9.12 shows the remarkable, if sporadic, growth in cultural proximity among key Asian countries and the United States in the

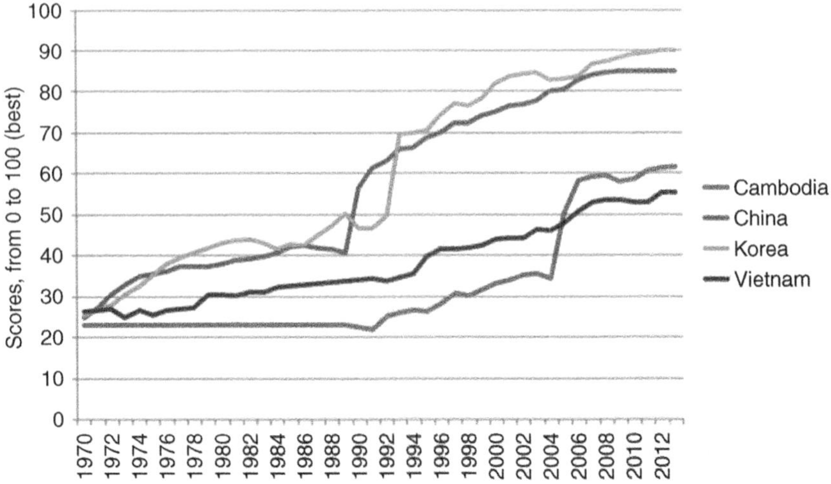

Graph 9.11 Political Globalization in key Asian countries 1970–2013

Source: Calculations by authors based on International Monetary Fund data, 2016

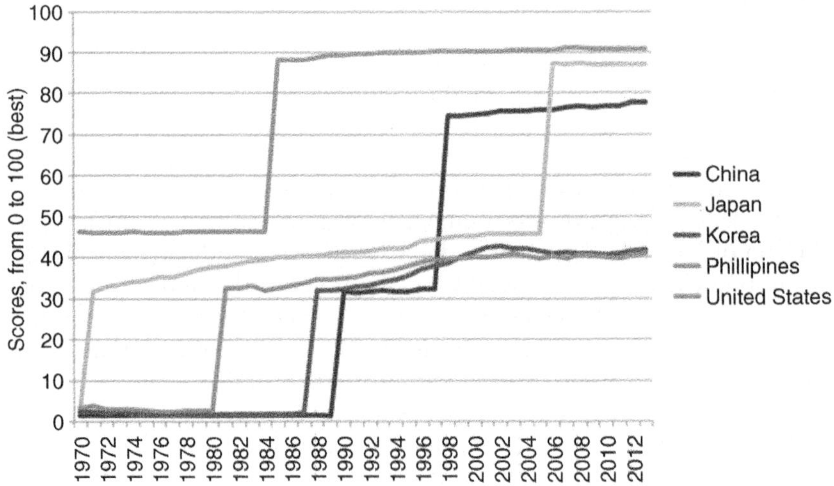

Graph 9.12 Cultural proximity in key Asian countries and the United States 1970–2013

Source: Calculations by authors based on International Monetary Fund data, 2016

1970–2013 time period. Whereas the United States starts off a score of just over 45 in 1970, and ends with a score of just over 90 in 2013, it is remarkable that Japan went from a score of less than 2 in 1970 to a score almost equal to that of the United States. The growing cultural proximity of Japan, with respect to the United States, is the clearest example of the positive influence of trade with a liberal, Western country for the development of a Third World country. For almost the first 20 years, China makes no improvements, then it makes a stutter step improvement after the end of the Cold War, and again at the end of the 1990s, ending with a score close to 80 in 2013, after having started off with a score very close to zero. Korea and the Philippines underperform Japan and China by almost 40 points.

Graph 9.13 shows the evolution of cultural proximity scores among key Asian countries and the member countries of the Pacific Alliance. Japan, followed by China, leads the pack, by over 35 points, with the exception of Costa Rica, an observer country to the Pacific Alliance, which scores 60 out of 100 in cultural proximity in 2013, compared to the 35–40 interval shown by the rest of the countries in the Pacific Alliance, along with Korea.

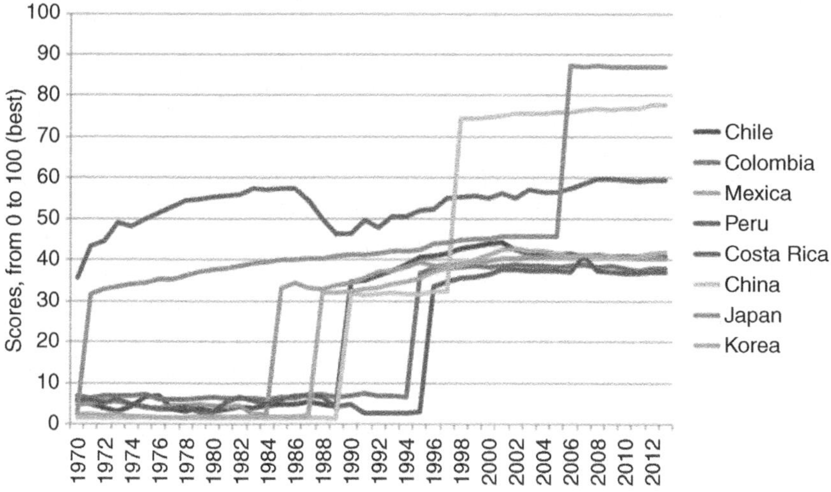

Graph 9.13 Cultural proximity in key Asian countries and the Pacific Alliance countries 1970–2013

Source: Calculations by authors based on International Monetary Fund data, 2016

The foregoing analysis of the evolution of the modern wave of globalization under the liberal world order established by the United States in the postwar era leaves little doubt that the benefits of greater and freer trade and movement of goods, capital, people, and ideas across the globe have been perceived by peoples of the world everywhere. Nowhere is this more evident than in the countries of the Pacific Alliance and in key Asian countries with whom they would be trading. The Pacific Alliance began as an endeavor inspired by the American free trade example, but not due to American diplomacy in any way. In the case of the Pacific Alliance, the United States may well become the late-comer seeking to join the party, regardless of who is the President of the United States.

Will the Pacific Alliance Produce Different Results than the other Latin American Trade Groups?

Will the Pacific Alliance provide a new path to real economic development for Latin America?

The countries of the Pacific Alliance have made significant progress over the years, not just in matters relating to globalization, but also democratization, macroeconomic stability, the establishment of relative fiscal and, especially important, monetary discipline. Just as the Asian economies are emerging as the future engine of economic growth in the world, the countries of Chile, Colombia, Mexico, and Peru have carved out a brand image as the Pacific Pumas, agile actors worthy of trading with the Asian Tigers. The clear, unabashed and seductively simple pro-free market and pro-trade message of the Pacific Alliance positions the bloc as a beacon, a modern model for development for the rest of the developing countries, not just in Latin America, but the world. On the basis of that there is strength in numbers and in unity, the economic integration of these key players in the region of Latin America and the Caribbean will make the Pacific Alliance a player to be watched on the international scene for years to come.

The obstacles that remain to be vanquished on the road to sustainable economic growth and human development go far beyond the traditional dependence on commodity exports. They include the resolution of the structural problems of persistent poverty, inequality before the law, and the problems that derive therefrom. As always in the Third World, the plagues of corruption, cronyism, and clientelism, the three negative C's hurt the three positive C's, competitiveness, commerce, and convergence (toward the American liberal political and economic norm). The member countries of the Pacific Alliance, Chile, Colombia, Mexico, and Peru, have each and all become leaders and beacons in their own right on how to achieve progress in Latin America, difficult as that may be, in no small part because intellectuals in Latin America are wont to sing the song that globalization exacerbates poverty rather than ameliorates it. The Pacific Alliance has the chance to prove that poverty and inequality and discrimination can be reduced by tying the Latin American economies to the more efficient international trade networks that span the globe.

It is here important to emphasize that it is not just free trade but economic integration that is the message that the Pacific Alliance holds for the region of Latin America and the Caribbean. It is through economic integration that the Pacific Alliance will achieve regional competitive advantage through greater economic specialization and trade within the group and, eventually, with the other members of the Pacific Alliance abroad, in the Asian region, or the North American region.

Positioned between Europe and Asia, the Pacific Alliance countries have a unique opportunity to leverage that strategic, geographical advantage and truly be a multiplying force for the accumulated wisdom of the West, both the United States and Europe, and greater economic dynamism shown by the developing market economies in Asia and Latin America over the last decades. This phenomena exists particularly in the light of the rise of nationalist movements in Europe and the United States, which have seemingly called into question the West's continued, credible commitment to the liberal world order. The Pacific Alliance countries stand ready to bridge the gap between the increasingly liberal Asian region and the decreasingly liberal Western region.

It is no exaggeration to say that the Pacific Alliance seems favored by economic history, particularly recent history. As has been emphasized elsewhere in this book, the Atlantic nations of Europe are seemingly in political and economic decline. Eight years after the economic crisis of 2008, the Eurozone countries still cannot escape the recurrent threats of recessions and tepid recuperations. Even the Latin American economy, as a whole, is in the doldrums, falling into recession again in 2016. The axis of world trade is moving toward the Pacific just at the time that the nations of Chile, Colombia, Mexico, and Peru decided to form the Pacific Alliance, of their own volition, without spirited US leadership. This is significant because prior Latin American trade agreements that have left out the US have been protectionist and antifree market, whereas the

Pacific Alliance frankly embraces liberal economic principles of free markets and free trade.

Will the Pacific Alliance provide a new path to real economic development in Latin America? Let us hope so. The Pacific Alliance differs substantially from other regional integration efforts in the Latin American region in that there is a credible commitment on the part of member countries to keep an aggressive export-oriented focus. This, in turn, will require a constant eye on national competitiveness on the part of policy-makers. With the region of Latin America and the Caribbean, as a whole, in recession in 2016, the Pacific Alliance is one of the few bright spots for the regional economy. As tragic as it may be, timing could not be better for the emergence of the Pacific Alliance as an alternative model to the New Socialism of the twenty-first century proffered by the collapsing Venezuelan regime for the rest of Latin America (George 2014).

Although Latin American countries generally trade relatively little among themselves, and the Pacific Alliance is no exception here, the Pacific Alliance nonetheless does manifest an important commitment to future trade liberalization. Its having liberalized 92% of internal trade among member nations, with an eye at 100% trade liberalization, the Pacific Alliance effectively stands to present concrete imitation benefits to the rest of the countries in Latin America. This credible commitment to free trade is a prime reason it has attracted over 40 observer states (Parish Flannery, Nathaniel 2016). The sheer number of observer states indicates a potential for expansion to include other countries some day in the Pacific Alliance, including Canada and the United States. Were this to happen, the Pacific Alliance would be a game-changer on a world order, not just regionally.

The export-oriented focus of the Pacific Alliance differs from the inward-looking focus of the regional trade blocs, such as Alba, Mercosur, among others. The outward focus will keep the member countries of the Pacific Alliance in competition with the rest of the world, thus spawning strong incentives to be agile and more competitive over time. The protectionist bent of other regional integration efforts in Latin America has always prevented precisely this incentive to compete (Villarreal 2016, p.12). As the competitive focus of the Pacific Alliance becomes a reality which most policy makers expect, it will provide strong concrete, tangible, and easily replicated lessons for the rest of the Latin American countries. Following these lessons, however, will require them to muster the political will to implement the needed changes despite the public choice obstacles that vested and mercantilist interest continue to pose among the national economies in Latin America.

The Pacific Alliance, as its name bears out, has a Pacific focus, that is to say that its focus is on Asia. The Pacific Alliance aims to function as a unified commercial entity, not just a group of countries. The Pacific Alliance boasts the region's largest stock market in terms of capitalization (the MILA, Mercado Integrado Latino Americano). The Doing Business scores and rankings of the member countries are all in similar range, among the top 60 in the world, whereas the Mercosur countries are not even among the top 90 in the world (Parish Flannery, Nathaniel 2016). These indicators reflect a real degree of economic and commercial maturity by the countries conforming the Pacific Alliance. They all want to do better on standard business climate indicators, not just human development ones. The focus is on business and trade. Once again, having a Pacific Ocean focus to it, it is only logical to wonder if one day the United States and Canada might not also join the Pacific Alliance.

Challenges remain for the member countries if the Pacific Alliance is to optimize and fulfill its potential. Maersk executives, for instance, point out that much investment is needed in port, road, and rail infrastructure, as well as improvements in streamlining port processes to optimize supply chain efficiencies. If this is done, it is believed that the Pacific Alliance holds promise to become the anchor of the Latin American economy (Maersk 2015). In fact, it is hoped that the Pacific Alliance becomes a sort of a political and economic model for the rest of Central and South America to emulate. Central America, in particular, has never really seen its regional economic integration efforts get off the ground, and Mercosur has yet to achieve the reality of a common market. Given the success of the Pacific Alliance, this model could serve as a wake-up call to the rest of the countries in Latin America to get on the free trade and markets train to prosperity and human development.

The Pacific Alliance countries do not just share language and inherited customs; they also share the values of free trade and economic liberalism, and a commitment by national leaders and a cadre of experts to put them into practice for the general goodwill of their respective nations. These shared values enabled the negotiations for the Pacific Alliance to proceed apace in the first place, and the goodwill among the four original member countries is evident (Villareal 2016, p.13). The negotiations to create and expand the Pacific Alliance have occurred at an astonishingly fast pace, a fact due to the overwhelmingly broad and deep commitments by national leaders and experts to the importance of free trade for the future economic growth and development of member nations (Parish Flannery, Nathaniel 2016).

Will the Pacific Alliance Provide the Incentives to Conquer Corruption, Cronyism and Clientelism?

Corruption hurts national development, both in economic and political terms, in what becomes a vicious cycle, whereby corrupt political institutions engender economic informality, tax evasion, bribery, which further weaken political institutions, which constitute the first pillar of Global Competitiveness according to the World Economic Forum. Weak institutions are the chief obstacle holding back Latin American countries from achieving sustained economic growth and political and social progress.

The Pacific Alliance's proof of mettle will be shown by the ability of its member countries to develop and fortify and nurture over time solid inclusive, productive institutions. The best possible combination would be First World institutions with Third World economic and commercial potential. This is what the best drawn free trade pacts offer, such as the Pacific Alliance offer, in fact. The Pacific Alliance, in point of fact, imports and adopts foreign principles and ideas of free markets and trade as the basis upon which to write into concrete trade pacts with other nations tangible commitments by one country to another. This empowers reformers domestically, who can point to the "positive" external influence pushing for this or that reform as a condition of membership in the Pacific Alliance. The inclusion of foreign audiences into national politics often involves just this type of positive pressure for beneficial reforms.

In a Trump world, the Pacific Alliance countries will do well to be able to prove the concrete benefits that accrue to a given country to pertain and sustain a trade agreement with other countries. The benefits will not only need to be large, they must be easily communicable. In the case of the Pacific Alliance, the project stands to win, inasmuch as it was written with a long run vision in mind. The goal should be substantial political and economic integration, whatever self-sustainability demands, while refraining from the imposition of progressive social norms shared by Latin American policy elites, but not by Latin American electorates. If the vantage point stays economic in the sense of greater efficiency, and concrete benefits in terms of jobs, pay, and worker share of profits, etc., then it can be said that well-regulated free trade agreement benefit the working class.

Mexico, Colombia, Peru, and Chile do not need to be perfect, nor will they be. But if they can continue their positive momentum, they will blaze a trail for the Pumas of Latin America to run with the Tigers of the East.

The Obstacles of Corruption, Cronyism and Clientelism

Third World corruption, clientelism, and cronyism endures because a den-of-thieves equilibrium pertains among the key actors involved, to the detriment of society as a whole. This is where free trade treaties can prove beneficial to the member countries, by providing a scapegoat, i.e., the alliance as a whole, as the party imposing reforms. From a public choice point of view, when political elites can point to politically immune actors as the agents of change, reform becomes more possible, inasmuch punishment becomes more difficult. From an institutionalist point of view (a la North), when positive change becomes possible, countries find themselves suddenly able to implement positive change, which had heretofore been found impossible.

The Importance of Institutions and External Institutions

Trade agreements are complex, which often leads to confusion about their role in reducing corruption among member countries to a trade pact (Brown 2014). Free trade has been both a cause and consequence of corruption. National industries might engage in corruption to prevent the entry of foreign competition. At the same time, multinational corporations might engage in corruption to escape the protectionist measures directed against them (Alard 2014).

Corruption is, in and of itself, a trade barrier. Mercantilist practices in developing nations may spawn corruption, as threatened national industries seek government favor in order to escape the competition from foreign companies in a freer market. As well, multinational corporations may well engage in corruption to circumvent such protectionist policies. For these reasons, it is often small and medium businesses that have a greater stake in a freer market, a factor that makes them the natural candidates to spur greater trade liberalization. This is why it is key that countries pertaining to the Pacific Alliance improve their Ease of Doing Business scores, particularly as they regard the facility of opening new businesses. Smaller businesses have a greater stake in reforming legal processes pertaining to the opening and expansion of a new business, as compared to established global enterprises that have the resources to bribe their way out of compliance with the same (Brown 2014).

Free trade agreements (FTAs) have been criticized for doing little to promote good governance and anticorruption practices. While FTAs might pay lip service to transparency and anticorruption standards, most countries in the Third World, particularly in Latin America, lack the strong institutions to make enforcement of such standards credible and real (Alard 2014). FTAs such as the Pacific Alliance should promote political and economic reform by incorporating the strictest anticorruption measures possible. This requires institutional reforms among the countries that are signatories to a free trade pact such as the Pacific Alliance, because, in the absence of anticorruption measures, FTAs would not introduce greater competition into their member countries, defeating the purpose of entering into such free trade blocs as the Pacific Alliance (Katulis 2004).

Inasmuch as the IMF promotes market economics on an international scale, it promotes free trade. In this guise, anticorruption is central to the IMF's mission of promoting economic and financial stability in the international economic system. To the extent that the world economy becomes increasingly globalized, the commitment of the IMF against corruption becomes more important (Shang-Jin, Wei 2001). The World Bank is another international organization that promotes globalization. The United Nations, of course, does the same, and for the region of Latin America, in particular, ECLAC, the Economic Commission for Latin America and the Caribbean, works hard on such matters as economic integration among countries in the region.

For its part, Transparency International has called for the strictest measures and interpretations of it in new trade agreements (Alard 2014). The general thrust behind new FTAs is to incorporate transparency and anticorruption measures into them, to create a virtuous self-feeding cycle of reforms. The benefits of belonging to an FTA run from greater economic opportunities, among countries with shared values. This is thought to be a greater inducement to move toward free trade than, for example, trade sanctions might be for countries that run afoul of international norms (Katulis 2004).

Key to the efforts to reduce corruption via FTAs are such factors as paying customs officials high wages and an independent judiciary that can enforce the international rules of the game (Brown 2014).

Discussion: Integrated Ordoliberal Solutions to Free Trade Challenges and Opportunities.

La estabilidad de las reglas económicas, políticas y sociales se evidencia en las siguientes situaciones:

1. Orden competitivo: Es un componente de la innovación que brinda soluciones a las necesidades de las personas en forma de productos, servicios e ideas.
2. Libre acceso a los mercados: esto garantiza que los precios sean reflejo fiel de la interacción entre la oferta y la demanda.
3. Propiedad privada: El derecho a la propiedad debe de ser útil para el bienestar social.
4. Libertad de contratación: Es una condición necesaria del orden competitivo, dotando de un marco de legalidad y seguridad a las relaciones contractuales de los individuos.
5. Imperio de la ley: No obstante la primacía del orden jurídico, éste tiene el objeto de proteger a los ciudadanos de arbitrariedades. Asimismo de dar certeza legal al desarrollo de la actividad económica.
6. Política económica estable: Provee un entorno de certeza a un fenómeno propiamente dinámico como lo es la competitividad.
7. Estabilidad monetaria: El cumplimiento de metas expresadas sobre nivel de precios por parte de las autoridades correspondientes es un indicador de confianza institucional.
8. Intervención estatal en caso de fallas de mercado: En especial en aquellos casos que los costos sociales, como los asociados a las externalidades que afectan a los recursos naturales, sean considerablemente altos y provoquen un daño sensible a la sociedad.
9. Balance social (Lauks et al. 2008[11]).

The social market economy envisioned by Ordoliberal economics emphasizes the following, among other factors[12]:

1. Monetary discipline
2. Fiscal discipline
3. Free movement of goods, capital, services, people, and ideas.
4. Correct pricing
5. Regulation over Intervention, i.e., rules over discretion.

As one can see, the recipes of Ordoliberalism are quite similar to the recipes of the Washington Consensus, the first order reforms which constituted the necessary, yet not sufficient, conditions for economic growth, the motor which permits the attainment of human development. While it is true that other, complementary, second-generation reforms need to accompany and/or follow the imposition of such gold standard rules as fiscal, monetary, and exchange rate discipline, it is nonetheless also true that few Third World countries can expect to go far for long without adopting these measures (Spillan et al. 2014). The Pacific Alliance countries have shown themselves as countries that have learned the valuable, if painful, economic, fiscal, monetary, and commercial lessons of the past.

Free trade is the way of the future. On this, the Pacific Alliance is right on track. Greater international competition brings the benefits of greater competition to domestic consumers, leaving aside considerations of economic nationalism. Greater free trade spawns greater specialization among nations according to their respective comparative advantages, producing a win-win situation among freer trading nations. In this light, the Pacific Alliance seems to fulfill the promise of well-ordered free trade.

Conclusions

We live in an uncertain world. Each day new events change our perspective on how we will live, how we will transact business, who we will trade with, and what mechanisms we will use to aid our pursuit of success. The Pacific Alliance, as a trading bloc, is a dynamic organization that is, as yet, in its infancy. It has a solid foundation with lots of support from respective governments and enthusiasm from business partners. How the changes in the world will affect the operation or even existence of the Pacific Alliance is yet to be seen.

The cause of globalization has been generally good for the world, particularly the developing world. Proof in the pudding has been the fact that an FTA such as the Pacific Alliance comes out of the Third World, rather than from the developed world for the Third World. This alone suggests that the cause of greater liberalization in the world, in economic and commercial terms, is likely to survive the election of a seemingly protectionist Donald Trump to the presidency of the United States, or the vote for exit by Britons of a defunct Union which has long since ceased to be European and more focused on the needs of Third World regions such as Northern Africa and the Middle East, to the detriment of the advanced countries of the EU.

The world, more than ever, needs true believers in the cause of greater globalization and trade, properly regulated, of course. Who would ever thought that Great Britain would leave the EU? Who would have thought that the United States would elect a candidate who openly criticized the free trade deals that have been made hallmarks of US foreign policy? Such notions would have been dismissed as nonsense a couple of years ago. We are in the early stages of an era wherein every regional trading bloc will have to prove its worth; it will no longer be assumed. Fortunately, all the preliminary indications for the Pacific Alliance seem positive. As stated in previous chapters of this book, time will tell.

Notes

1. In fact, the terrorism has continued until 2016 in such countries as Colombia, where FARC guerrillas have effectively tried to hold the country's development hostage to their demands for political representation, lest they continue with their violent campaigns of kidnappings, extortions, and drug trade.
2. In the foregoing analysis, we skip the years of 2009 and 2010, on the premise that these years are characterized by an unusually strong recession and (initial) "recovery." Including those figures would skew somewhat the data for basic comparison purposes.
3. Unless otherwise specifically cited, all quoted figures and averages mentioned in this chapter are computed by the authors using International Monetary Fund data, from the World Economic Outlook online database. Last accessed January 3, 2017. http://www.imf.org/external/pubs/ft/weo/2016/02/weodata/index.aspx
4. The terms of trade express a country' export prices in relation to its import prices (Obstfeld and Rogoff, 1996).
5. The massive inflows of new immigrants are coming from the Middle East due to the conflict in Syria and the barbarities committed by Islamic terrorists associated with ISIS, the Islamic State in Iraq and Syria. As a consequence of this conflict, Muslim immigrants have invaded Europe. Adding insult to injury, the ranks of the refugees have been infiltrated by terrorists who have already committed attacks in Europe. Sexual assaults and petty crimes by other refugees in Europe have contributed to anti-immigrant sentiment, which worked against the Remain (in the EU) camp.
6. The tables of indicators for the countries and regions pertaining to the Pacific Alliance included the scores of the different countries and regions on the KOF Index of Globalization, and its subcomponents.
7. http://globalization.kof.ethz.ch/

8. http://globalization.kof.ethz.ch/media/filer_public/2016/03/03/method_2016.pdf
9. http://globalization.kof.ethz.ch/media/filer_public/2016/03/03/method_2016.pdf
10. It includes such things as indicators for the number of Internet users, the share of households with a television set, and international newspapers traded. These are variables which proxy people's potential for receiving news from other countries, thus contributing to the global spread of ideas. http://globalization.kof.ethz.ch/media/filer_public/2016/03/03/method_2016.pdf
11. Lauks, Lydia; Ostry, Hardy; Schafer, Matthias; Schiomach, Gerrit. (2008). Freedom and Order for more Justice.
12. These other factors are quite important, including mechanisms of social compensation (assistance to the needy), social security safety nets, public investment to ensure a modicum of basic education, and health services. Properly provided, these services would be complementary to a well-functioning market economy, not a tax on the same.

References

Alard, M. (2014). Corruptions and the future of global trade: Risks and opportunities. July 10, 2014. Transparency International Blog, Transparency International. http://www.transparencyinternational.eu/2014/07/discussing-risks-and-opportunities-in-the-future-of-global-trade/

BBC, Mundo. (2016a). Three topics that define the referendum about saying or leaving the European Union, June 23,2016. http://www.bbc.com/mundo/noticias-internacional-36591052.

BBC, Mundo (2016b). Eight reasons why they won the referendum for leaving the EU, http://www.bbc.com/mundo/noticias-internacional-36619175.

Brown, F. (2014). The role of international trade agreements in fighting corruption. Corporate Compliance Trends. September 30, 2014. http://cctrends.cipe.org/the-role-of-international-trade-agreements-in-fighting-corruption/

George, S. (2014). *The Pacific Pumas: An emerging model for emerging markets.* Washington: Bertelsmann Foundation. http://www19.iadb.org/intal/intalcdi/PE/2014/14383.pdf.

Katulis, B. (2004). Use free trade agreements to fight corruption and promote democracy. Center for American Progress. http://www.americanprogress.org/issues/courts/news/2004/03/16/611/use-free-trade-agreements-to-fight-corruption-and-promote-democracy/

Lauks, L., Ostry, H., Schafer, M.,& Schiomach, G. (2008). Freedom and Order for more Justice.

Maersk. (2015). The Pacific Alliance: Latin America's economic anchor. Trade Update. Second Quarterhttp:http://www.maersk.com/~/media/publications/trade-reports/latin-america/2015-q2-maersk-line-trade-report_latin-america-english-version.pdf?la=en.

Montaner, C. A. 2016. Por qué gano Trump. Infobae. November 13, 2016. http://www.infobae.com/opinion/2016/11/13/por-que-gano-trump/.

Obstfeld, M., Rogoff, K. (1996). *Foundations of International Macroeconomics.* Cambridge, MA: MIT Press.

Oppenheimer, A. [1]. 2016. Imagining a Trump presidency. Miami Herald. March 4, 2016. http://www.miamiherald.com/news/local/news-columns-blogs/andres-oppenheimer/article64099112.html#storylink=cpy

Oppenheimer, A. [2]. 2016. Trump, Clinton would be very different on Latin America. Miami Herald. July 29, 2016. http://www.miamiherald.com/news/local/news-columns-blogs/andres-oppenheimer/article92550487.html#storylink=cpy

Parish Flannery, N. (2016). What should investors know about Latin America's Pacific Alliance? Forbes. May 30, 2016. http://www.forbes.com/sites/nathanielparishflannery/2016/05/30/what-should-investors-know-about-latin-americas-pacific-alliance/#3194e72d611c

Shang-Jin, W. (2001). Corruptions and Globalization. Brookings Institution's Report. Policy Brief 79. April 30, 2001. https://www.brookings.edu/research/corruption-and-globalization/.

Spillan, J. E., Virzi, N., & Garita, M. (2014). *Doing Business in Latin America: Challenges and Opportunities.* New York: Taylor and Francis.

Villarreal, M.A. (2016). The Pacific Alliance: A trade integration initiative in Latin America. Congressional Research Service. March 29, 2016. 7–5700.

CHAPTER 10

Some Final Words: Our Conclusions

The Pacific Alliance between Chile, Colombia, México, and Peru has already been wildly successful. These four countries represent an important part of the Latin American economy and their imports. This treaty, based on the principles of trade liberalization, has already achieved the first steps toward the freer circulation of goods, services, capital, and persons among its member countries, having eliminated 92% of tariffs between the member countries of the Pacific Alliance.

The following analysis using indicators of 2015–2016 illustrates why investing in the Pacific Alliance nations can be rewarding, not just for nations in Latin America, but for developed and developing nations in Asia, Europe, and North America as well.

Recapping Pacific Alliance Member Profiles

Chile

Chile is the Latin American country that teaches the benefits of market economics to the rest of Latin America and, indeed, the developing world. Chile is a country with a GDP of 240,796 billion, with a 2015 per capita GDP estimated at $13,312 by the Economic Commission for Latin America and the Caribbean (ECLAC) of the United Nations. Bearing in mind that the region of Latin America and the Caribbean is in recession, Chile is growing at a modest rate of 1.6% per annum, per last report, with

J.E. Spillan, N. Virzi, *Business Opportunities in the Pacific Alliance*,
DOI 10.1007/978-3-319-54768-8_10

per capita GDP growing at 0.6%, a relatively small difference in the overall GDP growth rate and the per capita GDP growth rate, reflecting a controlled population growth.[1] This permits productivity advances, which, in turn, enhance competitiveness.

The Chilean economy is quite modern. In value-added terms, over 26% of GDP is accounted for by the financial intermediation sector, an area where Chile performs well in the realm of global competitiveness (*vide infra*). Both manufacturing and wholesale and retail trade account for over 11% of national GDP. The mining sector approximates 10% of GDP, while construction comes in at over 8% of GDP. Transport, storage, and communications account for almost 7% of GDP, as of 2015, according to ECLAC data.

Chile's terms of trade have been slightly declining over the last five years, while its trade volume has grown steadily, but not at optimal rates. Chile's exports are dominated by precious metals. Exports of refined copper account for 23% of total exports for Chile, while ores and concentrates of copper account for 22% of total exports. Fish exports account for almost 6% of total exports, while wine of fresh grapes accounts for just under 3% of total exports. On the import side, intermediary goods account for 61.7% of imports, followed by capital goods with 20.5% of total imports, then consumption goods (11.9%).[2] Chile's strong endowment in precious metals and ores make it a potential strategic ally of just about any modern and modernizing economy in the world. The Asian diet will readily accommodate Chile's comparative advantage in high quality fish exports. With some cultural learning, Chilean wines may be a surprise sector in exports to Asia in the coming years.

Chile outperforms the average score for the region of Latin America and the Caribbean on all the twelve pillars of global competitiveness, according the World Economic Forum. Chile substantially outperforms the region on Institutions, Macroeconomic Environment, Higher Education and Training, Financial Market Development, and Technological Readiness.[3] Chile's excellent performance on Higher Education and Training gives that country a critical mass of human talent that foreign businesses would be only too happy to hire to run and execute operations not just in Chile, but throughout Latin America.

Colombia

Colombia is the United States' pet project and key ally in Latin America, especially as regards the war on drugs. Other benefits will derive from this relationship, chief among them American partnership in the fight against corruption, which Colombia needs badly. Having a close relationship with the United States State Department makes Colombia a key player in the region, on trade and other matters as well.

According to the ECLAC of the United Nations, Colombia is a country with a GDP of 292,080 billion, with a 2015 per capita GDP estimated at $6,056. Bearing in mind that the region of Latin America and the Caribbean is, as of 2016, in recession, Chile is growing at a modest rate of 2% per annum, per last report, with per capita GDP growing at 1.1%.[4]

The Colombian economy is relatively modern, though not quite as much as Chile's. In value-added terms, just over 21% of GDP is accounted for by the financial intermediation sector. Manufacturing accounts for over 12% of GDP while wholesale and retail trade account for over 13% of national GDP. The mining sector approximates 7.5% of GDP, while construction comes in at over 10.6% of GDP. Transport, storage, and communications account for about 6.9% of GDP, as of 2015, while agriculture accounts for about 6.8% of GDP, according to ECLAC data.

Colombia's exports are dominated by energy exports, making Colombia a potential strategic partner of just about any dynamic Asian economy, especially China, going into the future. Exports of crude petroleum account for 37.1% of total exports for Colombia; Coal exports account for 12% of total exports. Coffee exports account for about 7.4% of total exports, while cut flowers account for just roughly 3.7% of total exports. On the import side, intermediary goods account for 61.7% of imports, followed by capital goods with 20.5% of total imports, then consumption goods (11.9%).[5] Though the Asian countries are mainly characterized by their strong preference for tea over coffee, Colombian coffee is of high quality. The high quality of the Colombian coffee should make it attractive to customers in Japan, and the growing economic elite in China, as their consumer tastes, expand and become more westernized.

Colombia outperforms the average for the region of Latin America and the Caribbean on all the twelve pillars of competitiveness, according the World Economic Forum, but quite unevenly. In some areas, Colombia barely at all equals the generally poor scores of Latin America on the pillars of competitiveness, such as institutions, infrastructure. Colombia outperforms the region on Macroeconomic Environment, Financial Market Development, Technological Readiness, and Market Size.[6] Colombia's solid performance on Financial Market Development comes on top of Chile's even better performance in the same pillar of global competitiveness, indicating the economic potential of this sector, particularly if financial integration takes off within the Pacific Alliance.

Mexico

Mexico is the next Brazil. The difference between Brazil, the rising Latin American star of yesteryear, and Mexico, always an economic powerhouse in the region, is that Mexico has better prospects for staying power into the future thanks in no small measure to Mexico's commitment to free trade, as exemplified by its membership in NAFTA with the United States and Canada, and now, the Pacific Alliance. Right next door to the United States, Mexico stands as the most favored developing nation in the world, being a natural trading partner to the largest consumer market in the world, the United States. This will always remain so, no matter who is elected President of the United States, and no matter the vagaries of public opinion in the United States on matters of free trade. In fact, the ex-finance minister of Mexico, who was fired in September of 2016 for arranging the Trump visit with the president of Mexico,[7] Luis Videgaray, has been named in 2017 as Mexico's next foreign minister.[8] The message is clear; Mexico will do business with Trump. This is, undoubtedly, in recognition of the importance of the US relationship with Mexico.

Mexico is the largest country of the Pacific Alliance with a GDP of over 1.1 trillion, with a 2015 per capita GDP estimated at $9,213 by ECLAC of the United Nations. With the region of Latin America and the Caribbean in recession, Mexico growing at a modest rate of 2% per annum, per last report, with per capita GDP growing at 0.7% constitutes strong achievements.[9]

Mexico's terms of trade in normal terms have remained steady in recent years, and its trade volume has increased steadily since the 1990s. Mexico has a diverse export basket, with passenger cars accounting for 8.7% of total exports, Lorries and trucks account for 5.8% of total exports, while other parts for motor vehicles account for 6.7% of total exports. Crude petroleum accounts for 4.9% of exports, while television broadcast receivers' account for another 4.4% of exports.[10]

Mexico is more competitive than the average for the region of Latin America and the Caribbean on matters of Infrastructure, Macroeconomic Environment, Financial Market Development, Market Size, and Business Sophistication.[11] The greater business sophistication of Mexico is surely due to its membership in NAFTA and Mexico's strong and continued trade relationship with the United States. Financial market development, an area where Chile and Colombia scored relatively strong on, is appearing to be an area on which the Pacific Alliance should focus.

Peru

"Peru is an extraordinary success story" – Barack Obama.[12]

Peru is a Doctor Jekyll and Mr. Hyde country. Peru had a socialist past and a capitalist present, all with the same president, Alan Garcia, who presided over a disastrous leftist government from 1985 to 1990 and, by comparison, a more successful[13] government from 2006 to 2011. Although this is due to the fact that in the second contest, Garcia confronted on his left a candidate that was considered extremely radical and to the left (Ollanta Humala) of Garcia, who was able to shake off nervousness due to his own leftist failures of the past, due to the tangible presence of a [Hugo] Chavista threat to the status quo. Faced between a leftist, and a far leftist, Peru chose the candidate who most declared himself in favor of free trade and market economics.

With China, now its largest trade partner, gobbling up Peru's minerals and raw materials (such as copper, iron ore, and zinc), it experienced Chinese-level growth rates. Indeed, over the last decade, Peru expanded more than any other Latin American or Caribbean economy, and it saw wages rise at an annual pace of 6 to 7%. Meanwhile, between 2002 and 2011, the national poverty rate was virtually cut in half, dropping from 54.7 % to 27.8%.

Peru is a country with a GDP of 189,210 billion, with a 2015 per capita GDP estimated at $6,029 by ECLAC of the United Nations. Peru is growing at a solid rate of 3.9% per annum, per last report, with per capita GDP growing at 2.6%. Bearing in mind that the region of Latin America and the Caribbean is in recession, these are impressive results.[14]

The Peruvian economy is modernizing, with just over 11% of value-added GDP being accounted for by the financial intermediation sector. In value-added terms, agriculture accounts for 7.8% of GDP, while manufacturing accounts for 14.5%, and wholesale and retail trade account for 16.9% of national GDP. The mining sector approximates 8.8% of GDP, while construction comes in at over 7% of GDP, as of 2015, according to ECLAC data.

Peru's terms of trade in normal terms have declined steadily in the last few years, while its trade volume has increased consistently, year on year. Peru's exports are also heavily represented by precious ores. Ores and concentrates of copper account for 23.8% of total exports for Peru, while exports of refined copper account for 5.4% of total exports. Ores and concentrates of zinc account for 4.4%% of total exports, while ores and concentrates of lead account for 3.9% of total exports. Meat and fishmeal, unfit for human consumption, account for 4.3% of total exports.[15]

Peru slightly outperforms the average for the region of Latin America and the Caribbean some of the twelve pillars of competitiveness, according the World Economic Forum. Peru is at the regional poor score on institutions, actually behind in infrastructure, and behind in technological readiness. Peru performs stronger than the average for Latin America on financial market development, labor market efficiency, goods market efficiency, market size, and, quite substantially, on macroeconomic environment.[16]

The Pacific Alliance

The Pacific Alliance is "the most exciting thing going on today in Latin America," according to the famed Chilean economist and finance minister, Felipe Larraín (The Economist, 29 April 2013). Special conferences and forums uniting the ambassadors of each of the Pacific Alliance member countries with their Asian counterparts have been held in countries as far off as Malaysia, with the purpose of highlighting the traits that empower the Pacific Alliance, their individual and collective capabilities, and the organizational structure of the Pacific Alliance.[17]

One of the main reasons for doing press events on the Pacific Alliance is that, despite the golden opportunities for doing business between the Pacific Alliance member countries and Asia, there is a lack of knowledge about these opportunities. This knowledge gap effectively impedes investment between the Pacific Alliance countries and the Asian region.[18] Knowledge of the Asian region, as well as the Latin American region, in economic, social, demographic, and political terms is essential for foreign direct investments to succeed. This is true not only of the Pacific Alliance, but for other countries in other regions as well.

The Pacific Alliance as a Free Trade Signal

Categories such as Emerging Economies used by the International Monetary Fund are useful for data compilation and analyses, but foreign investors are expected to differentiate, categorize, and prioritize investment options. In this regard, the Pacific Alliance sends off strong, positive signals that should go far to assuage investors' rational fears. In many areas, a virtuous cycle may been entered, whereby political reforms have generated social equilibrium and greater governability, improved business and investment climates, job creation, growing income levels, all of which, in turn, feed positively into the democratic political system.

Given the huge potential promise of the Pacific Alliance, the trade bloc has received and will continue to receive press attention.[19] The press attention that the Pacific Alliance receives is definitely far more positive than negative, although stalwarts exist in both camps. Good reasons exist for this positive interest in a free trade agreement such as the Pacific Alliance. As the author has shown in other studies, free trade spawns greater innovation in Third World countries (Virzi and Monzon 2013).

The Pacific Alliance remains one of the positive developments emanating from the Latin American region since the economic contraction of 2009. Its chief positive attribute is that it is an outward-looking trade agreement, as opposed to the inward-looking trade agreements, which have long been characteristic of the Latin American region. In each of the original member countries, there exists a substantial consensus among policy and business elites on the issue of freer trade, and that free trade is the key to future economic development. In Chile, Colombia, Mexico, and Peru, the governments are reliably centrist and avoid the type of policy extremes that have landed the Venezuelan and Argentinian economies, for example, in hot water.[20]

Having coasts on the Pacific Ocean gives the countries of Chile, Colombia, Mexico, and Peru a strategic natural endowment that gives the Pacific Alliance a tremendous comparative advantage in terms of sheer geography. Given proper investments in port infrastructure, and roads, in the future, the Pacific Alliance can become a hub not only for trade between its member countries and Asia, but a conduit for connecting the movement of goods between Asia and those countries in Latin America that lack a Pacific coastline.

Geographical seafaring advantages are important for the Pacific Alliance, both to magnify their trade opportunities within the trade bloc, but also to connect with potential trading partners abroad. The economic opportunities are awesome, in no small part due to the low point from which the Pacific Alliance members start. The country of Colombia is a case in point. Colombia's largest trading partners are the United States, followed by the European Union. Even the Colombian government recognizes that Colombia is lagging behind on the matter of exploiting commercial opportunities in Asia.

In the words of Gabriel Duque, Vice-Minister of Foreign Trade for Colombia:

Our largest trading partners are the US and the EU. We have large trade relations with Latin America but we are lagging behind with regards to our interaction with Asia. We are aiming at being very risk averse and trying to diversify our trading partners. We are trying to reach further with Asia and that will be our priority. The objective for the next few years is really diversification. We are lagging behind in our exposure to the world. We are really coming from low levels of exports and investments. As a result, we want to diversify what we are doing with the rest of the world.[21]

Recognizing that Colombia is lagging behind with the internationalization of its economy, Colombia has a country strategy to catch up with the integration of its economy into the world economy. Importantly, the country strategy includes consulting regularly with the World Economic Forum standards and the Ease of Doing Business standards presented in this book because those publications and studies are seen as sources to identify where Colombia's priorities or actions should be. The country strategy also includes trade agreements, such as the Pacific Alliance, which ensures lower costs and greater certainty for national and foreign economic agents. The country strategy includes, for the future, investments in infrastructure, which is important if the country is to maximally exploit the opportunities presented by the Pacific Alliance.[22]

Port infrastructure is a huge, pending need among the Pacific Alliance countries, especially now given the commercial promise of the trade bloc. The Buenaventura port terminal of Colombia has seen its annual activity grow at a clip of 12.5% since the creation of the Pacific Alliance (Schipani, Andres and Benedict Mander 2014. Special Report: The New Trade Routes: Pacific Alliance Pacific Alliance opens doors for businesses in Latin America Positive steps in co-operation are being made in Latin America. Financial Times, https://www.ft.com/content/faf9f5fc-aec0-11e3-a088-00144feab7de).

For some sectors, such as wine, the trade treaties to which Chile is already a signatory member have already brought about the main benefits of free trade, among the countries of Latin America. However, when it comes to Asia, there are greater growth opportunities there. Colombian coffee is expected to continue to have a growing market in quality-conscious Japan. However, cultural learning will have to take place for its true market potential to be realized, as is the case with Chilean wines (Schipani, Andres and Benedict Mander 2014. Special Report: The New Trade Routes: Pacific Alliance Pacific Alliance opens doors for businesses in Latin America Positive steps in co-operation are being made in Latin America. Financial Times, https://www.ft.com/content/faf9f5fc-aec0-11e3-a088-00144feab7de). For such goods as Chilean Salmon, or Mexican Beef, cultural learning and consumer preference shifts are not so much of an issue.

For a time, in the mind-set of many Latin American businessmen, the Trans Pacific Partnership (TPP), a free trade treaty that was in the works between the United States and various Asian economies, outshined the Pacific Alliance. However, the election of Donald Trump killed the prospects for the TPP, which stood to reduce tariffs substantially on key products that Asian countries import from the Americas. If investments in port and road infrastructure take place, as needed in order to fulfill the promise of the Pacific Alliance, a boom is in prospect for the cement sectors in Latin America, and Central America, too, if that region eventually joins the Pacific Alliance.

One area where much work remains to be done is in financial integration, although there has been progress. "The Pacific Alliance is an opportunity for pension funds to diversify their investments in four different local markets, as long as it provides a more agile and flexible [investment] environment," says David Bojanini, chief executive for Sura, the Assets Management Company (Schipani, Andres and Benedict Mander 2014. Special Report: The New Trade Routes: Pacific Alliance Pacific Alliance opens doors for businesses in Latin America Positive steps in co-operation are being made in Latin America. Financial Times, https://www.ft.com/content/faf9f5fc-aec0-11e3-a088-00144feab7de). Referring to the TPP, which is in much the same spirit as the Pacific Alliance, Thomas Shannon, Counselor of the US State Department even commented on the eventual link between the Pacific Alliance and the TPP: "This is how we are building the connectivity that uses markets not just to create wealth but to address issues like financial inclusion.[23]

In order to develop the capital markets of the region, the stock exchange markets of the member countries of the Pacific Alliance countries are already integrated into the Mercado Integrado Latinoamericano (MILA),[24] which is already Latin America's largest stock exchange, although it has not been sufficiently used. The MILA is a financial innovation that needs to be maximally developed if the Pacific Alliance is to realize its true potential. This is a doable feat, bearing in mind that all of the member countries have reasonably development financial market sectors. Colombia, Peru, Chile, and México have to continue to take gradual, continuous measures to more fully integrate their financial markets. "The integration of financial markets is a big issue. The only way to get there is one step at a time. If you stop, you'll never get to the top," says Jorge Errázuriz, a prominent Chilean banker involved in promoting the Pacific Alliance (Schipani, Andres and Benedict Mander 2014. Special Report: The New Trade Routes: Pacific Alliance Pacific Alliance opens doors for businesses in Latin America Positive steps in co-operation are being made in Latin America. Financial Times, https://www.ft.com/content/faf9f5fc-aec0-11e3-a088-00144feab7de).

The world economic recession of 2009 made many international investors skeptical about investing in the Third World. Since then, a "flight to safety" has ensued, whereby investors park their investments in lower-yielding investments in developed countries such as the United States, the United Kingdom, and Germany. However, the developing economies cannot be overlooked.

Emerging markets offer more opportunity going forward that the developed parts of the world. The IMF estimates that emergent developing economies such as those found in Latin America are expected to grow two to three times faster than the developed countries. It is important to note that emerging developing economies are contained on both sides of the Pacific Alliance, among its Latin American member countries, and the Asian countries they seek to do more agile and aggressive business with (http://reports.worldfinance.com/investing-in-the-pacific-alliance/#part-5).

Particularly in Latin America, future prospects are promising. According to the World Bank, the Latin American middle class is burgeoning. In the past decade, the Latin American middle class grew by 50%, accounting for roughly 30% of the population. The reasons for this enlargement of the middle class, the consuming class, are economic growth and job creation over time.[25]

In a report on the Pacific Alliance, Scotia Banks surmised that growth prospects for Latin America were promising due to important, particular factors:

- positive political developments among key economic actors
- emergence of a prosperous middle class and large consumer markets
- technological advancement
- large reserves of raw materials[26]

The Pacific Alliance countries have undergone substantial political, legal, and structural reforms that improve their competitiveness. Chile underwent the neoliberal economic reforms that gave it its hallmark fiscal and monetary discipline. Trade treaties, such as NAFTA, may have provided the impetus for many of these reforms, particularly in countries such as Mexico. As a case in point, Mexico reformed its financial markets, labor markets, political processes, and fiscal policies after the peso crisis of 1994.

The geographical location of the Pacific Alliance countries gives it collectively a fundamental advantage, because each member country can trade easily with other member countries and, in particular, the Asian countries. Already the Pacific Alliance countries are benefitting from greater access to a wider variety of imports, at cheaper prices. If the integration of new Latin America countries in the Pacific Alliance proceeds apace, it would increase trade between the countries and also increment trade with other big markets situated in Asia. Led by the Pacific Alliance example, the Latin American economy can become even more competitive in the global markets.

The Pacific Alliance has a significant market size when compared with other economic blocs. Taken as a single economy, it would be in the top ten largest in the world. Making an economic "region" of this size more open and competitive promises to bring untold benefits to consumers all over the world. Led by the Pacific Pumas, Latin America can finally leave the protectionist, interventionist, pseudosocialist economic policies, for which Latin American trade pacts have been famous, behind them. By abandoning strategic trade practices in favor of liberal trade practices, human development goals will be better served, as freer trade and markets bring in more prosperity. Freer trade between countries also contributes to greater peace between them, as was discussed in chapter two of this book.

Central America

The Pacific Alliance could become an even more important economic bloc if the Central American countries eventually do join, particularly if they do so as an economically integrated region. All of the countries in the Pacific Alliance have a coastline and gateway to the Pacific Ocean. Although each of the countries can seek to enter the Pacific Alliance on its own, as Costa Rica has done, it would be more in the spirit of the Pacific Alliance if Central America proceeded as a region. Central America has been pursuing for years projects related to greater economic integration, without much success. The Pacific Alliance might be just the push the region needs. With a united, integrated Central America as a member of the Pacific Alliance, its strategic reach would be tremendously enhanced.

Central America is one of the regions in the world with the most economical potential due to its geographic location.

The geographic location of Central America makes it a strategic asset for the Pacific Alliance. The Central American Isthmus easily connects the Pacific and Atlantic Oceans, mainly through the Panama Canal; however, other regional canal initiatives arise from time to time.

Central America is important economically in its own right. In 2016 the six countries of Central America, Guatemala, El Salvador, Honduras, Nicaragua, Costa Rica, and Panama had a combined population of approximately 47.01 million people, a regional GDP of $241.67 billion, and a GDP per capita of $5,140.63. In value-added terms, much of Central America's production is based on services, 64.47%; another 26.94% is from industry and only 8.59% are agriculture-based products.

On the Global Competitiveness Index of the World Economic Forum, the region, if it were a country, would have a score of 4.20 (out of 7) on the global index score. With a score in the middle of the table, the pillar of Macroeconomic Environment is the more solid standout. Innovation and Institutions are still weak and there is a lot of work that can be done there.

If Central America were a country, the region would have a rank of 78 in the Index of Ease of Doing Business of the World Bank. Getting credit (17.73) and electricity (48.05) are areas of relative strength. However, starting a business (100.63) or insolvency (120.38) are areas where much improvement is still needed. Of course, this varies among the six countries that make up the region of Central America. Central America suffers from the same port and road infrastructural deficiencies as the member countries of the Pacific Alliance, and with relatively poor scores on Customs Burdens to boot.

Despite its weak points, the region of Central America would be a strong addition to the Pacific Alliance. On the Index of Economic Freedom the isthmus countries taken together score 63.66 out of 100, which indicates that free markets are prevalent in the region. The strong points on this index are low government spending, and solid fiscal and trade freedom. On the other hand, weak institutions make freedom from corruption and problems with the security of private property something that should be taken into account.

The Central American region is fairly globalized, scoring, as a whole, 61.75 out of 100 in the Globalization Index. In the Human Development Index, of the United Nations Development Program, scores 0.7 out of 1, which classifies the region as Medium High Development. If the safety from violence could be guaranteed, Travel and Tourism would be a strong point for the region, which today enjoys only a middling score in this area.

Incorporating Central America into the Pacific Alliance would be a logical move, both for the Pacific Alliance countries and the Central American countries, which would seek to join the Pacific Alliance. The Pacific economies of Asia hold out enormous potential economic promise to the Pacific economies of Latin America. In particular, the ASEAN free trade agreement is one of the most important treaties in Asia, and would provide greater incentives to the nations of the Pacific Alliance to make good on their promise to reduce duty rates between the countries that are part of it to zero. Philippines, just as the countries of Singapore, Thailand, Indonesia, and Malaysia have shown strong economic growth, and social and cultural progress, so, too, can the countries of the Pacific Alliance, which have the added advantage of sharing one common cultural legacy, and language.

Integrating Public Choice and New Institutional Economics into an Ordoliberal View of Trade

As was stated in chapter two of this book, Ordoliberalism seeks to make the free trade and free market ideals of Adam Smith into a reality. Ordoliberalism proposes an ordered liberty, where the State complies with certain basic functions that are essential to economic and political Freedom. The benefits of free markets and trade can best be reaped while there is a clear order of laws, rules and norms (Lazcano 2008). Free trade agreements such as the Pacific Alliance are excellent examples of just such commitments to impose rules of exchange for the overall, general benefit of participating parties.

The key trait of Ordoliberalism is order (Noejovich 2012). The visible hand of the State may well serve the operations of the invisible hand of the market. Ordoliberalism gives ample discretion for the state to design the legal structure that will best support operations of the free market (Lazcano 2008). Part of this legal structure may well include the Free Trade Agreements to which countries like Chile, Colombia, Mexico, and Peru have become signatories. This ties in the thrust given by the New Institutional Economics (NIE) on the clear establishment of the rules of the game and the institutions charged with their stipulation and compliance (North 1993).

The Pacific Alliance is a Free Trade Agreement. As such, it will bring in greater competition to local firms, especially ones that have market-dominance. This will make the economies of Chile, Colombia, Mexico, and Peru more competitive, more innovative, and more entrepreneurial, having been exposed to greater competition on account of the Free Trade Agreement.

The Ordoliberal preoccupation with the influence of big business in the State is a clear precursor to the concerns of the school of Public Choice founded by James Buchanan. Public Choice, again, studies the private interests of public agents and such matters as State capture by private interests. There can be no greater evidence of state autonomy in favor of free market logic than the fact of the celebration of a free trade agreement such as the Pacific Alliance, where the national economies of Chile, Colombia, Mexico, and Peru expose are deliberately exposed to international competition. This would improve the functioning of the national pricing mechanisms, another central preoccupation of Ordoliberal economics. Under an Ordoliberal perspective, in the Pacific Alliance the State does not assume the task of protecting national industries or companies. Rather the functions of the State are oriented toward the rule of law, the protection of property rights, market competition, and the provision of the basic public goods necessary for human development as well as the optimal functioning of the market economy (de Mascías 2003). Ordoliberalism exalts the freedom of business Enterprise, but this does not translate into particular businesses always getting their way (Llanos 2010). Ordoliberalism mandates competition, which is why it specifies the need to protect against monopolist practices and promotes ever-freer competition and trade. This is precisely what the Pacific Alliance represents. Under an Ordoliberal perspective, free trade agreements would also be a natural corollary to an Ordoliberal theory of trade, inasmuch as these free trade agreements expose the national markets to greater competition.

The Pacific Alliance proposes not just institutional reforms to make its member countries more competitive and free. The Pacific Alliance is itself a package of new institutions oriented toward free trade, above the national pressures for mercantilist policies, which the Public Choice School warns about, as was pointed out in chapter two of this book. The quality of institutions, in turn, determines whether or not a country develops according to something akin to its full potential (Acemoglu et al. 2012).

The NIE also reviewed in chapter two emphasizes the role of institutions in the success or failure of countries to develop (Miguez, G. C. 2002). Institutions are important because they influence in the formation and interrelationships of ideas and beliefs (De Azevedo, 329). One subset of the whole set of beliefs can be those of the benefits of free trade, obviously, and this is reflected in the belief system which underpins the Pacific Alliance.

The Pacific Alliance is important in that it transmits the strength of this belief system to international economic agents in credible ways that enhance the economic brand of the member countries. As was seen in chapter two of this book, the NIE School emphasizes the importance of the fact that economic agents possess incomplete information and limited mental capacity to process information. What countries in the emerging world are the best investment outlets? Invest in Venezuela, Argentina, or Chile? Economic agents need cognitive shortcuts in order to make decisions in a timely manner. It is for this reason that institutional restrictions are put upon the interactions of economic agents, to structure exchange and thus reduce the uncertainty (North 1993, 1–2). Free trade agreements, such as the Pacific Alliance, provide just this type of institutional restrictions that foment greater economic certainty. The Pacific Alliance constitutes now a credible commitment among the member countries because, by way of signed agreements among heads of state, they have locked in free trade as part of the economic policies of the country, making it very hard for any future president to simply undo the trade pact. This provides a greater degree of certainty as to the commercial policies a country signatory to a trade pact might take in the foreseeable future. International investors can take it for granted that the Pacific Alliance countries will make good on their commitments to free trade.

Institutions can be difficult to change, even when they work against the development of a country. As we saw earlier in chapter two of this book, the concept of "path dependency" explains how, once a country has gone on a suboptimal path of erroneous political and economic policies, institutions may form around these same, encrusting private interests in political and economic configurations that work against the collective good. Changing path dependency can be extremely hard (Ordónez, H. A. 2009). It is when it is obvious that a given institutional arrangement no longer serves the public good that institutional change becomes more probable (Durazo, A. 2010). As a case in point, when the Latin American economies crashed in the 1980s, they confronted a world recession with high inflation, high debt burdens, and noncompetitive economies. Having hit rock bottom, some nations took advantage to apply the first-order lessons of the Washington Consensus, to orient their national economies more in line with free market and sound government principles. Chief among these economies are the member countries of the Pacific Alliance.

The Pacific Alliance can, indeed, serve as an example of the benefits of the free trade to the rest of the region, which recurrently falls into the traps of socialist, interventionist economics. A case in point would be Venezuela, which is an example of a political and economic disaster due to political mismanagement by its socialist regime. This is precisely the type of economic history that the Pacific Alliance is moving away from. The hope is that the Pacific Alliance becomes an example of free trade for countries such as Argentina and Venezuela. Were Venezuela, for example, to change paths and adopt the Pacific Alliance model, it would serve its purposes of establishing macroeconomic stability. Reconstructing a country, in the end, would seem to be a lot easier that developing an undeveloped country (Alonso-Martínez, C. B. 2006). However, as NIE and Public Choice economics tell us, political and economic interests can coalesce around suboptimal arrangements, making positive change exceedingly difficult (North 1993, 3). What is needed is a change in the mental maps of the political and economic elites whose perceptions matter (North 1993, 7) in the elaboration of economic and trade policies. This change or shift in thinking needs to be in favor of an ideology of free trade, as borne out in the spirit and letter of the Pacific Alliance.

The precepts of NIE as discussed in this book are substantially congruent with those of Ordoliberalism. This is particularly so with regard to such themes of importance to free trade agreements such as the Pacific

Alliance, such as competition of interests, competitiveness, pro-market infrastructure, subsidiarity in the public administration, and transparency in government decision-making.

Public Choice economics is similarly congruent with Ordoliberalism. An integrated Ordoliberalism mindful of the lessons of the Public Choice School contributes to a greater understanding of the importance of the achievement of the Pacific Alliance. Public Choice seeks to link politics and economics via the State, emphasizing the private interests of public agents (Zúñiga 2011). Government action can make social, political, and economic problems worse (Shaw 1993). This has been the Latin American experience with interventionist, socialist governments. Public agents have used State coffers to benefit particular sectors, not the collective welfare. With these lessons in mind, Public Choice serves to promote the understanding of the interests for and against such free trade agreements such as the Pacific Alliance.

The very existence of the Pacific Alliance demonstrates that strong domestic interests in favor of protectionism have been defeated, on the hopes and promise of the economic benefits of free trade with Asian economies. The Pacific Alliance, as a free trade agreement, minimizes the political discretion that can wreak havoc on an economy. This is in compliance with the goal of Public Choice economics of establishing an institutional framework where discretionary political abuses are minimized (Zúñiga 2011).

An integration of Ordoliberalism, NIE and Public Choice leads to an analytical framework quite similar to the model of Social Market Economy of German inspiration. This is tremendously useful for understanding the importance of the benefits of greater competition, as granted by well-written competition laws, and free trade pacts, such as the Pacific Alliance. An integrated Ordoliberal model such as this puts a well-functioning free market in charge of producing prosperity (Von Hoegen, xi; Rodríguez 2009). A well-functioning market economy is characterized by domestic and foreign competition, because it is competition that makes the free market a superior economic paradigm (Quaas 2008; Müller-Armack 1967; Fritz 1979). The Pacific Alliance is an example of this type of Ordoliberal economic policy, as it is a free trade agreement between countries, each one of which has a competition law in its regulatory framework as well.

Under the Social Market Economy, the stability of economic policies is particularly important (Von Hoegen 1999). This is why it is important that the Pacific Alliance agreement grants just such stability and credence to the commercial policies, in particular, of the countries of Chile, Colombia, Mexico, and Peru. Were the countries of Central America take the example and work toward greater economic integration and seek to enter the Pacific Alliance as a regional entity, the credible commitment to free markets and open trade would be even greater.

Although not explicitly so, the Pacific Alliance would seem to represent the ideal economic and commercial policy from an integrated Ordoliberal perspective. The Ordoliberal commitment to freedom and functioning, competitive markets are obviously there. The NIE recipe for institutional arrangements that benefit the country as a whole over just private, sectorial interests is also there. The Public Choice recipe of removing discretionary power over commercial policy is also represented in the Pacific Alliance. The Pacific Alliance, in few words, has a solid theoretical foundation that predicts its continued success, especially as the economic benefits promised become tangible and grow in time.

The Challenges Ahead – Can They be Overcome?

One of the biggest challenges that some Latin America countries have is in the area of human development. Forty percent of the region lives in poverty, and malnutrition haunts many countries, hurting the economic and productive potential of millions of people. These problems don't escape the Pacific Alliance member countries, particularly Colombia, Mexico, and Peru. Lags in the area of human development means that some counties in Latin America are having difficulties in developing conditions so the people can have a proper education, a long and healthy life, and a decent standard of living earned by working productively over a lifetime. Given widespread national poverty, the national savings rates in Latin America are low, so investment potential is also low. Foreign direct investment is key to the future of Latin American development. There is no better way to Latin America countries to face this challenge of the cycle of poverty than by embracing free trade. The United Nations has declared that job creation is critical for equitable economic growth, poverty reduction, and gender equality. Well, trade makes the internal markets more efficient and creates more jobs, and this is precisely what the Pacific Alliance seeks to do.

The weak governments in Latin America also are also a challenge for many of Latin American countries, but some of them some time ago enjoyed of a healthy economy with trade involve, but these days

Venezuela using strategic trade theory policy have a crisis in economy and governability. Countries like Venezuela need to return the application of liberal trade theory based on free market, property rights, democracy, and peace.

Countries like China have overcome bigger challenges that the ones Latin America countries now face and now China is the second biggest economy in the world. China and the Asian Tigers have set the example for Latin America of the importance of the right application of trade policy to promote the economic growth and job creation upon which the conquest of poverty and the attainment of human development depend. It is fitting that the Pacific Alliance name harkens the Asian region that has provided the inspiration and source of opportunities for the Pacific Pumas to pounce on.

Conclusion

Four Pacific boomers have shown their commitment to democracy, economic stability, and global integration by forming the Pacific Alliance. At a time when the United States is rejecting the TPP, the Pacific Alliance Pumas of Latin America are leading the crusade for freer trade in the region.

The Pacific Alliance is a solid example of a strong economic bloc. It has the opportunity to demonstrate how free trade and economic integration can begin to end Latin American poverty. The Pacific Alliance promises to conquer the obstacle of distance. Even though the distance between the Pacific Alliance nations and the nations of Asia might seem to pose a great difficulty, all member countries have a Pacific Ocean coastline and ready access to the sea.

The Pacific Alliance member countries also share liberal principles and values, which has brought them together to trade more freely not only among each other, but also with other parts of the world. The lessons of free trade and market capitalism will have beneficial effects throughout the region of Latin America, which for too long has flirted with cheap versions of socialist, interventionist governance models.

The Pacific Alliance, viewed as a unit, has the intention to convert a series of small-sized to mid-sized economies into a global force. With 220 million people, the Pacific Alliance would be in the top 5 most populous countries in the world, ahead of Brazil. For Mexico, the Pacific Alliance represents the reintegration to Latin America, after almost 20 years of NAFTA's focus on the United States and Canada. Now, it is Latin American resources and commerce that may be the new promise for the free trade, whereas before it was the region of Asia (Borden 2014).

For Colombia, the Pacific Alliance enhances an opportunity to engage as a regional player. Thanks to its population and of course its significantly sized GDP, Colombia has a high potential of leading this continent, and nevertheless it has too many serious political problems. The guerrilla problem, fused with the War on Drugs, has generated instability and given pause to foreign investors. The Pacific Alliance has provided much needed credibility to Colombia, which saw investments increase after the signing of the Pacific Alliance.

For its part, Peru earns a measure of legitimacy in the Pacific Alliance. In fact the Alliance had its origins in this country. It was President Allan Garcia who initiated the Pacific Alliance. Chile is a small, but sophisticated, country, with strong prestige on account of its economic model, which is strongly based on the Social Market Economy model. Given its relative economic success, the errors of the current president Michelle Bachelet notwithstanding, Chile has become an example for the rest of the region not only on its political stability but also on the benefits that free trade gives. Its leadership role in the Pacific Alliance is sure to spawn copycats in the region, and that is a good thing.

It is important to recognize that the Pacific Alliance is not a panacea. The four countries that build it are not major trading partners. It faces some challenges for the future especially because of the change in governments. The Pacific Alliance could fall by the wayside, like so many other integration initiatives in Latin America in the past. One problem that this continent faces is instability. It has been difficult for these countries to achieve consolidated democracies. One important challenge for all the countries that want to join the Pacific Alliance is that they should be consolidated democracies and have free trade agreements with each founder country.

Nevertheless the Pacific Alliance has made its four member economies emerge as one, which is of enormous benefit to the entrepreneurs and investors who seek to find easier ways to commerce worldwide. If the tendency continues, more countries could be included. This could finally lead to Latin America emerging as a regional bloc without parallel. This is not an altogether far-fetched idea. It has always been part of the plan. As Colombia's president, Juan Manuel Santos, once said: "the Pacific Alliance is not a closed pact, we are open to new members who share the principal components with us."[27] Panama, Guatemala and Costa Rica have expressed interests in joining. As the failures of the Venezuelan socialist model become more apparent, the benefits of free markets and open trade are becoming more apparent. This is the message of the Pacific Alliance.

Notes

1. http://interwp.cepal.org/cepalstat/WEB_CEPALSTAT/perfilesNacionales.asp?idioma=i.
2. http://interwp.cepal.org/cepalstat/WEB_CEPALSTAT/perfilesNacionales.asp?idioma=i.
3. http://reports.weforum.org/global-competitiveness-index/#topic=data.
4. http://interwp.cepal.org/cepalstat/WEB_CEPALSTAT/perfilesNacionales.asp?idioma=i.
5. http://interwp.cepal.org/cepalstat/WEB_CEPALSTAT/perfilesNacionales.asp?idioma=i.
6. http://reports.weforum.org/global-competitiveness-index/#topic=data
7. https://www.theguardian.com/world/2016/sep/07/mexican-finance-minister-resigns-donald-trump
8. https://www.theguardian.com/world/2017/jan/04/mexico-foreign-minister-luis-videgaray-donald-trump
9. http://interwp.cepal.org/cepalstat/WEB_CEPALSTAT/perfilesNacionales.asp?idioma=i
10. http://interwp.cepal.org/cepalstat/WEB_CEPALSTAT/perfilesNacionales.asp?idioma=i
11. http://reports.weforum.org/global-competitiveness-index/#topic=data
12. https://hudson.org/research/9466-the-peruvian-miracle
13. Many say lucky, due to the fact that commodity prices were very high during the second Garcia Administration in Peru.
14. http://interwp.cepal.org/cepalstat/WEB_CEPALSTAT/perfilesNacionales.asp?idioma=i
15. http://interwp.cepal.org/cepalstat/WEB_CEPALSTAT/perfilesNacionales.asp?idioma=i
16. http://reports.weforum.org/global-competitiveness-index/#topic=data
17. https://alianzapacifico.net/en/the-forum-pacific-alliance-latin-america-malaysia-business-prospects-was-held-in-malaysia/
18. The Star Online. 2016. UM organises public forum on business prospects in Pacific Alliance. http://www.thestar.com.my/business/business-news/2016/05/25/um-organises-public-forum-on-business-prospects-in-pacific-alliance/

19. MacBride, Elizabeth 2015. Forget Brazil. This emerging market is on the rise. CNBC online. Thursday, 26 Mar 2015. http://www.cnbc.com/2015/03/26/pacific-alliance-trade-bloc-of-mexico-chile-colombia-peru-and-costa-rica-is-growing-fast.html
20. Parish Flannery, Nathaniel 2016. What Should Investors Know About Latin America's Pacific Alliance? Forbes. http://www.forbes.com/sites/nathanielparishflannery/2016/05/30/what-should-investors-know-about-latin-americas-pacific-alliance/#3ccf2e57611c
21. http://www.theprospectgroup.com/colombias-vice-minister-of-foreign-trade-gabriel-duque-on-facilitating-trade-export-development-81953/
22. http://www.theprospectgroup.com/colombias-vice-minister-of-foreign-trade-gabriel-duque-on-facilitating-trade-export-development-81953/
23. https://www.weforum.org/press/2015/05/despite-headwinds-in-the-global-economy-outlook-for-latin-america-still-looks-positive
24. http://mercadointegrado.com/integration/
25. http://www.worldbank.org/en/news/feature/2012/11/13/crecimiento-clase-media-america-latina
26. http://reports.worldfinance.com/investing-in-the-pacific-alliance/#part-5
27. https://alianzapacifico.net/juan-manuel-santos-la-alianza-del-pacifico-es-la-integracion-mas-exitosa/

References

Acemoglu, D., Robinson, J. A., & Woren, D. (2012). *Why nations fail: The origins of power, prosperity and poverty* (Vol. 4). New York: Crown Business.

Alonso-Martínez, C. B. (2006). Economía del subdesarrollo y subdesarrollo de la Economía. *Principios: estudios de economía política*, (4), 5–22.

Ayala, José. (2005). Economía del sector público mexicano. Universidad Nacional.

Borden, W. (2014). *The Pacific Alliance: United States Foreign Economic Policy and Japanese Trade Recovery 1985*. Global Economics Dynamics 2014. https://ged-project.de/

Bruce, S. (1999). *Una brevísima introducción a la sociología*. México: Océano.

De Mascías, Amalia Mattio. (2003). Políticas públicas. Transparencia y su incidencia en la construcción de la ciudadanía. VII Congreso Internacional del CLAD sobre la Reforma del Estado y de la Administracion Publica, Panama, 28–31 October 2003.

Durazo, A. (2010). Innovación y gobernabilidad en un Estado obsoleto. *En-claves del pensamiento*, *4*(8), 123–146.

Eguren, I. R. (2010) CAMBIO.

Fritz, U. (1979). Economía Social de Mercado. Ludwig-Erhard-Stiftung.

Global Economics Dynamics. (2014). The Pacific Alliance: Economic Developments in Chile, Mexico, Colombia and Peru 3. USA.

Horton, P. B., & Hunt, C. L. (1968). Sociology.
Lazcano, I. (2008). El Ordoliberalismo alemán y la Economía Social de Mercado. Universidad Nacional Autónoma de México, *34*, 38.
Llanos, C. R. (2010). El deber de estado en el ordoliberalismo de Walter Euchen: tradicion y coyuntura en el manejo politico-economico del estado. *Revista Chilena de Economia y Sociedad*, *4*(1), 15–20.
Mace, Gordon and Thérien, Jean-Philippe. (2012). *Canada and the Americas: Making a difference?* (Vol. 67). USA: Sage Publications, Ltd.
Miguez, G. C. (2002). El programa de la nueva economía institucional: lo macro, lo micro y lo político. *Ekonomiaz: Revista vasca de economía*, (50), 230–261.
Miralbell, I. (1996). La economía social de mercado de Ludwig Erhard y el futuro del estado de bienestar.
Muller-Armack, A. (1967). *Genealogia de los estilos economicas*. Fondo de cultura economica, Historia Economica, 338 pages.
Noejovich, H. (2012). Ordoliberalismo: ¿alternativa al «neoliberalismo»?. *Economía*, *34*(67), 203–211.
North, D. (1993). Institutions and Economic Theory, American Economist, Primavera, 1992, 1.
Ordónez, H. A. (2009). *La nueva economía y negocios agroalimentarios*. Buenos Aires, Argentina: Facultad de Agronomía de la Universidad de Buenos Aires-FAUBA.
Quaas, F. (2008). Social Market Economy History, Principles and Implementation – From A to Z. Social market economy: Social irenics. Pág. 416.
Resico, M. F. (2011). *Introducción a la economía social de mercado: edición latinoamericana*. KAS. Pág. 123.
Rodríguez, J. (2009). Economía Social de Mercado: ¿una propuesta para América Latina? Economía Social de Mercado, serie 3. Guatemala. Pág. 37.
Shaw, Jane S. (1993). Public choice theory, The Concise Encyclopedia of Economics. Library of Economics and Liberty. http://www.econlib.org/library/Enc1/PublicChoiceTheory.html.
Vicente, G. V. (2014). *Integración económica y apertura comercial en Centroamérica* (Vol. 54). México: El Colegio de Mexico.
Virzi, N., Monzón, H. (2013). Comercio internacional e innovación; una exploración estadística sobre el impacto de la globalización en las prácticas empresariales. *ECO Revista Académica*, *9* 34.
Von Hoegen, M. (1999). *Economía social de mercado: ¿una opción para Guatemala?* Guatemala: Universidad Rafael Landívar.
Zúñiga, C. (2011). Texto Básico de Economía Agrícola. Editorial Universitaria. Nicaragua. Pág. 20.
Zweig, K. (1980). *The origins of the German social market economy: The leading ideas and their intellectual roots*. London: The Adam Smith Institute. Pág. 8.

Appendix A

Peru

GDP (million current US$, 2015)	192 084	**Rank in world trade, 2015**	Exports	Imports
GDP per capita (US$, 2013-2015)	6 425	Merchandise	58	55
Current account balance (% GDP, 2013-2015)	-4.2	excluding intra-EU trade	41	37
Trade per capita (US$, 2013-2015)	1 484	Commercial services	69	67
Trade (% GDP, 2013-2015)	23.1	excluding intra-EU trade	44	47

MERCHANDISE TRADE

Million US$	Value 2015	Annual percentage change 2010-2015	2014	2015
Merchandise exports, f.o.b.	34 157	-1	-8	-14
Merchandise imports, c.i.f.	37 850	5	-3	-11

	2015		2015
Share in world total exports	0.21	Share in world total imports	0.23

Breakdown in economy's total exports

By main commodity group (2015)

Agricultural products	22.4
Fuels and mining products	46.4
Manufactures	12.0
Other	19.3

Breakdown in economy's total imports

By main commodity group (2015)

Agricultural products	12.5
Fuels and mining products	11.4
Manufactures	76.1
Other	0.0

By main destination (2015)

China	22.1
European Union (28)	16.0
United States	15.1
Switzerland	8.1
Other	38.7

By main origin (2015)

China	22.7
United States	20.6
European Union (28)	11.7
Brazil	5.1
Other	39.8

TRADE IN COMMERCIAL SERVICES

Million US$	Value 2015	Annual percentage change 2010-2015	2014	2015
Commercial services exports	6 070	11	1	6
Commercial services imports	7 794	6	1	4

	2015		2015
Share in world total exports	0.13	Share in world total imports	0.17

Breakdown in economy's total exports

By main services item (2015)

Transport	22.7
Travel	54.7
Other commercial services	22.6

Breakdown in economy's total imports

By main services item (2015)

Transport	35.7
Travel	21.7
Other commercial services	42.6
Goods-related services	0.1

J.E. Spillan, N. Virzi, *Business Opportunities in the Pacific Alliance*,
DOI 10.1007/978-3-319-54768-8

Basic Indicators

Peru economy presents the following indicators: (a) a GDP of 192,084 million current US dollars, (b) a current account balance with a deficit of -4.2 millions of US dollars, (c) a trade per capita of 1,484 US dollars, and (d) a trade to GDP ratio of 23.1%. In the world trade, the exports ranks of 223 countries for Peru are: 58 in merchandise and 69 in commercial services. On the other hand, the imports ranks are: 55 in merchandise and 67 in commercial services.

Merchandise Trade

The merchandise exports have an f.o.b. value of 34,157 million of US dollars, which grew at an annual rate of -1% in 2010–2015, -8% in 2014, and -4% in 2015. Its share in world's total exports is 0.23%. The breakdown in economy's total exports by main commodity group is: (a) 22.4% in agricultural products, (b) 46.4% in fuels and mining products, and (c) 12.0% in manufactures. On the other hand, the breakdown by main destination is: (a) 22.1% to China, (b) 16.0% to European Union, (c) 15.1% to United States, (d) 8.1% to Switzerland, and (e) 38.7% other regions.

The merchandise imports have a c.i.f. value of 37,850 million of US dollars, which grew at an annual rate of 5% in 2010–2015, -3% in 2014, and of -11% in 2015. Its share in world's total imports is 0.23%. The breakdown in economy's total imports by main commodity group is: (a) 12.5% in agricultural products, (b) 11.4% in fuels and mining products, and (c) 76.1% in manufactures. On the other hand, the breakdown by main origin is: (a) 22.7% to China, (b) 20.6% to United States, (c) 11.7% to European Union, (d) 5.1% to Brazil, and (e) 39.8% other regions.

Commercial Services Trade

The commercial services exports have a value of 6,070 million of US dollars, which grew at an annual rate of 11% in 2010–2015, 1% in 2014, and 6% in 2015. Its share in world's total imports is 0.13%. The breakdown in economy's total exports by principal services item is: (a) 22.7% in transportation, (b) 54.7% in travel, and (c) 22.6% in other commercial services.

The commercial services imports have a value of 1,171 million of US dollars, which grew at an annual rate of 6% in 2010–2015, 1% in 2014, and 4% in 2015. Its share in world's total imports is 0.17%. The breakdown in economy's total imports by principal services item is: (a) 35.7% in transportation, (b) 21.7% in travel, (c) 42.6.6% in other commercial services, and (d) 0.1% in goods-related services.

Basic Indicators

Mexico economy presents the following indicators: (a) a GDP of 1,144,331 million current US dollars, (b) a current account balance with a deficit of −2.4 millions of US dollars, (c) a trade per capita of 3,409 US dollars, and (d) a trade to GDP ratio of 33.6%. In the world trade, the exports ranks of 223 countries for Mexico are: 13 in merchandise and 39 in commercial services. On the other hand, the imports ranks are: 12 in merchandise and 33 in commercial services.

Mexico

GDP (million current US$, 2015)	1 144 331	**Rank in world trade, 2015**	Exports	Imports
GDP per capita (US$, 2013-2015)	9 847	Merchandise	13	12
Current account balance (% GDP, 2013-2015)	-2.4	excluding intra-EU trade	8	8
Trade per capita (US$, 2013-2015)	3 309	Commercial services	39	33
Trade (% GDP, 2013-2015)	33.6	excluding intra-EU trade	23	21

MERCHANDISE TRADE

Million US$	Value 2015	Annual percentage change 2010-2015	2014	2015
Merchandise exports, f.o.b.	380 772	5	5	-4
Merchandise imports, c.i.f.	405 280	5	5	-2

	2015
Share in world total exports	2.31
Share in world total imports	2.42

Breakdown in economy's total exports

By main commodity group (2015)

	Exports
Agricultural products	7.2
Fuels and mining products	8.5
Manufactures	81.9
Other	2.4

By main destination (2015)

Exports	
United States	81.2
European Union (28)	4.8
Canada	2.8
China	1.3
Other	9.9

Breakdown in economy's total imports

By main commodity group (2015)

	Imports
Agricultural products	7.0
Fuels and mining product:	8.9
Manufactures	81.0
Other	3.0

By main origin (2015)

Exports	
United States	47.4
China	17.7
European Union (28)	11.1
Japan	4.4
Other	19.4

TRADE IN COMMERCIAL SERVICES

Million US$	Value 2015	Annual percentage change 2010-2015	2014	2015
Commercial services exports	22 609	8	4	7
Commercial services imports	29 495	6	7	-3

	2015
Share in world total exports	0.48
Share in world total imports	0.64

Breakdown in economy's total exports

By main services item (2015)

	Exports
Transport	6.3
Travel	77.2
Other commercial services	16.5
Goods-related services	0.0

Breakdown in economy's total imports

By main services item (2015)

	Imports
Transport	43.4
Travel	34.2
Other commercial service:	21.6
Goods-related services	0.7

Merchandise Trade

The merchandise exports have an f.o.b. value of 380,772 million of US dollars, which grew at an annual rate of 5% in 2010–2015, 5% in 2014, and -4% in 2015. Its share in world's total exports is 2.31%. The breakdown in economy's total exports by main commodity group is: (a) 7.2% in agricultural products, (b) 8.5% in fuels and mining products, (c) 81.9% in manufactures, and (d) 2.4% in others. On the other hand, the breakdown by main destination is: (a) 81.2% United States, (b) 4.8% European Union, (c) 2.8% Canada, (d) 1.3% China, and (e) 9.9 others.

The merchandise imports have a c.i.f. value of 37,850 million of US dollars, which grew at an annual rate of 5% in 2010–2015, -3% in 2014, and -11% in 2015. Its share in world's total imports is 0.23%. The breakdown in economy's total imports by main commodity group is: (a) 7.0% in agricultural products, (b) 8.9% in fuels and mining products, (c) 81.0% in manufactures, and (d) 3.0% in others. On the other hand, the breakdown by main origin is: (a) 47.4% United States, (b) 17.7% China 11.1% European Union, (d) 4.4% Japan, and (e) 19.4% others.

Commercial Services Trade

The commercial services exports have a value of 22,509 million of US dollars, which grew at an annual rate of 11% in 2010–2015, 4% in 2014, and 7% in 2015. Its share in world's total imports is 0.48%. The breakdown in economy's total exports by principal services item is: (a) 6.3% in transportation, (b) 77.2% in travel, and (c) 16.5% in other commercial services.

The commercial services imports have a value of 29,495 million of US dollars, which grew at an annual rate of 6% in 2010–2015, 7% in 2014, and -3% in 2015. Its share in world's total imports is 0.64%. The breakdown in economy's total imports by principal services item is: (a) 43.4% in transportation, (b) 34.2% in travel, (c) 21.6% in other commercial services, and (d) 0.7% in goods-related services.

Basic Indicators

Colombia economy presents the following indicators: (a) a GDP of 292,080 million current US dollars, (b) a current account balance with a deficit of -4.8 millions of US dollars, (c) a trade per capita of 1,339 US dollars, and (d) a trade to GDP ratio of 18.3%. In the world trade, the

Colombia

			Exports	Imports
GDP (million current US$, 2015)	292 080	Rank in world trade, 2015		
GDP per capita (US$, 2013-2015)	7 329	Merchandise	56	47
Current account balance (% GDP, 2013-2015)	-4.8	excluding intra-EU trade	39	30
Trade per capita (US$, 2013-2015)	1 339	Commercial services	64	57
Trade (% GDP, 2013-2015)	18.3	excluding intra-EU trade	41	40

MERCHANDISE TRADE

Million US$	Value 2015	Annual percentage change 2010-2015	2014	2015
Merchandise exports, f.o.b.	35 691	-2	-7	-35
Merchandise imports, c.i.f.	54 058	6	8	-16

	2015		2015
Share in world total exports	0.22	Share in world total imports	0.32

Breakdown in economy's total exports

By main commodity group (2015)

Exports	
Agricultural products	19.4
Fuels and mining products	54.1
Manufactures	23.4
Other	3.1

By main destination (2015)

Exports	
United States	28.2
European Union (28)	16.9
Panama	6.7
China	6.3
Other	41.9

Breakdown in economy's total imports

By main commodity group (2015)

Imports	
Agricultural products	11.1
Fuels and mining products	11.1
Manufactures	76.5
Other	1.3

By main origin (2015)

Imports	
United States	28.8
China	18.6
European Union (28)	15.3
Mexico	7.1
Other	30.2

TRADE IN COMMERCIAL SERVICES

Million US$	Value 2015	Annual percentage change 2010-2015	2014	2015
Commercial services exports	7 150	7	0	5
Commercial services imports	11 084	4	6	-17

	2015		2015
Share in world total exports	0.15	Share in world total imports	0.24

Breakdown in economy's total exports

By main services item (2015)

Transport	22.3
Travel	59.4
Other commercial services	18.0
Goods-related services	0.3

Breakdown in economy's total imports

By main services item (2015)

Transport	22.9
Travel	39.0
Other commercial services	38.0
Goods-related services	0.1

exports ranks of 223 countries for Colombia are: 56 in merchandise and 64 in commercial services. On the other hand, the imports ranks are: 47 in merchandise and 57 in commercial services.

Merchandise Trade

The merchandise exports have an f.o.b. value of 35,691 million of US dollars, which grew at an annual rate of –2% in 2010–2015, –7% in 2014, and –35% in 2015. Its share in world's total exports is 0.22%. The breakdown in economy's total exports by main commodity group is: (a) 19.4% in agricultural products, (b) 54.1% in fuels and mining products, (c) 23.4% in manufactures, and (d) 3.1% in others. On the other hand, the breakdown by main destination is: (a) 28.2% United States, (b) 16.9% European Union, (c) 6.7% Panama, (d) 6.3% China, and (e) 41.9% others.

The merchandise imports have a c.i.f. value of 54,058 million of US dollars, which grew at an annual rate of 6% in 2010–2015, 8% in 2014, and of −16% in 2015. Its share in world's total imports is 0.32%. The breakdown in economy's total imports by main commodity group is: (a) 11.1% in agricultural products, (b) 11.1% in fuels and mining products, and (c) 76.5% in manufactures, (d) 1.3% in others. on the other hand, the breakdown by main origin is: (a) 28.8 United States, (b) 18.6 China, (c) 15.3 European Union, (d) 7.1% others.

Commercial Services Trade

The commercial services exports have a value of 7,150 million of US dollars, which grew at an annual rate of 7% in 2010–2015, 0% in 2014, and 5% in 2015. Its share in world's total imports is 0.15%. The breakdown in economy's total exports by principal services item is: (a) 22.3% in transportation, (b) 59.4% in travel, and (c) 18.0% in other commercial services.

The commercial services imports have a value of 11,084 million of US dollars, which grew at an annual rate of 4% in 2010–2015, 6% in 2014, and of −17% in 2015. Its share in world's total imports is 0.24%. The breakdown in economy's total imports by principal services item is: (a) 22.9% in transportation, (b) 39.0% in travel, (c) 38.0% in other commercial services, and (d) 0.1% in goods-related services.

Basic Indicators

Chile economy presents the following indicators: (a) a GDP of 240,216 million current US dollars, (b) a current account balance with a deficit of −2.4 millions of US dollars, (c) a trade per capita of 4,629 US dollars, and (d) a trade to GDP ratio of 31.8%. In the world trade, the exports ranks of 223 countries for Chile are: 41 in merchandise and 57 in commercial services. On the other hand, the imports ranks are: 44 in merchandise and 51 in commercial services.

Merchandise Trade

The merchandise exports have an f.o.b. value of 63,362 million of US dollars, which grew at an annual rate of −2% in 2010–2015, −1% in 2014, and −16% in 2015. Its share in world's total exports is 0.38%. The breakdown in economy's total exports by main commodity group

Chile

GDP (million current US$, 2015)	240 216	**Rank in world trade, 2015**	Exports	Imports
GDP per capita (US$, 2013-2015)	14 563	Merchandise	41	44
Current account balance (% GDP, 2013-2015)	-2.4	excluding intra-EU trade	27	28
Trade per capita (US$, 2013-2015)	4 629	Commercial services	57	51
Trade (% GDP, 2013-2015)	31.8	excluding intra-EU trade	37	35

MERCHANDISE TRADE

Million US$	Value 2015	Annual percentage change 2010-2015	2014	2015
Merchandise exports, f.o.b.	63 362	-2	-1	-16
Merchandise imports, c.i.f.	63 039	1	-9	-13

	2015		2015
Share in world total exports	0.38	Share in world total imports	0.38

Breakdown in economy's total exports

By main commodity group (2015)

Agricultural products	31.1
Fuels and mining products	54.0
Manufactures	13.7
Other	1.3

By main destination (2015)

China	26.3
European Union (28)	13.2
United States	13.0
Japan	8.6
Other	38.8

Breakdown in economy's total imports

By main commodity group (2015)

Agricultural products	9.7
Fuels and mining products	15.5
Manufactures	74.7
Other	0.1

By main origin (2015)

China	23.5
United States	18.7
European Union (28)	15.3
Brazil	7.7
Other	34.8

TRADE IN COMMERCIAL SERVICES

Million US$	Value 2015	Annual percentage change 2010-2015	2014	2015
Commercial services exports	9 737	-3	-12	-11
Commercial services imports	13 444	1	-7	-9

	2015		2015
Share in world total exports	0.20	Share in world total imports	0.29

Breakdown in economy's total exports

By main services item (2015)

Transport	35.2
Travel	24.7
Other commercial services	40.1
Goods-related services	...

Breakdown in economy's total imports

By main services item (2015)

Transport	36.2
Travel	15.1
Other commercial services	48.7
Goods-related services	....

is: (a) 31.1% in agricultural products, (b) 54.0% in fuels and mining products, (c) 13.7% in manufactures, and (d) 1.3% in others. On the other hand, the breakdown by main destination is: (a) 26.3% China, (b) 13.2% European Union, (c) 13.0% United States, (d) 8.6% Japan, and (e) 38.8% others.

The merchandise imports have a c.i.f. value of 63,039 million of US dollars, which grew at an annual rate of 1% in 2010–2015, –9% in 2014, and –13% in 2015. Its share in world's total imports is 0.38%. The breakdown in economy's total imports by main commodity group is: (a) 9.7% in agricultural products, (b) 15.5% in fuels and mining products, and (c) 74.7% in manufactures, (d) 0.1% in others. On the other hand, the breakdown by main origin is: (a) 23.5% China, (b) 18.7 United States, (c) 15.3 European Union, (d) 7.7% Brazil, and (e) 34.8% others.

Commercial Services Trade

The commercial services exports have a value of 9,737 million of US dollars, which grew at an annual rate of -3% in 2010–2015, -12% in 2014, and -11% in 2015. Its share in world's total imports is 0.20%. The breakdown in economy's total exports by principal services item is: (a) 35.2% in transportation, (b) 24.7% in travel, and (c) 40.1% in other commercial services.

The commercial services imports have a value of 13,444 million of US dollars, which grew at an annual rate of 1% in 2010–2015, -7% in 2014, and -9% in 2015. Its share in world's total imports is 0.29%. The breakdown in economy's total imports by principal services item is: (a) 36.2% in transportation, (b) 15.1% in travel, and (c) 48.7% in other commercial services.

Basic Indicators

Costa Rica economy presents the following indicators: (a) a GDP of 51,107 million current US dollars, (b) a current account balance with a deficit of -4.5 millions of US dollars, (c) a trade per capita of 10,503 US dollars, and (d) a trade to GDP ratio of 33.0%. In the world trade, the exports ranks of 223 countries for Costa Rica are: 86 in merchandise and 62 in commercial services. On the other hand, the imports ranks are: 82 in merchandise and 96 in commercial services.

Merchandise Trade

The merchandise exports have an f.o.b. value of 9,624 million of US dollars, which grew at an annual rate of 0% in 2010–2015, -3% in 2014, and -14% in 2015. Its share in world's total exports is 0.06%. The breakdown in economy's total exports by main commodity group is: (a) 44.9% in agricultural products, (b) 1.3% in fuels and mining products, (c) 53.2% in manufactures, and (d) 0.7% in others. On the other hand, the breakdown by main destination is: (a) 40.8% United States, (b) 18.8% European Union, (c) 5.8% Panama, (d) 5.5% Guatemala, and (e) 29.2% others.

The merchandise imports have a c.i.f. value of 15,503 million of US dollars, which grew at an annual rate of 3% in 2010–2015, -5% in 2014, and -10% in 2015. Its share in world's total imports is 0.09%. The breakdown in economy's total imports by main commodity group is: (a) 13.0%

Costa Rica

			Exports	Imports
GDP (million current US$, 2015)	51 107	**Rank in world trade, 2015**		
GDP per capita (US$, 2013-2015)	10 503	Merchandise	86	82
Current account balance (% GDP, 2012-2014)	-4.5	excluding intra-EU trade	61	59
Trade per capita (US$, 2013-2015)	3 462	Commercial services	62	96
Trade (% GDP, 2013-2015)	33.0	excluding intra-EU trade	39	70

MERCHANDISE TRADE

Million US$	Value 2015	Annual percentage change 2010-2015	2014	2015
Merchandise exports, f.o.b.	9 624	0	-3	-14
Merchandise imports, c.i.f.	15 503	3	-5	-10

	2015		2015
Share in world total exports	0.06	Share in world total imports	0.09

Breakdown in economy's total exports

By main commodity group (2015)

Agricultural products	44.9
Fuels and mining products	1.3
Manufactures	53.2
Other	0.7

By main destination (2015)

United States	40.8
European Union (28)	18.8
Panama	5.8
Guatemala	5.5
Other	29.2

Breakdown in economy's total imports

By main commodity group (2015)

Agricultural products	13.0
Fuels and mining products	10.6
Manufactures	76.2
Other	0.1

By main origin (2015)

United States	39.8
China	12.6
European Union (28)	9.3
Mexico	7.4
Other	30.9

TRADE IN COMMERCIAL SERVICES

Million US$	Value 2015	Annual percentage change 2010-2015	2014	2015
Commercial services exports	7 676	10	2	11
Commercial services imports	2 618	7	4	20

	2015		2015
Share in world total exports	0.16	Share in world total imports	0.06

Breakdown in economy's total exports

By main services item (2015)

Transport	3.6
Travel	42.7
Other commercial services	50.1
Goods-related services	3.6

Breakdown in economy's total imports

By main services item (2015)

Transport	36.3
Travel	20.8
Other commercial services	42.8
Goods-related services	0.1

in agricultural products, (b) 10.6% in fuels and mining products, and (c) 76.2% in manufactures, (d) 0.1% in others. On the other hand, the breakdown by main origin is: (a) 29.8% United States, (b) 12.6 China, (c) 9.3 European Union, (d) 7.4% Mexico, and (e) 30.9% others.

Commercial Services Trade

The commercial services exports have a value of 7,676 million of US dollars, which grew at an annual rate of 10% in 2010–2015, 2% in 2014, and 11% in 2015. Its share in world's total imports is 0.16%. The breakdown in economy's total exports by principal services item is: (a) 3.6% in transportation, (b) 42.7% in travel, (c) 50.1% in other commercial services, and (d) 3.6% in goods-related services.

The commercial services imports have a value of 2,618 million of US dollars, which grew at an annual rate of 7% in 2010–2015, 4% in 2014, and 20% in 2015. Its share in world's total imports is 0.06%. The breakdown in economy's total imports by principal services item is: (a) 36.3% in transportation, (b) 20.8% in travel, (c) 42.8% in other commercial services, and (d) 0.1% in goods-related services.

Basic Indicators

El Salvador economy presents the following indicators: (a) a GDP of 25,850 million current US dollars, (b) a current account balance with a deficit of –5.5 millions of US dollars, (c) a trade per capita of 1, 426 US dollars, and (d) a trade to GDP ratio of 34.7%. In the world trade, the exports ranks of 223 countries for El Salvador are: 103 in merchandise and 102 in commercial services. On the other hand, the imports ranks are: 93 in merchandise and 93 in commercial services.

El Salvador

			Exports	Imports
GDP (million current US$, 2015)	25 850	**Rank in world trade, 2015**		
GDP per capita (US$, 2013-2015)	4 107	Merchandise	103	93
Current account balance (% GDP, 2012-2014)	-5.5	excluding intra-EU trade	78	68
Trade per capita (US$, 2013-2015)	1 426	Commercial services	102	120
Trade (% GDP, 2013-2015)	34.7	excluding intra-EU trade	75	93

MERCHANDISE TRADE

	Value	Annual percentage change		
Million US$	2015	2010-2015	2014	2015
Merchandise exports, f.o.b.	5 485	4	-4	4
Merchandise imports, c.i.f.	10 416	4	-2	-1

	2015		2015
Share in world total exports	0.03	Share in world total imports	0.06

Breakdown in economy's total exports

By main commodity group (2015)

Agricultural products	20.5
Fuels and mining products	3.2
Manufactures	76.1
Other	0.2

By main destination (2015)

United States	47.0
Honduras	13.9
Guatemala	13.5
Nicaragua	6.6
Other	18.9

Breakdown in economy's total imports

By main commodity group (2015)

Agricultural products	18.9
Fuels and mining products	14.8
Manufactures	66.1
Other	0.2

By main origin (2015)

United States	39.4
Guatemala	9.6
China	8.1
Mexico	7.3
Other	35.6

TRADE IN COMMERCIAL SERVICES

	Value	Annual percentage change		
Million US$	2015	2010-2015	2014	2015
Commercial services exports	2 257	9	7	4
Commercial services imports	1 498	7	0	4

	2015		2015
Share in world total exports	0.05	Share in world total imports	0.03

Breakdown in economy's total exports

By main services item (2015)

Transport	21.6
Travel	36.2
Other commercial services	16.3
Goods-related services	25.8

Breakdown in economy's total imports

By main services item (2015)

Transport	41.4
Travel	19.6
Other commercial services	35.8
Goods-related services	3.2

Merchandise Trade

The merchandise exports have an f.o.b. value of 5,485 million of US dollars, which grew at an annual rate of 4% in 2010–2015, -4% in 2014, and 4% in 2015. Its share in world's total exports is 0.03%. The breakdown in economy's total exports by main commodity group is: (a) 20.5% in agricultural products, (b) 3.2% in fuels and mining products, (c) 76.1% in manufactures, and (d) 0.2% in others. On the other hand, the breakdown by main destination is: (a) 47.0% United States, (b) 13.9% Honduras, (c) 13.5% Guatemala, (d) 6.6% Nicaragua, and (e) 6.6% others.

The merchandise imports have a c.i.f. value of 10,416 million of US dollars, which grew at an annual rate of 4% in 2010–2015, -2% in 2014, and -1% in 2015. Its share in world's total imports is 0.06%. The breakdown in economy's total imports by main commodity group is: (a) 18.9% in agricultural products, (b) 14.8% in fuels and mining products, (c) 66.1% in manufactures, and (d) 0.2% in others. On the other hand, the breakdown by main origin is: (a) 39.4% United States, (b) 9.6% Guatemala, (c) 8.1% China, (d) 7.3% Mexico, and (e) 35.6% others.

Commercial Services Trade

The commercial services exports have a value of 2,257 million of US dollars, which grew at an annual rate of 9% in 2010–2015, 7% in 2014, and 4% in 2015. Its share in world's total imports is 0.05%. The breakdown in economy's total imports by principal services item is: (a) 21.6% in transportation, (b) 36.2% in travel, (c) 16.3% in other commercial services, and (d) 25.8% in goods-related services.

The commercial services imports have a value of 1,498 million of US dollars, which grew at an annual rate 7% in 2010–2015, 0% in 2014, and 4% in 2015. Its share in world's total imports is 0.03%. The breakdown in economy's total imports by principal services item is: (a) 41.4% in transportation, (b) 19.6% in travel, (c) 35.8% in other commercial services, and (d) 3.2% in goods-related services.

Basic Indicators

Guatemala economy presents the following indicators: (a) a GDP of 63,794 million current US dollars, (b) a current account balance with a deficit of -1.6 millions of US dollars, (c) a trade per capita of 1, 023 US

Guatemala

GDP (million current US$, 2015)	63 794	Rank in world trade, 2015	Exports	Imports
GDP per capita (US$, 2013-2015)	3 671	Merchandise	83	78
Current account balance (% GDP, 2013-2015)	-1.6	excluding intra-EU trade	58	55
Trade per capita (US$, 2013-2015)	1 023	Commercial services	99	89
Trade (% GDP, 2013-2015)	27.9	excluding intra-EU trade	72	63

MERCHANDISE TRADE

Million US$	Value 2015	Annual percentage change 2010-2015	2014	2015
Merchandise exports, f.o.b.	10 752	5	8	-1
Merchandise imports, c.i.f.	17 636	5	4	-4

	2015		2015
Share in world total exports	0.07	Share in world total imports	0.11

Breakdown in economy's total exports

By main commodity group (2015)

Agricultural products	46.1
Fuels and mining products	11.4
Manufactures	42.5
Other	0.0

By main destination (2015)

United States	35.8
El Salvador	11.5
Honduras	8.4
European Union (28)	7.9
Other	36.5

Breakdown in economy's total imports

By main commodity group (2015)

Agricultural products	15.7
Fuels and mining products	15.2
Manufactures	68.9
Other	0.2

By main origin (2015)

United States	37.1
Mexico	11.6
China	10.6
European Union (28)	7.5
Other	33.2

TRADE IN COMMERCIAL SERVICES

Million US$	Value 2015	Annual percentage change 2010-2015	2014	2015
Commercial services exports	2 644	4	11	-2
Commercial services imports	3 011	5	10	0

	2015		2015
Share in world total exports	0.06	Share in world total imports	0.07

Breakdown in economy's total exports

By main services item (2015)

Transport	16.0
Travel	59.7
Other commercial services	24.3
Goods-related services	...

Breakdown in economy's total imports

By main services item (2015)

Transport	45.9
Travel	25.1
Other commercial services	29.0
Goods-related services	...

dollars, and (d) a trade to GDP ratio of 27.9%. In the world trade, the exports ranks of 223 countries for Guatemala are: 83 in merchandise and 99 in commercial services. On the other hand, the imports ranks are: 78 in merchandise and 63 in commercial services.

Merchandise Trade

The merchandise exports have an f.o.b. value of 10,752 million of US dollars, which grew at an annual rate of 5% in 2010–2015, 8% in 2014, and –1% in 2015. Its share in world's total exports is 0.07%. The breakdown in economy's total exports by main commodity group is: (a) 46.1% in agricultural products, (b) 11.4% in fuels and mining products, and (c) 42.4% in manufactures. On the other hand, the breakdown by main destination is: (a) 35.8% United States, (b) 11.5% El Salvador, (c) 8.4% Honduras, (d) 7.9% European Union, and (e) 36.5% others.

The merchandise imports have a c.i.f. value of 17,636 million of US dollars, which grew at an annual rate of 5% in 2010–2015, 4% in 2014, and -4% in 2015. Its share in world's total imports is 0.11%. The breakdown in economy's total imports by main commodity group is: (a) 15.7% in agricultural products, (b) 15.2% in fuels and mining products, and (c) 68.9% in manufactures, (d) 0.2% in others. On the other hand, the breakdown by main origin is: (a) 37.1% United States, (b) 11.6% Mexico, (c) 10.6% China, (d) 7.5% European Union, and (e) 7.5% others.

Commercial Services Trade

The commercial services exports have a value of 2,644 million of US dollars, which grew at an annual rate of 4% in 2010–2015, 11% in 2014, and -2% in 2015. Its share in world's total imports is 0.06%. The breakdown in economy's total imports by principal services item is: (a) 16.0% in transportation, (b) 59.7% in travel, and (c) 24.3% in other commercial services.

The commercial services imports have a value of 3,011 million of US dollars, which grew at an annual rate 5% in 2010–2015, 10% in 2014, and 0% in 2015. Its share in world's total imports is 0.07%. The breakdown in economy's total imports by principal services item is: (a) 45.9% in transportation, (b) 25.1% in travel, and (c) 29.0% in other commercial services.

Basic Indicators

Honduras economy presents the following indicators: (a) a GDP of 20,152 million current US dollars, (b) a current account balance with a deficit of -8.5 millions of US dollars, (c) a trade per capita of 1,048 US dollars, and (d) a trade to GDP ratio of 43.1%. In the world trade, the exports ranks of 223 countries for Honduras are: 92 in merchandise and 100 in commercial services. On the other hand, the imports ranks are: 91 in merchandise and 112 in commercial services.

Merchandise Trade

The merchandise exports have an f.o.b. value of 7,810 million of US dollars, which grew at an annual rate of 5% in 2010–2015, 3% in 2014, and -3% in 2015. Its share in world's total exports is 0.05%. The breakdown in economy's total exports by main commodity group is:

Honduras

GDP (million current US$, 2015)	20 152	**Rank in world trade, 2015**	Exports	Imports
GDP per capita (US$, 2013-2015)	2 429	Merchandise	92	91
Current account balance (% GDP, 2012-2014)	-8.5	excluding intra-EU trade	67	66
Trade per capita (US$, 2013-2015)	1 048	Commercial services	100	112
Trade (% GDP, 2013-2015)	43.1	excluding intra-EU trade	73	85

MERCHANDISE TRADE

Million US$	Value 2015	Annual percentage change 2010-2015	2014	2015
Merchandise exports, f.o.b.	7 810	5	3	-3
Merchandise imports, f.o.b.	11 180	5	1	1

	2015		2015
Share in world total exports	0.05	Share in world total imports	0.07

Breakdown in economy's total exports

By main commodity group (2015)

Agricultural products	33.0
Fuels and mining products	1.2
Manufactures	59.5
Other	6.2

By main destination (2014)

United States	44.3
European Union (28)	18.0
El Salvador	6.1
Guatemala	5.0
Other	26.6

Breakdown in economy's total imports

By main commodity group (2015)

Agricultural products	14.4
Fuels and mining products	12.3
Manufactures	66.0
Other	7.2

By main origin (2014)

United States	40.8
China	11.3
Guatemala	7.5
European Union (28)	7.0
Other	33.4

TRADE IN COMMERCIAL SERVICES

Million US$	Value 2015	Annual percentage change 2010-2015	2014	2015
Commercial services exports	2 634	5	7	7
Commercial services imports	1 746	9	6	0

	2015		2015
Share in world total exports	0.06	Share in world total imports	0.04

Breakdown in economy's total exports

By main services item (2015)

Transport	3.6
Travel	24.7
Other commercial services	12.0
Goods-related services	59.7

Breakdown in economy's total imports

By main services item (2015)

Transport	58.2
Travel	23.2
Other commercial services	18.6
Goods-related services	0.0

(a) 33.0% in agricultural products, (b) 1.2% in fuels and mining products, and (c) 59.5% in manufactures. On the other hand, the breakdown by main destination is: (a) 44.3% United States, (b) 18.0% European Union, (c) 6.1% El Salvador, (d) 5.0% Guatemala, and (e) 26.6% others.

The merchandise imports have a c.i.f. value of 11,180 million of US dollars, which grew at an annual rate of 5% in 2010–2015, 1% in 2014, and 1% in 2015. Its share in world's total imports is 0.07%. The breakdown in economy's total imports by main commodity group is: (a) 14.4% in agricultural products, (b) 12.3% in fuels and mining products, and (c) 66.0% in manufactures, (d) 7.2% in others. On the other hand, the breakdown by main origin is: (a) 40.8% United States, (b) 11.3% China, (c) 7.5% Guatemala, (d) 7.0% European Union, and (e) 33.4% others.

Commercial Services Trade

The commercial services exports have a value of 2,634 million of US dollars, which grew at an annual rate of 5% in 2010–2015, 7% in 2014, and 7% in 2015. Its share in world's total imports is 0.06%. The breakdown in economy's total imports by principal services item is: (a) 3.6% in transportation, (b) 24.7% in travel, (c) 12.0% in other commercial services, and (d) 59.7 in goods-related services.

The commercial services imports have a value of 1,1746 million of US dollars, which grew at an annual rate 9% in 2010–2015, 6% in 2014, and 0% in 2015. Its share in world's total imports is 0.04%. The breakdown in economy's total imports by principal services item is: (a) 58.2% in transportation, (b) 23.2% in travel, and (c) 18.6% in other commercial services.

Basic Indicators

Nicaragua economy presents the following indicators: (a) a GDP of 12,693 million current US dollars, (b) a current account balance with a deficit of -8.9 millions of US dollars, (c) a trade per capita of 970 US dollars, and (d) a trade to GDP ratio of 49.5%. In the world trade, the exports ranks of 223 countries for Nicaragua are: 107 in merchandise and 120 in commercial services. On the other hand, the imports ranks are: 110 in merchandise and 113 in commercial services.

Merchandise Trade

The merchandise exports have an f.o.b. value of 4,839 million of US dollars, which grew at an annual rate of 8% in 2010–2015, 7% in 2014, and -6% in 2015. Its share in world's total exports is 0.03%. The breakdown in economy's total exports by main commodity group is: (a) 46.8% in agricultural products, (b) 1.0% in fuels and mining products, and (c) 42.1% in manufactures. On the other hand, the breakdown by main destination is: (a) 53.7% United States, (b) 11.1% Mexico, (c) 6.5% European Union, (d) 6.2% Venezuela, Bolivarian Rep. of, and (e) 22.4% others.

The merchandise imports have a c.i.f. value of 7,090 million of US dollars, which grew at an annual rate of 8% in 2010–2015, 4% in 2014, and 2% in 2015. Its share in world's total imports is 0.04%. The breakdown in economy's total imports by main commodity group is: (a) 14.9% in agricultural products, (b) 10.8% in fuels and mining products, and

Nicaragua

			Exports	Imports
GDP (million current US$, 2015)	12 693	**Rank in world trade, 2015**		
GDP per capita (US$, 2013-2015)	1 960	Merchandise	107	110
Current account balance (% GDP, 2013-2015)	-8.9	excluding intra-EU trade	82	85
Trade per capita (US$, 2013-2015)	970	Commercial services	120	140
Trade (% GDP, 2013-2015)	49.5	excluding intra-EU trade	93	113

MERCHANDISE TRADE

Million US$	Value 2015	Annual percentage change 2010-2015	2014	2015
Merchandise exports, f.o.b.	4 839	8	7	-6
Merchandise imports, f.o.b.	7 090	8	4	2

	2015		2015
Share in world total exports	0.03	Share in world total imports	0.04

Breakdown in economy's total exports

By main commodity group (2015)

Agricultural products	46.8
Fuels and mining products	1.0
Manufactures	42.1
Other	10.1

By main destination (2015)

United States	53.7
Mexico	11.1
European Union (28)	6.5
Venezuela, Bolivarian Rep.	6.2
Other	22.4

Breakdown in economy's total imports

By main commodity group (2015)

Agricultural products	14.9
Fuels and mining products	10.8
Manufactures	56.9
Other	17.3

By main origin (2015)

United States	18.0
China	14.4
Mexico	10.4
Costa Rica	8.2
Other	49.0

TRADE IN COMMERCIAL SERVICES

Million US$	Value 2015	Annual percentage change 2010-2015	2014	2015
Commercial services exports	1 342	10	5	3
Commercial services imports	902	6	-4	-9

	2015		2015
Share in world total exports	0.03	Share in world total imports	0.02

Breakdown in economy's total exports

By main services item (2015)

Transport	3.9
Travel	39.4
Other commercial services	12.9
Goods-related services	43.8

Breakdown in economy's total imports

By main services item (2015)

Transport	53.3
Travel	17.1
Other commercial services	29.6
Goods-related services	...

(c) 59.9% in manufactures, (d) 17.3% in others. On the other hand, the breakdown by main origin is: (a) 18.0% United States, (b) 14.4% China, (c) 10.4% Mexico, (d) 8.2% Costa Rica, and (e) 49.0% others.

Commercial Services Trade

The commercial services exports have a value of 1,342 million of US dollars, which grew at an annual rate of 10% in 2010–2015, 5% in 2014, and 3% in 2015. Its share in world's total imports is 0.03%. The breakdown in economy's total imports by principal services item is: (a) 3.9% in transportation, (b) 39.4% in travel, (c) 12.9% in other commercial services, and (d) 43.8 in goods-related services.

The commercial services imports have a value of 902 million of US dollars, which grew at an annual rate 6% in 2010–2015, -4% in 2014, and -9% in 2015. Its share in world's total imports is 0.02%. The breakdown in economy's total imports by principal services item is: (a) 53.3% in transportation, (b) 17.1% in travel, and (c) 29.6% in other commercial services.

Basic Indicators

Panama economy presents the following indicators: (a) a GDP of 52,132 million current US dollars, (b) a current account balance with a deficit of –8.6 millions of US dollars, (c) a trade per capita of 7, 465 US dollars, and (d) a trade to GDP ratio of 59.3%. In the world trade, the exports ranks of 223 countries for Panama are: 80 in merchandise and 53 in commercial services. On the other hand, the imports ranks are: 75 in merchandise and 79 in commercial services.

Panama

GDP (million current US$, 2015)	52 132	**Rank in world trade, 2015**	Exports	Imports
GDP per capita (US$, 2013-2015)	12 597	Merchandise	80	75
Current account balance (% GDP, 2013-2015)	-8.6	excluding intra-EU trade	55	52
Trade per capita (US$, 2013-2015)	7 465	Commercial services	53	79
Trade (% GDP, 2013-2015)	59.3	excluding intra-EU trade	34	56

MERCHANDISE TRADE

Million US$	Value 2015	Annual percentage change 2010-2015	2014	2015
Merchandise exports, f.o.b.	11 300	1	-11	-14
Merchandise imports, c.i.f.	18 770	2	-3	-11

	2015		2015
Share in world total exports	0.07	Share in world total imports	0.11

Breakdown in economy's total exports

By main commodity group (2015)

Agricultural products	5.7
Fuels and mining products	0.6
Manufactures	92.5
Other	1.2

By main destination (2015)

European Union (28)	27.5
United States	19.7
Costa Rica	7.7
China	5.9
Other	39.3

Breakdown in economy's total imports

By main commodity group (2015)

Agricultural products	7.7
Fuels and mining products	1.5
Manufactures	90.6
Other	0.2

By main origin (2015)

United States	25.9
European Union (28)	11.7
China	9.6
Mexico	5.1
Other	47.7

TRADE IN COMMERCIAL SERVICES

Million US$	Value 2015	Annual percentage change 2010-2015	2014	2015
Commercial services exports	11 176	12	7	4
Commercial services imports	4 357	10	-7	-4

	2015		2015
Share in world total exports	0.24	Share in world total imports	0.09

Breakdown in economy's total exports

By main services item (2015)

Transport	48.7
Travel	37.6
Other commercial services	13.6
Goods-related services	0.1

Breakdown in economy's total imports

By main services item (2015)

Transport	44.9
Travel	18.5
Other commercial services	36.4
Goods-related services	0.2

Merchandise Trade

The merchandise exports have an f.o.b. value of 11,300 million of US dollars, which grew at an annual rate of 1% in 2010–2015, -11% in 2014, and -14% in 2015. Its share in world's total exports is 0.07%. The breakdown in economy's total exports by main commodity group is: (a) 5.7% in agricultural products, (b) 0.6% in fuels and mining products, (c) 92.5% in manufactures, and (d) 1.2% in other. On the other hand, the breakdown by main destination is: (a) 27.5% European Union, (b) 19.7% United States, (c) 7.7% Costa Rica, (d) 5.9% China, and (e) 39.3% others.

The merchandise imports have a c.i.f. value of 18,770 million of US dollars, which grew at an annual rate of 2% in 2010–2015, -3% in 2014, and -11% in 2015. Its share in world's total imports is 0.11%. The breakdown in economy's total imports by main commodity group is: (a) 7.7% in agricultural products, (b) 1.5% in fuels and mining products, and (c) 90.6% in manufactures, (d) 0.2% in others. On the other hand, the breakdown by main origin is: (a) 25.9% United States, (b) 11.7% European Union, (c) 9.6% China, (d) 5.1% Mexico, and (e) 47.4% others.

Commercial Services Trade

The commercial services exports have a value of 11,176 million of US dollars, which grew at an annual rate of 12% in 2010–2015, 7% in 2014, and 4% in 2015. Its share in world's total imports is 0.24%. The breakdown in economy's total imports by principal services item is: (a) 0.1% in transportation, (b) 48.7% in travel, (c) 37.63% in other commercial services, and (d) 13.6 in goods-related services.

The commercial services imports have a value of 4,357 million of US dollars, which grew at an annual rate 10% in 2010–2015, -7% in 2014, and -4% in 2015. Its share in world's total imports is 0.09%. The breakdown in economy's total imports by principal services item is: (a) 44.9% in transportation, (b) 18.5% in travel, (c) 36.4% in other commercial services, and (d) 0.2% in goods-related services.

Reference

http://stat.wto.org/CountryProfile/WSDBCountryPFReporter.aspx?Language=E

Appendix B

Costa Rica

We are including Costa Rica in the Appendix B because it has been on the active observer status since about 2013 or earlier. At one time it made a decision to join the Pacific Alliance (PA) but because of internal political discussions questioning entrance into the Alliance, it has postponed joining the PA at this time. As such, it is important to include Costa Rica in any discussion of the PA expansion because this country has demonstrated major economic and political success and stability for a very long period of time.

Nevertheless, one can see why there is a desire to include Costa Rica as a member.

Over many decades, Costa Rica a Central American country has been a destination of many citizens from around the world due to its beauty, climate, tranquility, and good food. It has demonstrated in the short run and in the long run that it can successfully manage its economy. Its history and its strong human development infrastructure predict that the future is bright. If Costa Rica can continue on the same path that it has historically then the ability to be a major contributor to the PA will be achieved. Because of its stable economy and its ability to connect commercially with many countries around the world Costa Rica presents great promise for its partnership in the PA.

J.E. Spillan, N. Virzi, *Business Opportunities in the Pacific Alliance*,
DOI 10.1007/978-3-319-54768-8

Overview

Christopher Columbus found and named Costa Rica in 1502 (www.bbc 2016). Costa Rica is a small country located in the Middle of Central America. It has approximately 5 million inhabitants who are primarily employed as agricultural workers. It borders both the Pacific and Caribbean coastlines that provide lots of opportunities for economic activity (fishing and touristic adventure) and a leisure time endeavors. Costa Rica is a tropical country that has quite a few different climate zones. It has the major rainy season between May and November and then the dry season that begins in December and ends in April.

Over the last few decades Costa Rica has experienced a relatively stable environment. Costa Rica is one of the most prosperous countries in Central America. It does not have a standing army and has very little if any civil disorder. It is a very politically stable country with a high standard of living when compared to all of the other Central American countries. Tourism is a huge industry because Costa Rica has beautiful beaches, enchanting mountains, and considerable biodiversity, which attracts many people outdoors who just like the overall Costa Rican environment. One of its unique characteristics is the existence of a very open society, which supports open and free media expression without state intervention (Costa Rica Profile 2013).

Economic Summary

The LAC region or the Latin American and Caribbean area is at a crossroads. The dividends that were generated from the global commodities affluence have disappeared. Meanwhile the LAC governments have encountered increased social anticipations that result from an evolving middle class. This group of citizens are more linked with each other and with the outside world. They are more involved, and demanding more in goods and services.

The regional gross domestic product is anticipated to shrink 1.1% in 2016. This represents about a half percentage point decline from the 2015 level. Because its economic stability has been so good over the year, Costa Rica has developed a success story in many respects. By and large, Costa Rica is labeled as an upper middle-income country. It has experienced steady economic expansion over the past 25 years. The years after the 1980s found Costa Rica managing economic growth by using a strategy of outward-oriented development. This approach is based on openness to foreign investment and gradual trade liberalization.

Costa Rica has become a global leader for its environmental policies and accomplishments. These achievements have helped the country create it famous Green Trademark. The blend of political stability, a social compact, along with steady growth has resulted in one of the lowest poverty rates in Latin America and the Caribbean. The statistics indicate that only 1.6% of the population lives under the overall US$1.90 poverty line. Costa Rica's success across the past decades is echoed in its strong human development indicators. These indicators continue to be much higher than those of other countries in the region. All through the global crisis, real GDP growth slowed to 2.7% in 2008. Then in 2009 it contracted to 1%. The economy bounced back following the crisis and reached an average real growth rate of 4.9% between 2010 and 2012. The in 2013 growth decelerated to 3.5%. By 2015 economic growth increased to 2.8%. In 2016 it is projected to pick up to 3.3% and the outlook for 2017 is for an increase to 3.6%. Notwithstanding strong growth over the past decades, two persistent development problems stick out: (a) the deteriorating fiscal situation and (b) obdurate inequality. These challenges affect the basic foundations of development, which include growth, and sustainability (Worldbank 2016).

Graph 1 illustrates the ups and downs that Costa Rica has been through over the last decade. In the early part of the twenty-first century, Costa Rica had great growth rates up above 8%. This is remarkable for a small country. But as one views the chart, it also had a major fall around the Great Depression. It recovered somewhat but as one can see it has been taking another decline in the recent time frame. Costa Rica has always been a stable economy yet the impact of world economic turbulence has also affected this country. Costa Rica still has a growing economy (GDP) but not as robust as it did early on at the turn of the century.

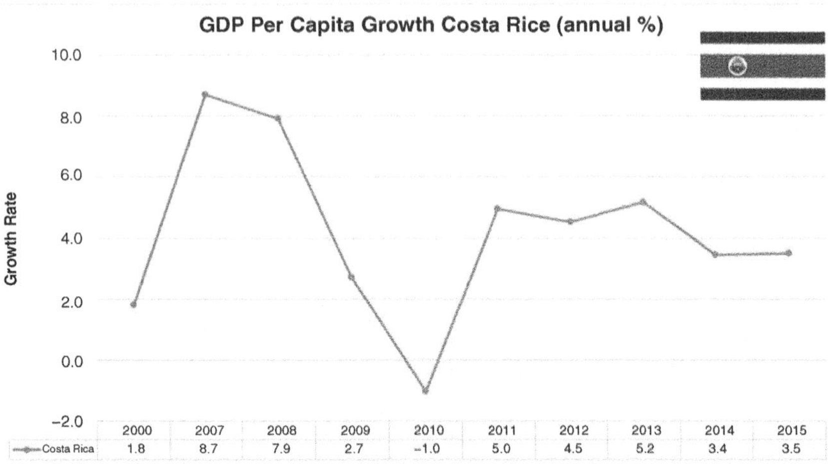

Graph Costa Rica

Source: Authors reconfiguration of CIA Factbook, 2016 GDP Data–https://www.cia.gov/library/publications/the-world-factbook/geos/xx.html

Educational, Social, and Political

Education

Costa Ricans are generally well-educated people with a 93% literacy rate among its citizens. This would rank Costa Ricans and the most literate population in Central America. There have been efforts over the last two decades to increase the educational standards with significant amounts of the public budget invested in education. Interestingly the Costa Ricans have implemented a requirement that all students take mandatory English. This has been done in order to support the technological and touristic industries (Doing Business 2014).

Social

A great majority of the Costa Rican population is essentially part of the middle class. While poverty exists it is not as severe and disabling as in other parts of Latin America. There is also a class of wealthy that exists in Costa Rica. This is composed of the traditionally rich people and those who have become rich in the most recent years. The society as a whole is primarily composed of middle class citizens.

Ninety percent of the Costa Rican population is affiliated with the Catholic religion while others participate in other organized religions that are germane to an indigenous culture. Finally, ninety-eight (98%) of the population is classified as white or mestizo. The rest are of black or indigenous classes (Social Class Costa Rica 2016).

Political

Costa Rica has three main branches of government similar to the United States. These branches consist of Legislative, Executive, and Judicial. It has presently five political parties that participate in periodic elections. The president is elected for a four-year term while the political parties are on staggered terms.

The Costa Rica legal system is based on a Civil Law originating from the Napoleonic Code (Doing Business 2014).

The map presented in Figure 1 shows how contiguous Costa Rica is to its neighboring countries. As mentioned earlier, the fact that it is bordered by the Caribbean on one side and the North Pacific Ocean on the other provides a huge asset that easily facilitates the import and export of trade. This visual portrayal of Costa Rica gives the reader a more realistic perspective as to how it could interact with all of the PA members but more interestingly with a close neighbor, Colombia. Easy trade with Colombia, Peru, Mexico, and Chile can be conducted using the major seaports along all of the countries coastlines.

The following section provides an outline of Costa Rica's strengths and weaknesses.

Strengths

- Stable democratic environment – Costa Rica has been recognized for a long time as a very stable country both politically and economically. This characteristic makes it an attractive partner for the PA relationship.
- Growing safe and attractive tourism around the country – Many tourists have been attracted to Costa Rica. Each year there are a large number of tourist excursions visiting Costa Rica and its surroundings and some of its neighbors. Good place to vacation.

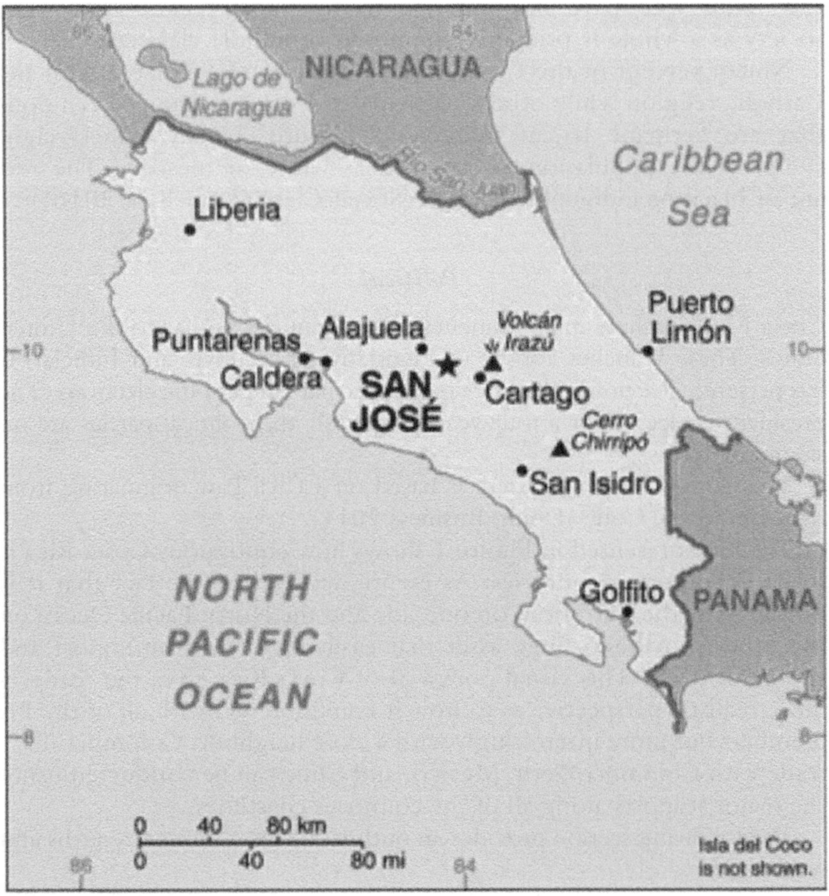

Map of Costa Rica

Source: The World Factbook – Central Intelligence Agency: Chile Map. (n.d.). Retrieved from https://www.cia.gov/library/publications/the-world-factbook/geos/ci.html

- Reasonable public debt – Costa Rica has been frugal and conservative in management of its internal and external debt. That approach has had a major impact on its economic and political stability.

- Foreign direct investment (FDI) has been substantial and continuous – Because of its stability, businesses and organizations are interested in investing in Costa Rica. The risk level is low and hence attractive for FDI.
- Substantial reserves that are good for unforeseen contingencies – With frugal and smart management of public budgets, Costa Rica has been able to create and maintain substantial reserves for the future.
- Very good social indicators for education and health – Health and education levels are higher than most Latin American countries and provide very good service levels for all the Costa Rican families.
- State-of-the-art industries – Another attractive area of business that can be real opportunity for those interested in this industry.
- Multiple trade agreements from companies around the world – Smart and strategic decision-making has allowed Costa Rica to have good trade relationships and good import and export business around the world.

Weaknesses

- Decreasing foreign exports – As the world economy goes so goes Costa Rica. As the preceding graph illustrated, Costa Rica was not exempt from the worldwide recession and has lost some trade opportunities over the last few years.
- Tax reform is needed due to expanding fiscal deficit – While Costa Rica policy makers have had a good record of fiscal management, the world economy along with some other macroeconomic decisions have allowed Costa Rica to experience some level of expanding deficits. These deficits must be conquered and resolved very soon.
- Too reliant on FDI from the United States – This is an issue of putting all their eggs in one basket. Costa Rica needs to diversify its FDI activity so it can more realistically manage the ups and downs of FDI activity.
- Vulnerable to natural disaster – Costa Rica being on two coasts can does have vulnerability. Proper precautions need to be made to address and mitigate the threat of a major natural disaster. Good planning and analysis can help reduce this vulnerability.
- Infrastructure is not suitable for efficient transportation of goods – This seems to be a major condition throughout Latin America. Not much

attention has been paid to the infrastructure. As Costa Rica gets more FDI it will be necessary to renovate and upgrade its infrastructure.

- Shortage of skilled labor for various industries – While Costa Rica has a good education system that is a foundation for skill development, there is no massive pool of skilled labor available. Costa Rica has to recognize this deficiency and begin to decide how it will address this recognized deficiency.

(*Source*: Costa Rica Risk Assessment and Sound Fundamentals, 2016).

Why Costa Rica Is a Good Partner?

The PA was developed as a means to enhance existing trade agreements among the Mexico, Peru, Chile, and Colombia The goal is to provide in Latin America a unified economic bloc to negotiate and trade with other countries. The PA's focus is to liberalize trade in goods and services, open foreign investment, and integrate securities markets. It also has a similar provision similar to the European Union where there is free movement of people among member countries. It also has shared values in regard to the respect for rule of law, democracy, and protection of human rights (M. Angeles Villarreal 2016).

Costa Rica's geographic position and its stable and strong economic situation make it a suitable partner for the PA. Its successful experience in FDI activity is a major asset to the Alliance. Since Costa Rica has good connections with foreign companies around the world, it can promote interconnected trade activity with its own partners and additional entities outside of the Alliance.

Discussion

Costa Rica is a country with solid economic, political, and social credentials to be involved in a trade partnership that will benefit all parties involved. Its strong economic and political foundation is an important feature that can sustain the dynamic interactions of trade and globalization. Just about every indicator that is important for sustaining a strong partnership in the PA exists in Costa Rica. The decision to include Costa Rica in the PA is strategically and practically a good decision. The present members of the PA have recognized that Central America has many attributes that can contribute to the strength and success of the PA. While only time will tell and everything does change in the long run, it is clear now that the inclusion of Costa Rica in the PA will enhance the structure and the operations of the PA.

Conclusion

Costa Rica has demonstrated in the short run and long run that it can successfully manage its economy. Its history and its strong human development infrastructure predict that the future is bright. If Costa Rica can continue on the same path that it has historically then the ability to be a major contributor to the PA will be achieved. Time will tell how successful Costa Rica will be as a member of the PA. Hopefully the positive indicators that now exist will continue into the future and give Costa Rica the chance to continue its robust economic development trajectory over the next decade. This is a goal and a major challenge and opportunity for its people and its leaders.

References

Costa Rica Profile (2013).http://www.bbc.com/news/world-latin-america-19414705, accessed on 10/8/16.

Doing Business: A Guide for Costa Rica. January, 2014, www.Pwc.com/interamericas. Accessed on 10/8/16.

Social Class Costa Rica (2016). Incostarica.weeby -http://incostarica.weebly.com/social-class.html, accessed on 10/8/16

Villarreal, M.A., (2016). The Pacific Alliance: A Trade Integration Initiative in Latin America, CRS Report, Prepared for Members and Committees of Congress, Congressional Research Services, 7-5700, www.crs.gov, R43748.

World Bank. (2016). http://www.worldbank.org/en/region/lac, September 19, 2016.

Index

J.E. Spillan, N. Virzi, *Business Opportunities in the Pacific Alliance*,
DOI 10.1007/978-3-319-54768-8

The manufacturer's authorised representative in the EU is Springer Nature Customer Service Centre GmbH, Europaplatz 3, 69115 Heidelberg, Germany. If you have any concerns regarding our products, please contact ProductSafety@springernature.com

Printed and bound by CPI Group (UK) Ltd, Croydon, CR0 4YY
30/09/2026
02225216-0006